I.C.C. LIBRARY

Illinois Central College
Learning Resources Center

Women, Women Writers, and the West

Women, Women Writers, and the West

by

L. L. Lee

and

Merrill Lewis

The Whitston Publishing Company
Troy, New York
1979

PREFACE

It is something of a commonplace in American literary history to say that the central significance of regional writing in late nineteenth-century may not have been America's literary discovery of place—or local color—or the regionalists' contributions to literary realism, regardless of how important those discoveries and contributions were. The major significance of such writing may have been—indeed was—the opportunities it gave writers, especially women writers, to render the condition of women in American society or to explore the woman's perception of reality. While this argument undoubtedly gains its major support from the work of Sarah Orne Jewett and Mary Wilkins Freeman in New England and Kate Chopin in the South, the evidence presented by the eighteen essays in this collection indicates that the judgment may well stand in the case of midwestern and western writing as well, even though everyone recognizes that that society—at least in its frontier stages—was predominantly masculine in character.

That masculinity, Richard Bartlett has observed in *The New Country, A Social History of the American Frontier, 1776-1890* (Oxford, 1974), has been so much taken for granted that it has hardly been questioned, let alone analyzed. But as Leslie Fiedler has made clear in *Love and Death in the American Novel* and elsewhere, questions of masculinity cannot be separated from questions of femininity. That is a beginning. But for the most part the contributors to this volume share few other assumptions with Fiedler. Indeed, both the significance of women writers within the tradition of regional literature and the questionable relevance of Fiedler's famous paradigm of classical American literature are addressed cogently by Susan Armitage in her opening essay, "A New Perspective on the Frontier Myth." Armitage argues tellingly that the relationship of women to the "savage" and the "wilderness" discloses truths every bit as important as those embedded in the relationship between men and the savage wilderness. Variations on Armitage's statements are central to almost every essay in this book.

The editors recognized these lively possibilities in the subject only dimly in the fall of 1975, when they suggested to the membership of the Western Literature Association that one of the special topics at the annual meeting scheduled for Western Washington University in October, 1976, would be "Women, Women Writers, and the West." The response, as we have said elsewhere, was overwhelming. The final program included two sessions on that theme; and eleven other papers were either on the image of women in western writing or the work of women writers living in the west or using western material.

We already had plans afoot to publish a bicentennial collection of essays, *The Westering Experience in American Literature* (Western Washington University, 1977), but the interest in women writers and the West was so intense that the only adequate response was to propose a companion volume,—this volume—also as a part of, albeit a delayed celebration of, the nation's two-hundredth birthday. The eighteen essays collected here include ten of the papers read at that meeting plus eight solicited between then and the fall of 1977.

In selecting the essays for the volume we made no attempt to choose or assign certain topics in order to assure a full coverage of the subject. In fact, it is not at all clear what "full coverage" would be, since so much work needs to be done, as Professor Armitage says. Nevertheless, the essays that were selected do fall into at least five categories—determined for the most part by the critic's primary interest. And so we have divided them in the book. Some essays concern themselves primarily with the social, mythical, and literary milieu within which the woman writer chose or was forced to work. Working from the point of view of social historian and psycho-historian respectively, Ann Ronald and Jeannie McKnight explore the external and internal forces at work upon the woman writer on the raw frontier. One thing they both note is the variety of literary vehicles with which the women writers worked—from the humble diary and letter to social history and novel. The essays by Elinor Lenz and Helen Stauffer demonstrate, further, that the best as well as the most common writing by women does not necessarily find its expression in the traditional and status forms. Carol Bangs' essay

"Women Poets and the 'Northwest School,' " brings the writer's milieu and the writer's choices together and demonstrates—as do all the essays in the first major section—that if we are going to understand the woman writer and take a fair measure of her contributions to literature we must meet her on her own ground, and that means on the ground of her own experience and within the literary forms of her own choosing.

Inevitably, there are a number of essays that undertake to study the image of women in western fiction. The work of Gertrude Atherton belongs here because her fiction is shaped by her conception of the "new" woman. But predictably, perhaps, most of these essays concern male writers such as Garland, Rølvaag, Conrad Richter, Vardis Fisher, Wallace Stegner, and Ken Kesey. And, again, predictably perhaps, we find the critic centering his or her interest on the relationship between the writer's women characters and the success (or failure) of his art. And by now a certain difference between the women and men writers begins to emerge. Typically, the male writers who treat of the western experience choose to see man (and humankind) as akin to the natural, animal world—perhaps even animal in the good sense; whereas the women writers see humankind as a social animal. There are exceptions, to be sure, but even these prove instructive.

Almost all the essays which investigate the work of women writers concern themselves with how these women looked upon themselves as writers and solved—for better or worse—a writing problem that arose from the fact of their being women. But several of the essays address this question in such a way as to suggest a third grouping of essays, The Woman *as* Writer. The difference between the essays in group two and those in group three can be measured in part by comparing two observations made by Bernice Slote and Kerry Ahearn in connection with the writing of Willa Cather and Wallace Stegner—two novelists of kindred spirit if there ever were (at least we know Stegner's enthusiasm for Cather; we can only guess that Cather would reciprocate). Ahearn approaches Stegner by way of a major theme of his fiction. Slote approaches Cather by way of Cather's solution to certain novelistic problems. Ahearn argues that "in the deepest sense, Stegner's fiction is in the West but not of it." And he goes on to demonstrate how Stegner's abiding theme— "how shall a good man conduct himself"—involves a putting down (or a putting aside) the western man with the "neo-romantic creed" or "a grandiose plan." Slote likewise argues that Cather is not a regional writer in the sense that she "attempt[s] to interpret [the] region." Rather, Cather attempts to give the land a past, a history, and consequently a dignity. "The history of every country" Alexandra Bergson says in *O Pioneers!*, "begins in the heart of a man or a woman." Cather's stories are "the gathering together of the consciousness of a man" such as Father Latour in *Death Comes for the Archbishop*.

The essays by Lou Rodenberger and Sylvia Lee are perhaps equally instructive in giving us insights into just how the woman writer's material shapes the story she has to tell. Virginia Sorensen's *The Evening and The Morning* demonstrates the *kind* of novel a Mormon novel *must* be if it hopes to render the Mormon world justly and completely. That novel must capture the peculiar sense of community of the Mormons at the same moment that it recognizes that males dominated the society. So, Lee argues, it is important to see it from a woman's point of view —and from an apostate's point of view—that is, from the point of view of someone who is both inside and outside that special community.

We must admit, however, that our arrangement of the essays has an arbitrary element about it. After all, the problems Gertrude Atherton tried to solve as a novelist are close enough to those faced by Cather and Sorensen that she belongs with them as much as she belongs in company with Hamlin Garland. Some readers will undoubtedly wish to bring together McKnight's historical investigation of the mental life of pioneer women with Sylvia Grider's account of Beret Hanson's madness in Rølvaag's *Giants in the Earth* and Barbara Quissell's account of Dorothy Scarborough's attempt "to write a story which would show the effect of the wind and sand on a nervous, sensitive woman." Still others will pick up the implicit invitation—we hope—to compare Ronald's "Tonopah Ladies" with "Conrad Richter's Southwestern Ladies," by Barbara Meldrum. And if they go that far, they are bound to notice that Elinore Stewart's life in Wyoming which Elinor Lenz writes about in "Homestead Home" is not the life of a lady by either standard. Or they will notice that Meldrum's account of the differences between the masculine and feminine *ethos* in the West varies significantly from that initially proposed by Armitage. But this is all to the good, since the collection is intended to mark a beginning to that task outlined by Armitage.

The last two essays in the collection introduce women writers who are not American. The fiction of Ethel Wilson and the poetry of Judith Wright takes shape among the landforms of British Columbia and the Australian Out Back, not the plains of West Texas or the goldfields of Leadville, Colorado. Obviously their work is exposed here for the sake of comparison. But the capacity of their work to move readers unfamiliar with these particular geographical and cultural settings indicates that the Pierian springs continue to be fed by sources other than regionalism or the circumstances of one's sex.

It is in the context of these permanent, human concerns that it is appropriate to speak of the first selection in the book: Clarice Short's poem, "The Old One and the Wind." Written by a woman who for years resided in and used materials native to the Rocky Mountain Region, "The Old One and the Wind" is first of all and foremost the insight, human and humane, of an excellent poet. Professor Short, a great teacher and a warm friend, died while we were preparing this book for publication. The book is, in a way, an offering to her and the excellence she demanded of all of us.

ACKNOWLEDGEMENTS

We wish to thank the following publishers and institutions who have granted us permission to reprint material to which they hold copyright or ownership.

The Automobile Club of Southern California for permission to reprint "Homestead Home," by Elinor Lenz, printed in *Westways*, 1977, copyright © 1977 by the Automobile Club of Southern California.

Heritage of Kansas for permission to reprint "Westering and Woman: A Thematic Study of Kesey's *One Flew Over the Cuckoo's Nest* and Fisher's *Mountain Man*," by Joseph M. Flora; and "Folk Narrative in Caroline Gordon's Frontier Fiction," by M. Lou Rodenberger, both printed in *Heritage of Kansas: A Journal of the Great Plains*, 10 (Summer 1977), copyright © 1977 by *Heritage of Kansas*.

Itinerary for permission to reprint "Gertrude Atherton's California Women: From Love Story to Psychological Drama," by Charlotte S. McClure, printed in *Itinerary Seven*, copyright © 1978 by Robert T. Early.

The Nevada Historical Society for permission to reprint "The Tonopah Ladies," by Ann Ronald, printed in the *Nevada Historical Society Quarterly*, Vol. XX (Summer 1977), copyright 1977 by the Nevada Historical Society.

Baylor University for permission to use material from the Emily Dorothy Scarborough Papers, The Texas Collection, Baylor University, which is cited in "Dorothy Scarborough's Critique of the Frontier Experience in *The Wind*," by Barbara Quissell.

The Western Humanities Review for permission to reprint "The

Women, Women Writers, and the West

TABLE OF CONTENTS

Table of Contents

I

INTRODUCTION

The Old One and the Wind

Clarice Short

She loves the wind.
There on the edge of the known world, at ninety,
In her tall house, any wildness in the elements
Is as welcome as an old friend.
When the surgically patched elms and sycamores
Crack off their heavy limbs in the freak snow storm
Of October, she rejoices; the massy hail
That drives craters into her groomed lawn
Stirs her sluggish heart to a riot of beating.

A cluster of cottonwood trees in the swale
Of the prairie, oasis now in a desert of wheat fields,
Is all that is left of the home place. No one
Is left to remember the days there with her:
The playhouse sheltered behind the cowshed,
The whirlwinds that made a column of corn shucks,
Winters when snow brushed out all the fences,
Springs when the white of the snow turned to daisies,
Wind-bent as were the urchins who picked them.

To her in her tall house in the tame town, the wind
That escapes the windbreaks of man's constructing
Blows from a distance beyond the young's conceiving,
Is rife with excitements of the world's beginning
And its end.

WOMEN'S LITERATURE AND THE AMERICAN FRONTIER:
A NEW PERSPECTIVE ON THE FRONTIER MYTH

Susan H. Armitage
University of Colorado

The frontier myth is the great American myth, the story of how we made this land "our land." The stages of the process are familiar to us all: the encounter with wilderness, the risk, challenge and commitment, the final slow surrender of freedom to advancing civilization. In the west, even today, our frontier heritage is always present, as near as the stark and beautiful landscape which surrounds us.

The frontier myth *is* evocative, but it contains some deeply disturbing elements. The frontier myth is a male myth, preoccupied with stereotypically male issues like courage, physical bravery, honor, and male friendship. While these are important themes, they by no means encompass the reality and complexity of the frontier experience.

The frontier, Frederick Jackson Turner said, was the boundary between savagery and civilization. In the frontier myth, these two extremes are represented by the Indian, symbol of savagery, and the white woman, symbol of civilization. Usually, however, they remain secondary characters, for the white male hero occupies the space between them. As Leslie Fiedler formulates it, the white male himself becomes the boundary between the Indian-occupied "Wilderness" on the one side, and the woman-occupied "Clearing" on the other. The conflict between savagery and civilization is played out in the persona of the white male hero.[1] Because of this persistent focus on the white male, Indians and women rarely achieve full, authentic stature in frontier literature.

Nor is this all. At its deepest level, the frontier myth is concerned with violence and conquest—over the land, over the native inhabitants of that land, over fear of the unknown—and finally, over the temptation to succumb to wilderness and revert to savagery.[2] To justify this violence, the historical reality of Indians and women has been distorted.

According to the frontier myth, the confrontation between savagery—Indians—and civilization—white women—was violent and terrible. Captivity narratives, a major form of popular literature dating from Puritan times, told and retold the gruesome story. The Indians attacked fiercely and without cause, pillaging, burning and killing. The survivors, helpless women and children, were taken off into captivity. Few captives escaped or were rescued—many died, were lost, or, interestingly enough, became so assimilated to Indian culture that they didn't want to return.

The captivity narrative was originally preoccupied with the religious question of God's grace for those who escaped the wilderness. In addition, the early narratives often expressed interest in, and attraction to, Indian culture. As early as 1800, authentic captivity narratives had been replaced by immensely popular, melodramatic literature, full of hatred of Indians. These accounts, often totally fabricated, told of savage, irrational Indian violence against ever more helpless white women.[3] As the frontier expanded, this projection of the urge to violence onto the Indian provided a splendid rationale for white retaliation. Protection of white women, the symbols of civilization, and the extermination or removal of Indians went hand-in-hand.

The frontier myth, then, quite deliberately dramatized the stark dichotomy between savage Indians and civilized white women. But in so doing, the myth seriously misrepresented the frontier reality.

What was the reality? To answer that question, let us go directly to women's sources—to the diaries, letters, memoirs and novels women wrote about their experience on the trans-Mississippi frontier. These sources tell us of a very different confrontation between Indians and women.

The woman and her children are alone and "unprotected"— because the white man is elsewhere—when the Indians arrive. The result is not a massacre. The Indians want food, not scalps.

The woman, while afraid of the Indians, is even more afraid to refuse their demands. She cooks the requested item, or regretfully offers up a scarce store-bought food. The Indians leave peacefully. When the white man returns home, he praises the woman for her courage and commonsense.

This same scene appears again and again in women's writings. Clearly, this anxious domestic encounter was much more common than the notorious, popularized stories of massacre and captivity. Why, then, has the reality been so ignored?

To answer that question, let us return to our female sources and look at the domestic encounter in more detail. First, women were alone, and thrown upon their own resources. Mollie Dorsey Sanford's first encounter with Indians came on the wagon train from Nebraska to Colorado. She was alone, driving the family wagon, happily enjoying a respite from incompatible fellow-travellers, when a band of passing Indians saw her. They threatened her, apparently playfully—they gestured at cutting off her braids, and she feared scalping. Then they demanded food. Her fear was palpable: she let them have all of her precious, irreplacable sugar, and drew from the episode the lesson that she could never again seek personal independence from the wagon train.[4]

Other, more settled and experienced women responded differently to Indian demands. Amelia Buss, settled in Fort Collins, Colorado, in 1866, was frightened but exasperated, and peremptorily told the local Indians that she had no more food to spare.[5] Flora Hunter of Nebraska, aware that an entire tribe was camped around her cabin, at first fearfully gave two Indian braves six loaves of newly-baked bread, and then lost her temper at her wasted work, and shooed them out of her kitchen.[6] Other women resorted to cunning and doctored the food, adding something so unpleasant that the Indians never came back for more.[7]

Initially, of course, most women were afraid for their lives, for they all knew massacre and captivity stories. Significantly, in the female sources I have consulted, there is not a hint of sexuality. There are no fears of rape—although there are of scalping—and there is not the slightest suggestion of sexual interest in the "noble red man." The common female response to male Indians was one of repugnance, not of attraction. To most women, Indians remained frighteningly alien—dirty and smelly, incomprehensible and annoyingly inquisitive.[8]

Some few women moved beyond fear to observation and even sympathy. Flora Hunter was interested and amazed to see that her six loaves of bread were divided and shared among the entire tribe, from the smallest baby to the most elderly.[9] Nannie Alderson of Montana, who lived in close proximity to the once-fearsome Northern Cheyenne, became very friendly with several members of the tribe, and pitied the once self-reliant people who were now reduced to begging for food.[10]

Nannie's sympathetic presence was elsewhere on the unfortunate day when a hired hand decided to brag about his marksmanship by shooting off the hat of the tribal chieftain. For this insult, the Indians promptly turned against their erstwhile friends and burned the cabin to the ground.[11]

Women reacted to Indians with fear and anxiety, for very female reasons. Their fears were not sexual, but stemmed instead from new strains on their traditional female role. The Indians walked right into the kitchen. On the frontier, not even the domestic sphere, woman's special space, was private. Women were indeed very vulnerable. Although they usually had guns, they could not use them because they were alone and outnumbered. Finally, Indian demands for food could jeopardize the entire family.

The complaint of Caddie Woodlawn's mother now seems merely amusing: "Johnny, my dear. . .those frightful savages will eat us out of house and home."[12] The Woodlawns lived on a settled frontier (Wisconsin) and did indeed have food to spare. However, an inconvenience on a settled frontier was a major deprivation on a new frontier. Laura Ingalls Wilder recalled that, when her family lived on the Kansas-Oklahoma border, visiting Indians took all of the family's cornmeal and tobacco, which could not be replenished without a four-day round-trip journey to the nearest store. Nevertheless, when informed of the Indian visit, Mr. Ingalls reassured his wife, "You did the right thing. . . We don't want to make enemies of any Indians."[13]

Here is one major source for the anxious female response to

Indians.   The pioneer woman's major role was that of domestic provider and sustainer.   She was responsible for feeding and clothing her children and her husband.[14]   For her, the Indian demands posed a frightful choice: between the needs of her immediate family and the wider social demand for peace with the Indians.   She had to silence her domestic instincts and training and give away scarce, often irreplaceable food supplies.   She had to adapt her role to the new reality.

It is a fact, of course, that Indians did occasionally kill and capture, and white men and women were always afraid of that possibility.   The frontier myth dealt with this fear by emphasizing the white response, glorifying the violent, individual conflict with wilderness.   While the frontier myth had great psychological appeal, it was not a guide for action, for the reality was much more complex and ambiguous than the myth admitted.   Let us summarize the ways in which the female version complements the myth with the authenticity of real experience.

First, actual contact demonstrated that not all Indians were brutal, irrational savages.   Certainly they were frightening and unpredictable.   But they could also be pitiful: they begged for food.   It was impossible to regard all Indians as vicious, implacable, inevitable enemies.

But this potential understanding was largely vitiated for women because the nature of the cultural contact provoked such great anxiety.   Indian demands for food underlined the precariousness of white frontier existence.   White families were not yet self-sufficient in food, nor close enough to other settlers to form new interdependent communities.   The Indian demand for food was thus a constant reminder to whites that their frontier experiment might fail.

Furthermore, the domestic encounter demonstrated that violence was seldom an appropriate response to Indian demands. The adaptive, accommodating responses of women had the full support of their husbands.   Realistically, frontier homesteaders were too isolated and outnumbered to risk violence against the Indians, as the Alderstons learned to their regret.   The Indian presence was often irritating.   Nevertheless, the individual violence celebrated by the frontier myth was inappropriate to the circumstances.   The only possible answer was adaptation.   Al-

though women might be frightened, white men could not always
be present to protect them from the Indians. Women had to
learn how to cope on their own, and men had to learn to support
them.

Frederick Jackson Turner understood that his famous
"frontier as process" was in fact two processes, not only the
famous recreation of civilization (i.e. the defeat of "savagery")
but an earlier, more informal process of adaptation to a new
reality. This process of adaptation, which was not heroic, and
not violent, included the anxious response to Indians which I
have described. In most frontier areas, the early uncertain
period of settlement was quite short. Crops grew, new settlers
moved in, the Indians were killed or confined to reservations by
soldiers. But the memoirs of the early days remained, and are
rediscovered today in women's literature.

The frontier myth glorifies the deepest, most violent emotions aroused by the encounter with the new land and the unknown—that is why it is myth. Myths begin with reality, although they eventually transcend that reality. As I have shown,
the frontier myth does not accurately reflect the reality for
women and Indians, and therefore misrepresents the experience
of the families who settled on the boundary between savagery
and civilization, the frontier.

The foregoing brief analysis of the domestic encounter is
just one small example of the ways in which women's literature
can begin to complement our understanding of the frontier
myth. Women's literature will illuminate the private, domestic,
interior side of the frontier experience which the myth has
ignored. Women's literature will have much to tell us about
other non-heroic aspects of the encounter with wilderness:
responses to isolation, to hardship and failure, and more positively, about informal, cooperative efforts at community building.

My examples need not be limited to the frontier west. In
every region of the country, we now know, there are vast accumulations of women's literature in every form—diaries, letters,
journals, memoirs, novels, poems, children's books. This neglected material is of major importance. We have just begun the effort of recovery and analysis, but we can already say confidently

that when the process is complete, female voices will change our present understandings of American history and American literature.[15]

NOTES

[1]Leslie Fiedler, *The Return of the Vanishing American* (New York: Stein and Day, 1968), p. 50. Fiedler's analysis, while illuminating, is characterized by such persistent anti-female bias that some parts of the book are simply ridiculous.

[2]Richard Slotkin, *Regeneration Through Violence* (Middletown, Connecticut: Wesleyan University Press, 1973) thoroughly examines the stages of the creation of the violent frontier myth.

[3]Roy Harvey Pearce, "The Significances of the Captivity Narrative," *American Literature* XIX (March 1947), pp. 1-20 and Dawn Lander Gherman, "From Parlour to Tepee: The White Squaw on the American Frontier," unpublished Ph. D. dissertation, University of Massachusetts, 1975.

[4]*Mollie: The Diary of Mollie Dorsey Sanford* (Lincoln: University of Nebraska Press, 1959), pp. 123-124.

[5]Diary of Amelia Buss, 1866-67 (typescript copy), Western History Archives, University of Colorado, Boulder, Colorado.

[6]Berna Hunter Chrisman, *When You and I Were Young, Nebraska!* (Broken Bow, Nebraska: Purcell's Inc., 1971), pp. 40-42.

[7]Sheryll and Eugene Patterson-Black encountered many versions of this story while researching their forthcoming annotated bibliography, *Pioneer Women From the Missouri to the Sierras and Beyond* (Crawford, Nebraska: Cottonwood Press).

[8]These matter-of-fact accounts stand in sharp contrast to the lurid, and largely undocumented, picture of rape and fears of rape painted by Dee Brown in *The Gentle Tamers* (New York: Bantam, 1958).

[9]Chrisman, p. 41.

[10]Nannie T. Alderson and Helena Huntington Smith, *A Bride Goes West* (Lincoln: University of Nebraska Press, 1942), pp. 47-48.

[11]*Ibid.*, pp. 101-103.

[12]Carol Ryrie Brink, *Caddie Woodlawn* (New York: Macmillan, 1935), p. 7.

[13]Laura Ingalls Wilder, *Little House on the Prairie* (New York: Harper and Row, 1935), pp. 132-143.

[14]In rural families, this usually involved food growing (vegetable gardens) and processing (canning, preserving) in addition to cooking. By the nineteenth century, home weaving was uncommon, but home sewing was still customary. Susan H. Armitage, "Housekeeping Before 1930: The Oral History Record," paper presented at West Coast Conference of Women Historians, spring 1977; and Marjorie Kreidberg, ed., *Food on the Frontier: Minnesota Cooking 1850-1900* (St. Paul: Minnesota Historical Society Press, 1975).

[15]All over the country, scholars are engaged in the recovery of women's literature. One important, cooperative national effort is the PHIPSE-supported grant administered by the Modern Language Association, "Teaching Women's Literature From a Regional Perspective." The grant supports research and teaching of fifteen scholars and their students across the country; the author and her students at the University of Colorado are among them.

II

WOMEN, WRITING, AND THE WESTERN EXPERIENCE

THE TONOPAH LADIES

Ann Ronald
University of Nevada/Reno

Eighty years ago northern Nevadans spoke of "going down into the desert," implying that the lower half of their state was some kind of infernal region. Insufferably hot in summer, freezing in winter, windswept and nearly unpopulated, the land attracted only those few prospectors who still dreamed of another Comstock. Then one man's dream came true. On May 19, 1900, Jim Butler stumbled across a bonanza, and by the next spring a major mining rush was on, with people flocking to what had been the middle of nowhere—the new boomtown of Tonopah—hoping to find their fortunes in silver and gold. Some succeeded and others failed, while Tonopah and its sister city of Goldfield had success and failure too, first undergoing rapid growth and then years of slow abandonment. In short, Nevada's twentieth-century mining story differs little from thousands of others throughout the west.

Most of what we know about such booms and busts has come from the voices and pens of men. We've all listened to old-boy tall tales, read some factual histories, devoured some thrillers, and perhaps plodded through too many dry mineral statistics. About Tonopah and Goldfield, though, we can find out some different things. From these two towns comes a surprising amount of writing by women—first-person non-fiction narratives by Mrs. Hugh Brown, Mrs. Minnie Blair, and Anne Ellis; third-person non-fiction accounts by Zua Arthur, Helen Downer Croft, and Lorena Edwards Meadows; magazine articles by Clara Douglas; novels by Zola Ross and B. M. Bower; even children's stories by Aileen Cleveland Higgins.[1] These works, some written in the midst of the boom and others reconstructed lovingly after the fact, some telling of first-hand experience and others drawing imaginatively from library research, suggest some important notions about how women in general saw themselves and how they perceived the quality of their lives while the West was being won.

By 1900 mining was attracting professional men—engineers, assayers, attorneys, bankers, stockbrokers—men "whose grub-stake was the college diploma" (Brown, 38). They came from San Francisco and Philadelphia, from Stanford and Yale, and they brought their wives, ladies who were equally well-educated and well-traveled. Less advantaged women obviously lived in Tonopah and Goldfield also, but since they weren't as prominent we hear little about them or from them. Probably they were too busy at the time, and then less inclined to share their experiences later. Anne Ellis's *The Life of an Ordinary Woman* is the exception, but her title indicates a point of view quite different from her contemporaries' for, on the whole, women who came to southern Nevada thought of themselves as ladies. The O.E.D. defines the late nineteenth-century "lady" as "a woman whose manners, habits, and sentiments have the refinement characteristic of the higher ranks of society," and this is precisely what Tonopah and Goldfield ladies had in mind. In fact, two of their book titles—*Lady in Boomtown* and *Tonopah Lady*—predicate that overriding concern. Being a lady was of utmost importance.

Many amenities unheard of in the previous century encouraged such a posture. Tonopah, for example, had, in its first year, a weekly newspaper, a school, and church services; by 1902 (its second year), it had a piped water supply and electricity; by 1903, automobiles; by 1904, a railroad; and by 1907 some of the fanciest homes in the state stood where, only a decade earlier, had been nothing but sagebrush and sand. *Lady in Boomtown* covers its author's life from early 1904 when she went to Tonopah as a young bride until twenty years later when she and her husband returned to California. Their first home was only a three-room cottage, but "thank goodness," she writes, it "had electric light and a telephone" (Brown, 17); that is, it was a place where she could be a lady. She reports that her mother had "insisted that no lady should ever be seen doing menial labor" (Brown, 56), but within a few days Mrs. Brown—as she always refers to herself—knows this is ludicrous in a three-room cottage in Nevada. Still, she confesses, she sent all her laundry to be done in Reno, a three-week round trip. Furthermore, despite the inappropriateness of her trousseau, of her wedding presents, and of her furnishings, she emphasizes that she would never have traded her treasures for more practical things. "Tonopah was a community of city people," she explains, "who lived in roughboard houses and walked unpaved streets, but who dressed and acted as they would in San Francisco or New York" (Brown, 37); the lady from boomtown wanted it no other way.

Her fellow Nevadans, men as well as women, concurred. The weekly newspaper, for example, heralded Mrs. Brown as "a distinct acquisition to the social circle of Tonopah, being a lady of many accomplishments." And even more proprietary is the husband's point of view narrated by Minnie Blair, who joined the desert society after her 1909 marriage to a Goldfield banker. When she wanted to watch the formal shutdown of gambling in October, 1910, "Mr. Blair was quite shocked." He went downtown alone, but found that "just about all of [her] lady friends were there." The next day, when her devout Methodist neighbor remarked on her absence, Mrs. Blair, "with great humility," had to admit that she hadn't been allowed to go "because [her] husband said it wouldn't be any place for a lady" (Blair, 30). Half a century later, though, she still could quote his comment with pride.

The significance of being a lady in Tonopah occurred to another researcher too, Zola Ross, who fictionalized early twentieth-century Nevada life in a novel she called *Tonopah Lady*. The heroine, a former vaudevillian seeking social status, marries and settles in Tonopah only to learn that her husband is both a bigamist and a fraud. "I'm going back to show business" she announces emphatically, "I'm all through pretending to be a lady" (Ross, 252). Ironically, neither a husband nor social position necessarily would have made Judith a lady; despite her theatrical career and her peculiarly unmarried state, she had always been one, as the denouement of the novel proves.

Not needing to overcome the stigma of false marriages or illegitimate children, but wanting to assure their reputations, the real-life Tonopah women found other ways to make themselves known as ladies. Their activities, quite different from what occupied the men, are central to their writing. They formed sewing circles and women's clubs, built and decorated lavish homes, but they worked hardest to bring culture to their communities and to advance worthwhile causes. Mrs. Brown proudly tells of helping to establish the Tonopah public library, and later details her Red Cross achievements during World War I. Mrs. Blair mentions her war efforts too, while further indicating an interest in women's suffrage. Sometimes the ladies gathered for strictly cultural reasons—to read Shakespeare aloud, to play the piano, to sing—but more often they filled the evenings with parties. In particular, they meshed their social life with the desert environment. For example, Mrs. Brown fondly describes a dance held three hundred feet down in a mine shaft, while Mrs. Blair rather impishly recalls decorating her home to resemble a casino when hosting a party with a gambling motif. The ladies also recount their travels; Death Valley seems to have been the favorite nearby vacation spot, while San Francisco beckoned to them from afar.

One description of a visit to that city, however, unwittingly exposes a limitation of retrospective writing: it is all too easy to remember the good and repress the bad. Mr. and Mrs. Brown were asleep in San Francisco's Palace Hotel when suddenly they were "awakened by a strange rumbling that grew louder and angrier" (Brown, 119). Glass shattered while "plaster and soot showered down," and the great 1906 earthquake had struck the city. Although Mrs. Brown narrates what happened next, she seems more concerned with saving her sewing machine and more upset by losing her layette than by witnessing the destruction of a city. Clearly, time had alleviated her horror. By comparison, she appears disproportionately unnerved by the Tonopah bank failure of 1907 when the Browns did lose a million dollars, but all on paper. Her lady friends laughed it off, her husband showed no regrets, and even she knew "the gambler's code is not to squeal when he loses" (Brown, 132). Still, she fell into a period of severe depression eased only by a rest cure at a distant ranch. So not only does the lady have a selective memory, but she indicates a remarkable ordering of her emotional priorities.

This is not the case, of course, with all pioneer women, as *The Life of an Ordinary Woman* so starkly reveals. Written, too, about twentieth-century mining camps, it describes what life was like on the other side of the tracks. Unlike Mrs. Brown, Mrs. Ellis didn't marry the man of her dreams; instead, she married men who were available. When her first husband died in a mining accident, she regretted his death chiefly because she had learned "to manage him." After a second marriage she moved to Goldfield where, in quick succession, her husband lost his job, she had a miscarriage, and her daughter died from diphtheria. Her comment about the tragic series of events is both terse and stoic: "Fate was slapping me hard, trying to knock some sort of woman into shape" (Ellis, 268). A "woman" as defined by Mrs. Ellis and a "lady" as we have defined her, although of similar pioneer stock, are not synonymous. She demonstrates the real difference between the two after her husband left her in Nevada with sick, hungry, cold children while he looked for work elsewhere. She then explains how and why she stole, not firewood and not food, but a white stone step from the local school to make a tombstone for her daughter Joy's grave. No single episode so clearly marks the gap between what an ordinary woman might do and what would never occur to a lady to do. The ordinary woman gives a different emphasis to her writing too. Neither Mrs. Brown nor Mrs. Blair share much about their children, while by contrast the reader knows Mrs. Ellis's son and daughters intimately. Children seemed the ordinary woman's unconscious means of dealing with her own mortality. The blows dealt by life could best be eased by dreaming for the future, for one's children, rather than by struggling against the present. This accounts for the importance placed upon the memorial to mark a child's grave, since only in that way could Mrs. Ellis be certain of achieving any kind of immortality, either for herself or for her family. By contrast, the ladies had many ways of making their marks—through their husbands' careers, their own charitable works, their social successes—so they had no need to display their feelings or children to their readers.

The Brown, Blair, and Ellis accounts have more in common with each other, however, than they do with the Arthur, Croft, and Meadows books. The latter three were written by women who themselves experienced none of the events they narrate but who wished to create memorials to certain men. Mrs. Meadows reconstructed her father's role as a Tonopah merchandizer in its pre-railroad days; Mrs. Arthur wrote of her husband's adventures as a prospector; while Mrs. Croft told of her husband's career as the chief assayer in Goldfield. Although these three books have women authors, they view southern Nevada through masculine eyes, and they analyze far different subjects than did the Tonopah ladies. From the men's pages the reader learns how to prospect, how to assay, how to run a business. Factual details of Nevada history are given, labor disputes examined, the Gans-Nelson fight described, and a wealth of tall tales narrated. With

such different content, one would hardly know that these three
books were written about the same boomtowns as the previous
three under discussion; obviously, pioneer men and women
thought about different things. It's not superfluous, though, to
note that a woman's book displays a masculine aura when a
man is the inspiration but retains a distinctly female air when the
source is the woman herself. In other words, the male interests
displace the female. As a corollary, there are few western accounts written by men where the female interests displace the
male.

Like most of the women's non-fiction, the Tonopah fiction
is distinctly feminine in flavor. What makes it different is the
manner in which the novelists blend imagined scenes and people
with the real. Aileen Higgins, after seeing Tonopah first-hand on
a 1906 visit, returned home to convert that reality into a fairy-
tale milieu. By contrast, Zola Ross reconstructed the town
from library research alone, and yet her account is far more
realistic than Higgins's. Carl Glasscock's 1932 publication,
Gold in Them Hills, apparently was Ross's primary source for
Tonopah Lady. His record of the southern Nevada boom—like
the Arthur, Croft, and Meadows books—reports only details
attractive to male readers. Ross takes his information and then
reworks it for a female audience, often with advantageous dramatic results. For example, in January, 1902, an epidemic hit
the men of Tonopah. Glasscock cites a number of facts about
the siege—the unseasonable heat, the black and spotted corpses,
the need for more white shirts in which to clothe the dead, the
end of the plague when fresh snow finally falls—and Ross re-
peats the identical grouping. However, she uses those facts, not
solely for historicity, but to further the characterization of the
heroine. She establishes Judith's reputation by showing her
nursing some men back to health, burying others, and inspiring
still more when she shaves the corpses. Thus she shows how a
character behaves when historical circumstances force her to
adapt, while simultaneously revealing how a lady appears to the
men around her.

A less successful borrowing from Glasscock occurs during
and just after one of the novel's climactic scenes. First Ross
adroitly mixes setting and plot so that, in the midst of a fierce
electrical storm, Judith learns her husband is a bigamist. Then,
in the scene's aftermath and for a transition on the next page,

Ross tells how "the Key Pittmans had cashed in on their amateur photography" that night by taking "a picture of Mount Brougher and the worst lightning flash," and she further describes how "the Reynolds home had been struck. . . . A bolt had melted the stove, burned a hole in the floor and blasted a hole in the earth" (Ross, 248). Glasscock had devoted three pages to the August 10, 1904 storm, to the photographs taken by the Pittmans, and to the bolt which had struck the Reynolds home and "passed into the kitchen where it melted part of an iron stove, burned a ragged hole in the floor and blasted a hole a foot deep in the earth below" (Glasscock, 131). Several sources—an oral history by Harry Atkinson in the UNR Library, for example— confirm both the storm and the Pittman photograph, but obviously Ross took her information from Glasscock, since her paragraph borders on plagiarism.

Such an offense, unfortunately only one of several, detracts from Ross's professionalism. On the positive side, she blends fact and fiction with little distortion or pedantry; but on the negative, she leans too heavily on a single source and then polishes off her story with a simplistic ending. The latter problem is characteristic of all three pieces of Tonopah fiction: since each was written primarily as an escape vehicle, each solves its dilemmas too glibly to be taken seriously. Furthermore, each moralizes so egregiously that any historical value is overshadowed. *The Parowan Bonanza*, written by B. M. Bower (pen name for Mrs. Bertha "Muzzy" Sinclair) is the worst offender. It moves from a real landscape (Goldfield) to an imaginary one (somewhere near Death Valley), leads its protagonist through a series of misfortunes that appear and disappear miraculously, and then preaches that all woes will some day vanish (if one has faith). Any factual information about prospecting for gold or about developing a mining claim gets lost in its absurdly make-believe world.

Aileen Higgins's book is as one-dimensional as Bower's, but at least she designed it for children. For our purposes, The Rainbow Lady, an imaginative recreation of Mrs. Brown, is *A Little Princess of Tonopah*'s most intriguing feature. The Rainbow Lady reminds the little princess "of ring-doves, and dew and a pink rosebud in the morning, and fringes of starlight on the water, and peacock feathers and soap bubbles in the sun—and the inside of sea-shells—and all those things" (Higgins, 82). Seen through rose-colored glasses, here is the same lady who refused to wash windows in front of the neighbors and who sent all her laundry to Reno. Mrs. Brown's own comment about the book reveals that she understood what her friend had done: "of course," she wrote, "Miss Higgins romanticized everything" (Brown, 92). What Mrs. Brown did not understand was that she had done exactly the same thing too. In fact, the Tonopah fiction sounds no less flowery than Douglas's *Sunset* magazine articles or Blair's recollections, or even Ellis's reminiscences. On every dusty street corner and behind every clump of sage, these ladies found romance. Tonopah sits wedged between treeless, barren mountains. Yet Mrs. Brown remembers "the fascination of the pastel landscape" where "under the desert moonlight the hills looked as if they had been cut out of cardboard" (Brown, 19), which is no less idealistic than "the white stretches of in-crusted alkali" that the little princess imagined "looked like silver shallows of water in ripple" (Higgins, 43). And not only did the ladies idealize, but they fantasized. Higgins, for example, extends sea imagery to the desert in her descriptions, while Brown stresses subtle and subdued tones. It is as if they were sub-conciously depending upon inappropriate details to fill voids— that is, metaphorically they were bringing water to the desert.

Actually, the Tonopah ladies did that consistently. They romanticized their existence to make life seem not only tolerable but enjoyable. Mrs. Brown remarks, "you could almost tell by looking at the brides whether they would be able to stick it out"; those who did, "were successors to that wonderful race of pioneer women who have been scattered over the West since the Western trek began" (Brown, 51-52). Since the Tonopah ladies comprised the socially elite, we cannot quite call them typical; but we can view their writing as exemplary. They reveal exactly those abilities and concerns that all women must have had as they helped civilize the west. They transcended the mundane because they valued what they were doing and they survived because they kept their dreams. Their most significant contribu-tion was an ability to see beauty that others ignored while bring-ing culture to a society that had none. Indeed, this is the contri-bution made by most pioneer women. Read in this sense, not just the Tonopah ladies' but all women's writing from the west-ward movement opens a new dimension of the pioneer experi-ence.

NOTE

[1]To make life simpler for the reader, I include here a slightly annotated, complete bibliography of the Tonopah Ladies' writing. To make life
simpler still, there will be no further footnotes; all citations will be included
in the text.

I.   Non-fiction

    A.   First-hand experience, recounted in retrospect.
        Blair, Minnie P. "Days Remembered of Folsom and Placerville,
           California; Banking and Farming in Goldfield, Tonopah, and
           Fallon, Nevada." UNR Oral History Project, 1968.
        Brown, Mrs. Hugh. *Lady in Boomtown* (New York: Ballantine
           Books, 1968).
        Ellis, Anne. *The Life of an Ordinary Woman* (Boston: Houghton
           Mifflin, 1929).

    B.   First-hand experience, magazine articles.
        Douglas, Clara E. "What Tonopah's Gold has Wrought," *Sunset,*
           16 (February 1906), 350-354.
        Douglas, Clara E. "Those Nevada Bonanzas," *Sunset,* 17 (Sep-
           tember 1906), 262-265.
        Douglas, Clara E. "The Father of Tonopah," *Sunset,* 27 (August
           1911), 165-167.

    C.   Heard from husband.
        Arthur, Zua. *Broken Hills* [The Story of Joe Arthur, Cowpunch-
           er and Prospector, Who Struck It Rich in Nevada] (New
           York: Vantage Press, 1958).
        Croft, Helen Downer. *The Downs, The Rockies—and Desert Gold*
           (Caldwell, Idaho: Caxton, 1961).

    D.   Heard from father.
        Meadows, Lorena Edwards. *A Sagebrush Heritage* [The Story of
           Ben Edwards and his Family] (San Jose, California: Harlan-

Young Press, 1973).

E. Heard from women who lived in Tonopah or Goldfield during the
    boom.
    Mitchell, Sharon. "A Pioneer Nevada Woman," unpub. mss.,
    Nevada Historical Society, n.d. [a number of these unpub-
    lished accounts are available; apparently classes have done
    interview projects and then deposited their findings in the
    historical society's archives].

II. Fiction

A. Children's story, based on author's visit to Tonopah.
    Higgins, Aileen Cleveland. *A Little Princess of Tonopah* (Phila-
    delphia: The Penn Publishing Co., 1909).

B. Novels for adults, based on author's research.
    Bower, B. M. *The Parowan Bonanza* (Boston: Little, Brown, &
    Co., 1923).
    Ross, Zola. *Tonopah Lady* (New York: Bobbs-Merrill, 1950).

AMERICAN DREAM, NIGHTMARE UNDERSIDE: DIARIES, LETTERS, AND FICTION OF WOMEN ON THE AMERICAN FRONTIER

Jeannie McKnight
Lewis and Clark College

I have lived in isolation
from other women, so much

in the mining camps, the first cities
the Great Plains winters

Most of the time, in my sex, I was alone.

—Adrienne Rich, "From an
Old House in America"

In the summer of 1887 and again in 1889, Hamlin Garland travelled to his parents' Dakota farm homestead, where he was confronted by the "ugliness, the endless drudgery and the loneliness of the farmer's lot." But what especially appalled him was seeing the grim and lonely conditions under which the farm woman, particularly his own mother, lived. "The lack of color, of charm, in the lives of the people anguished me," he wrote. "I wondered why I had never before noticed the futility of woman's life on the farm." For when he arrived home, there was his mother, "imprisoned in a small cabin on the enormous sunburnt, treeless plain, with no expectation of ever living anywhere else."[1]

No doubt this realization motivated Garland to write the stories of *Main-Travelled Roads,* to portray women as bedraggled drudges, locked into lives of hard work, isolated from the doings of the world, from their husbands, from each other. If the stories of that book reveal Garland's anguish at realizing the empty, rigidly-circumscribed lives of farm women, such as his own mother, other writers too hint at an essential truth about frontier life in general that I wish to pursue here: something in the frontier conditions themselves provoked insanity, particularly in women.[2] The landscape itself became part of those conditions—consider, for instance, Beret Hansa, in O. E. Rŏlvaag's *Giants in the Earth,* for whom the windy and brooding Great Plains were an eerie kind of hell, "some nameless abandoned region."[3]

Now, to view women *only* as victims is as hazardous as it is misleading. Some specific women responded to life on the Western frontier in different ways. Depending upon health, level of education, cultural or religious background, proximity to family, relationships, the immediate circumstances of her life, a woman might be more or less resilient to the hardships that inevitably arose. It is safe to assume that many if not most pioneer women were strong, did adapt to the harshness of homestead or farm life, and did survive the wearying loneliness that had to be endured when, say, the Great Plains winters settled in with a nasty, longlasting vengeance.

Indeed, female strength in the face of frontier adversity is legendary. Certainly one of the most remarkable accounts of such strength is revealed in Laura Ingalls Wilder's autobiographical rendering of the difficulties encountered in her early married life to Almanzo Wilder. In *The First Four Years,* we learn of the difficulties the Wilders had to face while living on their Dakota homestead: losing an infant son shortly after his birth, losing what few possessions they had in a sudden house fire, watching, for three years in a row, sudden hailstorms or grasshopper plagues wipe out their crops—only a few of their demoralizing experiences. Despite this, and despite a debilitating disease which caused Almanzo to be semi-paralyzed, Laura nevertheless chooses to help him realize his dream of farming.

> Winter was coming on, and in sight of the ruins of their comfortable little house they were making a fresh start with nothing. Their possessions would no more than balance their debts, if that. If they could find the two hundred dollars to prove up, the land would be theirs, anyway, and Manly thought he could. It would be a fight to win out in this business of farming, but strangely

she felt her spirit rising to the struggle.[4]

Yet even the optimistic Laura betrays an awareness of the other side of frontier life. In *These Happy Golden Years,* she tells of her experiences boarding with the Brewster family on their isolated land claim so that she could teach school. For no reason she can fathom, Laura finds herself at odds with Mrs. Brewster, who plainly hates everything—the Dakota prairie which she calls "this dreadful country," Mr. Brewster, and Laura herself. Driven to desperation by an unpleasant spell of frigid weather, Mrs. Brewster takes up a butcher knife in the middle of a cold night, threatening her husband. "If I can't go home one way," she threatens, "I can another." Cowering behind the thin curtain which divides her sleeping room from the Brewsters' bleak and loveless boudoir, Laura overhears what must have been a common domestic quarrel. "I won't go over that again, this time of night," Mr. Brewster responds. "I've got you and Johnny to support and nothing in the world but this claim."[5]

Mrs. Brewster's intense longing to leave the Dakota claim and return East was a familiar one. And so we can only account for her murderous but pathetically ineffective rage in terms of a kind of insanity. For if we define insanity not only as the kind of severe and enduring psychosis which would have resulted in commitment[6] in a more civilized and settled region, but also as the kind of intermittent flareups of bizarre behavior (such as Mrs. Brewster's homicidal rage), and/or the kind of feeling disturbances such as melancholia and depression so common to women's writing, then my assertion makes perfect sense. The wives of the farmers (or homesteaders or pioneers), for reasons I shall discuss later, viewed the whole frontier enterprise differently, and protested the enterprise at times in indirect as well as direct ways. Insanity was one such response.

Lillian Krueger, in an article entitled "Motherhood on the Wisconsin Frontier" (1946), sums it up, "It must have taken all the self-control the mother could muster to appear stout-hearted." When her days were busiest, nostalgia may have lost its acuteness to return with a vengeance when she snatched a moment here and there to think and feel. "And sometimes," she continues, "indulgence in the thought of her loneliness and the monotony of her Herculean struggle brought on prolonged mental illness."[7]

It is tempting to hypothesize that in Mrs. Brewster's case, such self-control one day (one very cold day) snapped, and she could no longer keep at bay all the longings and anger and conflict she doubtless expended a great deal of energy trying to suppress. (Laura describes her as listless and apathetic, depressed. How else to make sense of her depression except as her great effort to keep all her emotions held tightly in?) For who knows how hard she and others like her fought to keep feelings under control? Laura, an outsider in this situation, does not say. That Mrs. Brewster did not keep a diary is our loss in trying to comprehend female experience on the frontier.

But there is other writing to explore. For as much as life on the newly opening frontier offered families the stuff American dreams were made of, for women, as I have suggested, the dream had a nightmare underside.

This is certainly one of the themes of Rölvaag's *Giants in the Earth:* while Per Hansa, household head and empire-builder, dreams his dreams of conquering the tough prairie sod and getting rich, his wife, Beret, has nightmares about her utter loneliness in the new land.

> As her eyes darted nervously here and there, flitting from object to object and trying to pierce the purple dimness that was steadily closing in, a sense of desolation so profound settled upon her that she seemed unable to think at all. It would not do to gaze any longer at the terror out there. . . . Suddenly, for the first time, she realized the full extent of her loneliness, the dreadful nature of the fate that had overtaken her.[8]

The contrasts between male and female are vividly implied in this passage: Per Hansa has a "vision" but Beret is becoming less and less able to see at all. The dimness she experiences existentially encloses her. All she can "see" in fact is the terror, the horror of a half-envisioned life; her loneliness is more real than anything else. (As Willa Cather reminds us, in *O Pioneers!*, "A pioneer should have imagination, should be able to enjoy the idea of things more than the things themselves."[9])

Beret's insanity in *Giants in the Earth* manifests itself first as free-floating anxiety, which begins with and is exacerbated by each mile the family treads into the New Land. Of significance in Rölvaag's saga is his awareness of "the human cost of empire-building,"[10] that is, that Beret's mental breakdown is a response to her powerlessness over her fate. "I will go no farther!" she insists, as her husband and children move relentlessly westward. "I will go no farther!" For her, the prairie is an evil place, inhabited by trolls, evil spirits; but these spirits are, in reality, projections of her own "evil" and angry feelings at her fate.

> I am not the wheatfield
> nor the virgin forest
>
> I never chose this place
> yet I am of it now.
> —Adrienne Rich, "From an Old House. . ."

It is because most women did not *choose* westward migration that their attitudes differed from those of men. Economic advancement was clearly part of the frontier's lure; and because economic considerations in the nineteenth century fell to males, men had the final say in moving. This fact alone sets male experience apart from that of the female, for having freely chosen to undertake the great adventure, men were often prepared to take their lumps in a way women were not. Consequently, as Johnny Faragher and Christine Stansell so eloquently argue, men "viewed drudgery, calamity, and privation as trials along the road to prosperity, unfortunate but inevitable corollaries of the rational decision they had made."[11]

What this lack of free choice has meant in all its complexity can only be speculated on. Certainly women's writing reveals a quality of resignation, of female submission to fate. Yet sometimes resignation turned upside down; acts of rebellion often constituted this nightmare underside as well.

How else to comprehend the actions of Mrs. Brewster? How else, indeed, to make sense of the puzzling and destructive behavior of "Mrs. Marcum" which is recorded in the diary of Mrs. Elizabeth Dixon Smith Geer (1847), kept during the overland migration to Oregon:

> This morning one company moved on except one
> family. The woman got mad and would not budge, nor

let the children go. He had his cattle hitched on for three hours and coaxing her to go, but she would not stir. I told my husband the circumstance, and he and Adam Polk and Mr. Kimball went and took each one a young one and crammed them in the wagon and her husband drove off and left her sitting. She got up, took the back track and traveled out of sight. Cut across, overtook her husband. Meantime he sent his boy back to camp after a horse that he had left and when she came up her husband says, "Did you meet John?" "Yes," was the reply, "and I picked up a stone and knocked out his brains." Her husband went back to ascertain the truth, and while he was gone she set one of his wagons on fire, which was loaded with store goods. The cover burnt off and some valuable articles. He saw the flames and came running and put it out, and then mustered spunk enough to give her a good flogging. Her name is Marcum. She is Adam Polk's wife.[12]

And how else to decipher the motive for the homicide in Susan Glaspell's one-act play, "Trifles," in which a farm woman, Mrs. Wright, has apparently murdered her husband while he slept—for reasons which are not comprehensible at first? But two neighbor women, Mrs. Hale and Mrs. Peters, who arrive at the Wright house to gather some of Mrs. Wright's things, intuit the motive for the strangulation murder. By piecing together the "trifles" of Mrs. Wright's life, they find suggestive evidence for the crime. Going through Mrs. Wright's sewing basket, these women discover her beloved pet canary, wrapped up in silk fabric scraps, arrayed for burial, its neck wrung. They also discover what looks like recent sewing on a quilt, but the stitches are all awry—more evidence of domestic chaos. What gets pieced together at last is the scene surrounding the crime: Mrs. Wright, apparently having discovered the mutilation of her songbird, stitches furiously on her quilt, trying to quell her rage. But the rage is "written" in the stitchery; the neighbor women realize it and rip out the incriminating "trifle." But in the play, Glaspell's brilliant image of the dead song bird, strangled by Mr. Wright, becomes a suggestive metaphor: this destructive gesture symbolizes Mr. Wright's destruction of his wife's lively, bird-like spirit. As Mrs. Hale muses, "She used to wear pretty clothes and be lively when she was Minnie Foster, one of the town girls singing in the choir. But that—oh, that was thirty years ago."[13]

Such examples illustrate extremes of behavior; murderous impulses, insanity, homicidal actions were exceptional acts of what must have been desperate women. It would, furthermore, be misleading to conclude that such acts occurred that much more often on the frontier than today.

Yet we must view such behavior as an extreme manifestation of a much more common female ambivalence toward the whole frontier venture, toward the loneliness of that venture. "Trifles" reveals on one level a kind of classic "cabin fever" as motivation for the homicide—after all, the Wrights are cooped up on their dreary farm; they have no children; and the once-lively Minnie Foster has chosen to marry a man who curbs her natural and necessary spontaneity. Yet to me, the issue of interest is what Minnie Foster lost when she became Mrs. Wright. Not only did she lose her vitality—the real tragedy of this woman who has been driven to homicide is that she lost the society of other women. "I could've come," Mrs. Hale chides herself. "I stayed away because it weren't cheerful—and that's why I ought to have come. I—I've never liked this place. Maybe because it's down in a hollow and you don't see the road. I dunno what it is, but it's a lonesome place and always was." She continues, musing about Mr. Wright, "He was a hard man, Mrs. Peters. Just to pass the time of day with him—like a raw wind that gets to the bone."[14] That is, whether they lived on farms, on homesteads, in sod houses or log cabins, whether, in fact they "lived" for a time on the Overland Trail, women's lonely voices, speaking in many ways, are often heard as a longing to return to the familiar world of female companionship: "Most of the time, in my sex, I was alone."

In her diary of the Overland journey to California, Lavinia Honeyman Porter records her anguish at parting from that female world, in this case her "dear sister." "We were the eldest of a large family," she writes, "and the bond of affection and love that existed between us was strong indeed." She describes her final parting from her sister as an intensely painful experience that divided her loyalties and wrenched her from a familiar, loving, and safe world: "As she with the other friends turned to leave me for the ferry which was to take them back to home and civilization, I stood alone on that wild prairie," she recalls, setting up an important distinction between "home" and "civilization" and the unknown "wild prairie."

> Looking westward I saw my husband driving slowly over
> the plain; turning my face once more to the east, my
> dear sister's footsteps were fast widening the distance
> between us. For the time I knew not which way to go,
> nor whom to follow. But in a few moments I rallied my
> forces. . .and soon overtook the slowly moving oxen
> who were bearing my husband and child over the green
> prairie.[15]

What I am struck by in this diary entry is Porter's absolute conflict of loyalties, her utterly schizophrenic dilemma: "I knew not which way to go, nor whom to follow." How often did women know that feeling, of standing utterly alone on the windy brooding prairie, having to make such a difficult choice?

Even more significant, how many women, like Lavinia Porter, had to hide their grief after such painful leave-takings? One must, as Lavinia Porter knew, be cheerful, brave. But those feelings sometimes burst through the most stoic resolve. "The unbidden tears would flow in spite of my brave resolve to be the courageous and valiant frontierswoman," she confides in her diary. "I would make a brave effort to be cheerful and patient until the camp work was done. Then starting out ahead of the team and my men folks, when I thought I had gone beyond hearing distance, I would throw myself down on the unfriendly desert and give way like a child to sobs and tears, wishing myself back home with my friends and chiding myself for consenting to take this wild goose chase."[16]

Women's felt need to suppress and contain their feelings is an important issue which will be discussed later. At this point, however, I am concerned with what Lavinia Porter's diary so poignantly expresses—that is, the inescapable consequences of following a husband wherever he desired to go, at the ultimate expense of, in this case, a beloved sister. This precarious balance between gain for her family ("it is better farther on"[17]) and personal loss is a classic female dilemma. As the diary of Charlotte Pengra relates, "I felt that indeed I had left all my friends, save my husband and his brother, to journey over the dreaded Plains, without one female acquaintance even for a companion. Of course I wept and grieved about it but to no purpose."[18] But where Lavinia Porter and Charlotte Pengra were both able to pinpoint the source of their grief, Mary Richardson Walker could not. "My health at present is rather feeble," she writes in her diary. "I find it difficult to keep up a usual degree of cheerfulness. If I were to yield to inclination, I should cry half my time without knowing what for."[19]

This inability to locate the source of depression, melancholia, and grief may seem at first glance to be naive; yet Mary Walker's poignant confession reveals women's ignorance of the magnitude of their loss in the great uprooting. Frontier psychosis, melancholia, depression—all aspects of the same phenomenon —had their origin in the irreparable loss of what feminist historian Carroll Smith-Rosenberg has defined as a "female world" which existed and flourished prior to and well into the nineteenth century, in which women, "whether friends or relatives, assumed an emotional centrality in each others' lives." Essentially, Smith-Rosenberg argues, the kind of nineteenth century female friendship and support provided certain important emotional functions: "Within this secure and empathetic world women could share sorrows, anxieties, and joys, confident that other women had experienced similar emotions." Furthermore, she continues, "this was, as well, a female world in which hostility and criticism of other women were discouraged, and thus a milieu in which women could develop a sense of inner security and self-esteem."[20]

Adrienne Rich, drawing upon Smith-Rosenberg's work, concludes suggestively that female experience on the frontier was radically altered from the kind of life women had previously known. "Instead of giving birth and raising children near her mother or other female relatives," Rich speculates, "the frontier mother had no one close to her whom to share her womanly experiences." What such isolation from other women meant was that women had to, as Rich describes it, go through the "rituals of death and mourning on their own." As a result, she argues, "loneliness, unshared grief and guilt often led to prolonged melancholy or mental breakdown." And so, despite any gains they made on the frontier, women assuredly lost a great deal. "If the frontier offered some women a greater equality and independence, and the chance to break out of more traditional roles, it also, ironically, deprived many of the emotional support and intimacy of a female community; *it tore them from their mothers*."[21] (Italics mine.)

In other words, what was lost was a source of emotional stability and support of which women may not have been consciously aware when they enjoyed its benefits, but which was assuredly missed when such support was lost to them. For the first time in their lives, many women were made to feel this isolation when they found themselves up-rooted, alone, out of touch with their usual female support world, and unable to share their experiences with their husbands.

"Nobody knows what the loss of a baby means to a mother," writes homesteader Emma Just, trying to cope with a life of isolation and tragedy on the Blackfoot River, Idaho Territory. "Every minute of the day and of the night I miss her. Nels and the boys come in and look at the empty cradle with a pang, but when they go out, they forget while my loneliness is always with me."22

Emma's letters, written to her father in the late 1800's, and later collected and published by her daughter, reveal a grim reality underneath pioneer romance. "The West is so unkind to its women," she writes on one occasion. And the unkindnesses are catalogued in these remarkably explicit letters: divorce from a drunken husband, remarriage in her early twenties to a man she did not love, the burdens of raising a growing family under harsh frontier conditions, the emotional hardships of losing five infant daughters in succession, the ever-present danger of Nez Perce Indian attack, all these, compounded by loneliness and an inability to communicate to her husband, had to be endured.

But it was her problematic relationship to her husband which, according to the letters she has left us, exacerbated Emma's troubles. Upon discovering that she married a man for whom she did not "feel anything more sacred than respect," Emma took to thinking of suicide and worrying about her sanity. "My Dear Father," she writes,

> The months have passed and I have neglected you. Neglected writing to you, but O, never neglected thinking of you. Day after day thinking of you and praying that in some way your love for me will guide me aright. I have tried to write cheerfully to you, but if something should happen to me before we meet again, I should like to feel that you understood. Sometimes in the months just past

> I have felt that I might lose my mind, or even lose myself
> in the friendly river that I once feared.[23]

Many of Emma's letters reveal to what extent the spectre of insanity haunted her life; often, in fact, it seems that the despair
was more deeply felt when Emma's relationship to Nels was
particularly bad. During one of her tragic, unfulfilled pregnan-
cies, for instance, she writes of knowing, as only a woman can
know her own body, that the child she was carrying had died,
yet Nels paid little heed to her fears.

> Somehow I dragged through the weary months of summer
> but about a month before we expected the baby I realized
> that something terrible was wrong. I had not over-exer-
> cised nor over-worried but I knew that the life had gone
> from the body beneath my heart. I knew that my own
> body that had been a temple where reposed a precious
> life, had suddenly and mysteriously been transformed
> into a morgue. And oh, the grewsomeness of that cer-
> tainty![24]

When she tries to share her fears with her husband, he rebuffs
her with the reply, "Woman's imagination." But Emma, begging
him to call for a doctor, had to suffer the double pain of knowing of the child's death and knowing her own husband did not
believe her. She attempts to rationalize Nels' behavior, but does
not succeed:

> I begged him to call a doctor but he did not see any need
> of it. I guess I should not blame him for how can any one
> but a mother know what a difference there is between
> a living child, with its sensitive little muscular body re-
> sponding to her every emotion, and the leaden weight of
> a child that no longer moves. To him duty is everything
> and he strives to do his full duty but there are times
> when a little tenderness would count for so much more,
> and his indifference at this time I feel was one of the
> cruelest blows he has ever dealt me.[25]

Yet Emma's troubles began much earlier, her problems
with Nels often getting deflected onto problems of coping in
general. On one occasion, frantic over an impending (or so she
thought) Indian attack, Emma relates a fantasy of doing away

with her four boys by taking them to the river to drown rather than have them fall into savage hands. Although, in this particular instance, Emma insists on the rational logic which has prompted what appears to me to be a Medea-like plot her words betray her. "Dear Father," she writes, "Tell me father, is it a mark of insanity for one to wish to take his own life? My husband says it is, but I insist that it is perfectly sensible, so we shall expect you to cast the deciding vote. I have been on the point of killing my children and myself that we might be spared a more terrible fate, and before you agree with Nels that my mind is becoming unbalanced, I want you to know how logical it all appears to me."[26]

But her logic, flawless as she first insists it to be, has a peculiar quality; it is deadpan; it is bizarre. The only anguish betrayed is her worry that Nels has begun to question her mental balance. "He called me crazy and said he would never trust me alone again and I am not sure that I blame him. The solitude must be getting on my nerves," she writes. "I need a neighbor. I need companionship. I never seem to feel lonesome for I am always busy, but I have had too much of my own society."[27]

It doesn't take much imagination to piece together Emma's experience. Unlike many of her pioneer sisters, she does not seem constrained to paint a brave and stoic picture of herself. While it is unarguable that few women had to confront problems the magnitude of Emma Just's, nevertheless it seems to me that no matter what the circumstances, women were on the average reluctant to plumb the depth of their feelings; so much appears to have been left unsaid. This obsession with restraint must certainly have pervaded not only diary-keeping but also interpersonal relations—where Emma hid little from her father, she must have learned the painful lesson of keeping her anxieties to herself and not sharing them with Nels. This necessity to withhold, addressed by Lillian Krueger's essay, raises all sorts of speculation about a mother's relation to her children as well. How often did they become targets for her deflected anger? Where did all her held-back feelings get vented?

> *What would happen if one woman told the truth about her life?*
> *The World would split open....*
>
> (Muriel Rukeyser)

Often the need to curtail unacceptable emotions seems to have meant that a woman prevented herself from sharing her feelings with her husband, a fact which could not possibly have enhanced intimacy and closeness. Thus Mollie Dorsey Sanford writes, "I am ashamed to be so homesick. Of course I do not *say* all that I inscribe here. This is my 'confidence.' I try to be cheerful for By's sake, for fear he might think I wasn't happy with him. He hasn't the family ties that I have and cannot understand."[28]

One way to make sense of this restraint is to realize the extent to which, in the nineteenth century, female conduct was highly and tightly circumscribed. Female norms for conduct depended in large part upon standards set by husbands; these, in turn, reflected societal standards. It is in fact quite likely that Mollie had read William Alcott's book, *The Young Wife,* which prided itself on its norms of conduct for wives. Even if she had not read Alcott, however, Mollie would have absorbed his conduct by virtue of subscribing to nineteenth century mores: "By her union with her husband," Alcott's book maintains, "by becoming bone of his bone and flesh of his flesh according to the divine intention—she promised to follow his destiny—to rejoice when he should rejoice—and to weep when he should weep."[29]

What then, did it mean to a woman who found herself the wife of a man who did not weep, did not rejoice? How frankly would such a woman record emotions which ran counter to those her husband deemed unacceptable? This question has broad implications for female identity in general, which space does not permit me to explore in depth here. Nevertheless, a woman who found herself in the position of having to negate real feelings because they ran counter to what was expected of her, must have been a woman who could not trust her own feelings. Indeed, I am often struck by the extent to which these diaries reveal women to be at war with themselves; I sense a forcefulness used at times to suppress "undesirable" feelings—feelings which Mollie Sanford in one instance judges as "wrong and useless."

Here's Mollie, recording in her journal, in what is for her rather atypical flowery prose, her despair over such recurrent bouts with homesickness. "I do not feel entirely amiable today," she notes.

> My heart has been like a turbulent stream, whose waters rush on in querulous motion. My little bark dashes out on the turbid waves today. It should have moored in a quiet harbor. I sit listlessly with dripping oars, and heed not its wayward direction. Over the dark river I see the bright sunshine I can behold but not reach! Must I thus recklessly dash along without one effort to make the brighter side? Must I remain in the shadow when I might reach the sunshine? Rouse, faint heart. Does not everything of beauty beckon me ashore?
>
> There! My effort has saved me. I leave the troubled waters behind. I know how wrong and useless it is to feel blue. Well for me it is, my good angel lifts me out of these momentary fits of despondency. I guess I get too tired, or too something. Why don't I hear from home?[30]

What I am intrigued by in this particular entry is Mollie's indirection and evasiveness. If Mollie harbors unacceptable wishes to give in to the turbid waves, she seems to have to try to disguise them from herself. Her understandable desire to abandon the struggle against despondency emerges as metaphor: "I sit listlessly with dripping oars," she writes. I am tired of rowing. But if I don't row, what horrible things will sweep me away? *Despair would.* So Mollie musters up all the energy she has and "saves" herself, or at least believes that by writing in her journal she has summoned the "good angel" which keeps her from drowning.

This particular journal entry of Mollie's raises other issues as well: what "effort" of Mollie's saved her? At what cost to her psychological health did Mollie so repress her real feelings—in this case, of homesickness ("Why don't I hear from home?")—that even she believed them to be eliminated? And if she could not be entirely truthful in her "little Journal," then where could she express the truth about her life?

Even when she records the death of her first-born child in infancy, Mollie omits and suppresses. "This was my first great grief," she writes of its death. "We dare not murmur at our loss, altho a great disappointment, for *my* life was spared. As soon as I was able I came to Dora [Mollie's sister], where I now am. By has returned to the mountains."[31] That Mollie and By dared not indulge in excessive grief after the infant's death makes sense philosophically—the "count your blessings" ethic became a way of dealing with the cruelties of frontier life. Yet to not murmur or grieve openly makes bad psychological sense. How much longer did the process of mourning last if it were constantly suppressed?

If Mollie had Dora to turn to in her grief, how much did she suppress even then? For it is tempting to speculate that the severe toothaches and swollen jaws she describes as plaguing her after the death of her child were triggered by unresolved emotion. Mollie's own experience is lost to us because she shuns exploring her feelings; suffice it to say that the depth of Mollie's grief is suggested by its omission. Mollie reveals a lot by concealing: neither the infant's name, sex, or the circumstances of its death are revealed in her journal.

Who knows how much was tempered, denied, or in the case of published writing, edited altogether from women's works? In Mollie's case we know she recopied her journal with the intention of bequeathing it to her grandson. "I trust what is worthy of emulation he may profit by," she writes in the introduction. "It is of more value to me than it could possibly be to my children, but I desire that it shall be kept in the family and treasured as a relic of by-gone days, not from any especial merit it possesses, but because I do not want to be forgotten."[3 2]

With such motives, that her journal bear witness to her life, it is entirely feasible that Mollie herself edited what she might have considered unworthy of emulation. But Mollie destroyed the original; her life remains in some respects a tantalizing mystery as a result.

Despite Mollie's sins of omission, despite her cautious restraint at looking too closely at her bad feelings, her journal, too, is in many ways testimony to the pervasive battle which needed to be fought against despondency and homesickness. During the summer and early fall of 1860, during the first year of her marriage to Byron Sanford, and during the first years away from her family, Mollie's journal entries, restrained though they are, reveal her to be grief-stricken and hopelessly homesick. As she writes, for instance, in August, "I am in a room alone, and believe I feel more sad and homesick than ever before in my life. . . .I believe one reason of my homesickness is that I do not hear from home. They must have written, but our mails come every way, or *any* way. 'Little Book!' do you think I'm naughty? *Do* you suppose I'm morbid? I have a horror of either."[33]

Essentially, I read Mollie's fear in this entry, as in other similar entries, that she might not be in touch with reality: "naughty" and "morbid" in this context seem to be euphemisms for "not in my right mind."

Of course, what Mollie meant exactly only she knew; in this context it seems she is addressing her perennial problem of not having the "right" feelings. More noticeable, however, is her relating to her journal as something separate from herself: her "Little Book" fulfills what must have been an intense longing to have someone with whom to communicate. "Little Book" can at least hear Mollie, although it can't talk back.

The need to be heard, acknowledged; the need to share emotional burdens and joys; the need to be supported, to establish self-esteem; the need to come to terms with this new and isolated, utterly changed life was for women during the frontier era a terrible need. For while men and women alike were uprooted from the familiar, women, whose needs and expectations differed, had different burdens to bear. For even the most optimistic and highspirited, under the best of circumstances (Mollie, we remember, was in love with Byron Sanford; no doubt their good relationship made things easier for her), the frontier presented a gap, a great discontinuity in the way of doing things, a transformation which we are now only beginning, by examining what women have written, to understand.

> What would happen if one woman told the truth about
>   her life?
> The world would split open
>   —Muriel Rukeyser, "Kathe Kollwitz"

NOTES

[1]Hamlin Garland, *Main-Travelled Roads* (New York: Harper, 1930), p. vi, in foreword.

[2]Hamlin Garland, *Other Main Travelled Roads* (New York: Harper, n.d. [copyright 1892]), p. 102. See G. J. Barker-Benfield, *The Horrors of the Half-Known Life: Male Attitudes Toward Women and Sexuality in Nineteenth Century America* (New York: Harper and Row, 1976), p. 6.

[3]O. E. Rölvaag, *Giants in the Earth,* trans. Lincoln Concord and O. E. Rölvaag (New York: Harper and Row, 1955), p. 37.

[4]Laura Ingalls Wilder, *The First Four Years* (New York: Harper and Row, 1971), p. 133.

[5]*These Happy Golden Years* (New York: Harper and Row, 1971), pp. 65-66.

[6]Given the prevalent nineteenth century disease model of mental illness, I think it unlikely that a diagnosis of "insanity" would have assisted in its treatment. For a comprehensive discussion of the subject of women in nineteenth century medicine, see Barbara Ehrenreich and Dierdre English, *Complaints and Disorders: The Sexual Politics of Sickness* (New York: The Feminist Press, 1973). See also Barker-Benfield, *op. cit.*

[7]See Lillian Krueger, "Motherhood on the Wisconsin Frontier," *Wisconsin Magazine of History,* Vol. 29, No. 3, 1946, p. 239.

[8]*Giants,* p. 38.

[9]Willa Cather, *O Pioneers!* (New York: Houghton-Mifflin, 1913), p. 48.

[10]See Lincoln Concord's introduction to *Giants,* p. xi. "Rölvaag is preoccupied with the human cost of empire building, rather than with its

glamour and romance," he asserts.

11Johnny Faragher and Christine Stansell, "Women and their Families on the Overland Trail to California and Oregon, 1842-1867," *Feminist Studies,* Vol. 2, No. 2/3, 1975, p. 151. Faragher and Stansell's article discusses in depth the kinds of changes in life-style, the alteration in woman's culture, that took place on the overland trail. Unlike many writers on the subject, Faragher and Stansell do not romanticize woman's life; theirs is feminist scholarship of the highest quality.

12"Elizabeth Dixon Smith Geer, Diary." *Transactions of the Oregon Pioneer Association,* 1907, p. 165. I am indebted to Amy Kesselman for bringing this quotation to my attention.

13Susan Glaspell, *Plays* (Boston: Small, Maynard & Co., 1920). "Trifles" was first performed in 1916.

14Glaspell, pp. 21-22.

15Lavinia Honeyman Porter, *By Ox Team to California: A Narrative of Crossing the Plains in 1860* (Oakland, California: author, 1910), p. 7. Cited in Faragher and Stansell, p. 153.

16Porter, p. 41.

17Laura Ingalls Wilder, in *The First Four Years* (New York: Harper and Row, 1971), relays the "Creed of [her] pioneer forefathers, that 'it is better farther on.' " See p. 134.

18Charlotte Emily Pengra, "Diary of Mrs. Byron J. Pengra" (unpublished typescript in Lane County Historical Society, Eugene, Oregon, n.d.). Cited in Faragher and Stansell, p. 160.

19"The Diary of Mary Richardson Walker, June 10-December 21, 1838." Edited by Rufus A. Coleman, *Sources of Northwest History,* No. 15 (Missoula: University of Montana), p. 3.

20See Carroll Smith-Rosenberg, "The Female World of Love and Ritual: Relations Between Women in Nineteenth Century America," *Signs,* Vol. 1, No. 1, pp. 14-15.

21Adrienne Rich, *Of Woman Born* (New York: Norton, 1976), p. 234. What Rich's wording implies here is a new way of looking at this female uprooting and its subsequent emotional toll on women; that is, what is suggested is the kind of anxiety and mental breakdown psychoanalyst John Bowlby defines as "separation anxiety"—the three-stage pattern of *protest, despair* and *detachment* which occurs in infants and children when they are "torn" from their mothers. Certainly, what Smith-Rosenberg's research points to is a new way to understand the complex pattern of grief, despair, rebellion and insanity, which I describe. See John Bowlby, *Attachment and Loss,* Vols. I and II (New York: Basic Books), 1973.

[22]Emma Just's letters, collected and published by her daughter, Agnes Just Reid, under the title *Letters of Long Ago* (Caldwell, Idaho: Caxton Printers, 1932) are unfortunately out of print. These letters are indeed testimony to pioneer strength and endurance, a reminder of the incredible hardships the pioneer/homesteader had to face. I am especially grateful to my colleague, William Ramsey, for bringing these letters, part of his family's private collection, to my attention.

[23]Undated letter, p. 29.

[24]Letter of December 12, 1882, p. 83.

[25]*Ibid.,* pp. 83-84.

[26]Letter of September 14, 1887, p. 45.

[27]*Ibid.,* p. 48.

[28]*Mollie: The Journal of Mollie Dorsey Sanford in Nebraska and Colorado Territories, 1857-1866* (Lincoln, Nebraska: University of Nebraska Press, 1959), p. 145.

[29]William A. Alcott, *The Young Wife of Duties in the Marriage Relation* (Boston: George Light, 1837. Reprinted, New York: Arne Press and New York Times, 1972). Cited in Amy Kesselman, *Diaries and Reminiscences of Women on the Oregon Trail: A Study in Consciousness.* Unpublished Master's Thesis, 1974.

[30]*Mollie,* p. 143.

[31]*Mollie,* p. 157.

[32]*Mollie,* Introduction to *Journal.*

[33]*Mollie*, p. 139.

HOMESTEAD HOME

Elinor Lenz
University of California at Los Angeles

An April day in 1909. A stagecoach is traveling over roads rutted by spring rains from the railroad station in Utah to a ranch in Burnt Fork, Wyoming. Jouncing along on the stage are three passengers: Elinore Pruitt, a buxom, energetic young woman recently widowed, on her way from Denver to a job as a house-keeper for a cattle rancher; her two-year old daughter, Jerrine; and Clyde Stewart, her new employer who had come to fetch her at the station and who, as Elinore recounts it, let out a "hoot" every time the stage struck a rock or rut "until I began to wish we would come to a hollow tree or a hole in the ground so he could go in with the rest of the owls."

The evanescent moment is caught and preserved, like a butterfly in amber, in *Letters of a Woman Homesteader*,[1] written over a span of five years by Elinore Stewart to her former em-ployer, Juliet Coney. A revealing account of homesteading during the early years of the century, the letters sketch a portrait of a woman bountifully provided with vitality, joie de vivre and love of adventure together with an apparently unlimited capacity for hard work. "I have done most of my cooking at night," she remarks offhandedly, "have milked seven cows every day and have done all the haycutting, so you see, I have been work-ing."

Elinore belongs to that breed of women whose roots go deep into the frontier and whose role in the winning of the West was a quiet one—nothing to tempt TV writers looking for blood and thunder and derring-do—but it provided the stuff of daily living and shaped the values that continue to permeate the Western consciousness. Born in the Indian Territory of Okla-homa, one of six children who were orphaned when the parents died within a year of each other, she learned in her early years that her survival kit had better include keenness with rod and rifle and the ability to improvise in the face of scarcity and danger. It was a childhood that was lived on intimate terms with woods and fields and animals and that took its strength from a sense of family closeness. When relatives offered to share the parentless children among them, "we refused to be raised on the halves and so arranged to stay at Grandmother's and keep together."

From this experience, Elinore acquired a largely do-it-yourself education which made no concessions to her tender years or female gender. "We had no money to hire men to do our work . . .consequently, I learned to do many things which girls more fortunately situated don't even know have to be done." Of formal schooling there was none at all. "I never went to a public school a day in my life," she writes, "there was no such thing in the Indian Territory part of Oklahoma where we lived, so I have had to try hard to keep learning." It was learning in true frontier style, somewhat short on the classics and other refinements, but it gave a solid underpinning to the many difficult and precarious times of her life.

Poverty and tragedy were, in fact, twin companions of her young years. She married and bore a child but the home and family of her own that seemed to offer a way out of loneliness and dependency were snatched away when her husband was killed in a railroad accident and she was left penniless with an infant to support. In Denver, where she went to find work, she hired out as a housekeeper and laundress—she refers to herself as a "washlady"—and it was during this time that she met Juliet Coney who employed her as a part-time domestic. But while her arms were immersed in grimy soapsuds, she dreamed her dreams—and they carried her far beyond the snug domestic existence which was considered the only appropriate aim for women in her situation at the time.

"I wanted to knock about foot-loose and free to see life as a gypsy sees it," she confesses in one of her letters. "I had planned to see the Cliff-Dwellers home; to live right there until I caught the spirit of the surroundings enough to live over their lives in imagination anyway. I had planned to see the old missions and to go to Alaska; to hunt in Canada. I even dreamed of

Honolulu. Life stretched before me one long happy jaunt. I aimed to see all the world I could, but to travel unknown by-paths to do it.

"But first," she adds, "I wanted to try homesteading." She saw homesteading as an escape from the oppressive confines of urban poverty and, though hardly an early advocate for women's rights, she recognized that here was an opportunity for women to expand their possibilities. "I am very enthusiastic about women homesteading. It really requires less strength and labor to raise plenty to satisfy a large family than it does to go out and wash, with the added satisfaction of knowing that their job will not be lost to them if they care to keep it."

But while she dreamed of homesteading and traveling over unknown bypaths, her practical side was at work, and she decided to prepare for a civil service examination in the hope of improving her prospects. Her tutor was a clergyman, Reverend Father Corrigan, who became the galvanizing force that propelled Elinore out of her washtubs toward her cherished goal of 160 acres and independence. It all happened, as she relates it, when she developed a severe pain in her side as a result of carrying a heavy load of coal to the furnace in the nursing school where she worked as a housekeeper. Arriving for her lesson, the pain gnawing at her nerves, she was "so blue that I could hardly speak without weeping, so I told the Reverend Father how tired I was of the rattle and bang, of the glare and the soot, the smells and the hurry. I told him what I longed for was the sweet, free open and that I would like to homestead."

Father Corrigan urged her to put an ad in the Sunday paper, which promptly yielded results in the form of a visit from a Wyoming rancher, Scotsman Clyde Stewart. He had been spending a few days in Boulder and, seeing Elinore's ad, had come to interview her for a job as housekeeper. The reserved Scotsman and the vivacious young widow must have hit it off quickly, or so subsequent events would suggest. In any case, it took her very little time to "size him up" and accept his offer.

Life at the ranch in Burnt Fork lived up to all of Elinore's expectations from the beginning. She describes her situation as "very comfortable" and Mr. Stewart as "absolutely no trouble for as soon as he has his meals he retires to his room and plays

on his bagpipe, only he calls it his 'bugpeep.' It is 'The Campbells Are Coming' without variations at invervals all day long and
from seven till eleven at night. Sometimes I wish they would
make haste and get here."

Instead, sometime during the next few weeks, the arrival of
the Campbells was indefinitely postponed as the rancher and his
housekeeper discovered a growing pleasure in each other's company. Six weeks after Elinore's arrival, they were married in a
makeshift ceremony that had to be "chinked in" between planting oats and other early spring chores. "Ranch work seemed to
require that we be married first and do our sparking afterward,"
Elinore remarks and, admitting to some embarrassment about the
hasty nuptials, she is quick to add, "I have no cause to repent.
That is fortunate since I have never had one bit of leisure to repent in."

The transition from housekeeper to housewife made very
little change in the essential Elinore. There is always, like a
bright thread running through the letters, her irrepressible sense
of fun. "I am a firm believer in laughter. I am real supersititous
about it. I think if Bad Luck came along, he would take to his
heels if someone laughed right loudly." And there is her ability
to impale her fellow creatures on the sharp points of her deadly
accurate observations, yet without this twenty-twenty vision
detracting in the slightest from her fondness for most of the
people who came her way. "Mr. Lane is a powerful good husband," she writes of a neighbor whose wife bore twin girls during
a November blizzard while coming across the overland trail. "He
waited two whole days for his wife to gain strength before he re-
sumed the journey, and on the third morning he actually carried
her to the wagon. Just think of it! Could more be asked of any
man?"

Throughout these chatty accounts of the friends, neighbors
and happenings that make up her new world, she vividly evokes
Wyoming ranch life, with its hardships and isolation, but also its
rich neighborliness, family warmth and enjoyment of nature in
all its aspects. "Everything, even the barrenness, was beautiful,"
she writes of a winter just ending. "We have had frosts, and the
quaking aspens were a trembling field of gold as far up the stream
as we could see. . . . We could see the silvery gold of the willows,
the russet and bronze of the currants, and patches of cheerful

green showed where the pines were. The splendor was relieved
by a background of sober gray-green hills, but even on them gay
streaks and patches of yellow showed where rabbit-brush grew."

There are reports of rituals and celebrations, of visiting and
gossiping and lending a hand, of the pleasures of garden and
children and cooking up great feasts for friends and ranch hands.
Preparing a Christmas dinner for twenty-four sheepherders, "We
roasted geese, boiled three small hams and three hens. We had
besides several meat loaves and links of sausage. We had twelve
large loaves of the best rye bread; a small tub of doughnuts;
twelve coffee-cakes, more to be called fruitcakes, and also a
quantity of little cakes with seeds, nuts, and fruit in them—so
pretty to look at and so good to taste. I had thirteen pounds
of butter and six pint jars of jelly, so we melted the jelly and
poured it into twelve glasses." Her comment on this culinary
feat: "I never worked so hard in my life or had a pleasanter
time."

These descriptions of the events and preoccupations of
ranch life convey a clear sense of the way women like Elinore
were able to make a warm and familiar world out of an essentially hostile terrain, where harsh climate and vast distances between
ranches and towns wore down the endurance of many homesteading families. "We are sixty miles from the railroad," Elinore
writes. "When we want anything we send by the mailcarrier for
it, only there is nothing to get."

The Homesteading Act of 1862 required settlers to live on
their claims for five years in order to complete their titles, or
"prove out," but there were families who abandoned their
claims within the first year rather than face the loneliness and
the cruel climate. ("There are three seasons here," Elinore com-
ments, "winter, and July and August.") Mental breakdowns
occurred among some who stayed on, and the drudgery, the relentless consuming struggle to wrest a living out of 160 acres of
stubborn soil had provided the raw material for innumerable
homesteading sagas.

None of these trials or discouragements, of which the
Stewarts had their fair share, was able to diminish Elinore's
exuberant enjoyment of the life around her. Nor did she ever
abandon her determination to homestead on her own. "I should

not have married if Clyde had not promised I should meet all my land difficulties unaided. I wanted the fun and the experience. For that reason I want to earn every cent that goes into my own land and improvements myself." Her house joined on to the Stewart house and her boundary lines ran within two feet of the ranch. . .an arrangement she resisted at first, for fear it might jeopardize the "separate but equal" status she wanted to establish for herself, but "I see the wisdom of it now," her practical side concedes.

What she was attempting would certainly have deterred anyone with less than superhuman energy and motivation. In addition to her full range of duties on the Stewart ranch, which took in running the household, mothering a growing family and helping with the chores, she developed and operated her neighboring claim, doing the plowing, planting, irrigating and cultivating almost entirely by herself.

Her newly cleared land now yielded an abundance of vegetables, berries and fruits. She freely indulged her urge to experiment, with often gratifying results. "I have experimented and found a kind of squash that can be raised here. . . . They told me when I came that I could not even raise common beans, but I tried and succeeded. . . . I found that I could make catchup, as delicious as that of tomatoes, of gooseberries."

In carrying out the herculean tasks she had set for herself, she was responding to a profound inner need to "prove out" not only on her land, but on herself, on her desire for an identity of her own—and, beyond that, as a woman showing the way to other women. "Any woman who can stand her own company, can see the beauty of a sunset, loves growing things, and is willing to put in as much time at careful labor as she does over the washtub, will certainly succeed; will have independence, plenty to eat all the time, and a home of her own in the end." Yet, she admits that "temperament has much to do with success in any undertaking, and persons afraid of coyotes and work and loneliness had better let ranching alone."

Since she was addressing her remarks primarily to single women, those who were trapped in urban poverty, as she had been, for whom homesteading offered, as she saw it, a secure future, she was careful to point out how little assistance she had received or, rather, accepted from her husband. But Clyde Stewart's understanding and support of his wife's activities offer a variant view of the familiar picture of frontier family life in which the woman was confined to kitchen, children and chickens while the man took on the more arduous and demanding tasks of the farm. Elinore's sparse and somewhat reticent references to her husband reveal him as shrewd and good-humored, a family man who took pride in his wife's accomplishments. The reluctance to say more about him than she does Elinore attributes to her fear that, in talking about him, she might appear to brag.

It was a marriage in which there was much affectionate give-and-take and sharing of work and responsibility. From the beginning, Elinore had demonstrated that she was not to be influenced by prevailing attitudes that labeled some activities "man's work." One time, shortly after she had taken up her duties as housekeeper, Clyde found himself in need of a man to run the mowing machine. Since it was haying time, help was scarce, and while Stewart was off searching for an available ranch hand, Elinore went down to the barn, took out the horses and set to work mowing. "I had enough cut before he got back," she writes, "to show him I knew how, and as he came back manless, he was delighted as well as surprised." So delighted and surprised, in fact, that he paid her the compliment of admitting she had "almost as much sense as a mon," "an honor," says Elinore in her dry, teasing way, "I never aspired to even in my wildest dreams."

One can't help wondering whether it was this incident that quickened the Scotch rancher's pulses and put thoughts of matrimony in his head. Certainly, it must have given him a clear inkling of this young woman's yard-wide streak of independence . . .independence that coexisted in Elinore with an equally strong impulse toward something else that has had a less definable place in Western psyche—"the sense of community." The people from diverse and unrelated cultures and backgrounds brought together by the development of the West were linked less by their beliefs and traditions, as Daniel Boorstin points out, than by common effort and experience, by the events of their daily lives and their way of thinking about themselves. But these linking threads were fragile and the conditions of life, of economics and geography, tended toward separation rather than cohesion.

The particular function that women like Elinore performed was a knitting together of the disparate human strands, a slow and intangible weaving process that created a sense of belonging among loners, misfits and people who were simply homesick and longed for the society of others but lacked the ways and means of achieving it. For this role, Elinore's temperament was perfectly suited. She enjoyed people, and she had a gift for offstage managing that, by her own admission, could only be characterized as meddling.

There was, for example, "the charming adventure" with Zebulon Pike, a kinsman of Pike of Pikes Peak fame. Elinore entered his life during a severe blizzard, the kind that comes up suddenly and swiftly in Wyoming, often trapping unwary campers. It was round-up time, and with the men gone, Elinore decided to go off with Jerrine on a camping trip in the mountains. They were about forty miles from home and settled snugly in a rocky crevice when the snow began falling and continued steadily, "big as dollars," through the night.

In the early morning, with the snow showing no signs of abating, they started down the trackless mountainside, Jerrine perched on Jeems, the packhorse. As the horse stumbled along, Elinore searched for signs of life, but it was hours later, with darkness gathering and her usual fortitude beginning to be shaken, before she spied a trickle of smoke and heard the baying of hounds. They had come to a small log house in a clearing "and I knew by the chimney and the hounds that it was the home of a Southerner. A little old man came bustling out, chewing his tobacco so fast and almost frantic about his suspenders, which it seemed he couldn't get adjusted."

When he had determined that Elinore was neither a spy for the game warden, checking up on the deer he had killed, nor a competitor for the gold mine he had discovered, he invited her to take shelter in his cabin. "How I enjoyed it all!" reports Elinore. "He had a big, open fireplace with backlogs and andirons. We feasted on some of the deer killed 'yisteddy' and real cornpone baked in a skillet on the hearth. He spread down a buffalo robe and two bearskins before the fire for Jerrine and me. . . . I spread blankets over them and put a sleepy, happy little girl to bed. . . ."

In the morning, Zebbie introduced his guests to the glory of a sunrise in the Wyoming mountains: "fancy to yourself a big jewel-box of dark green velvet lined with silver chiffon, the snow peak lying like an immense opal in its center and over all the amber light of a new day."

Zebulon Pike now became a friend of the Stewart family; and when Elinore learned that, though he longed to visit his home in Arkansas, he never heard from his family and never wrote to them—"I am not an eddicated man"—she indulged in a little of her well-intentioned meddling. A letter was dispatched to Mrs. Carter, Zebbie's sister. "I told her all I could about her brother and how seldom he left his mountain home. I asked her to write him all she could in one letter, as the trips between our place and his were so few and far between." As a result, Zebbie received an invitation to spend Christmas with his family in Yell County, Arkansas, a culmination that prompted Elinore to count herself a very lucky woman "in finding really lovely people and having really happy experiences. Good things are constantly happening to me."

Her penchant for rearranging human affairs included an occasional fling at matchmaking that would have done credit to Thornton Wilder's Dolly Levi. The daughter of neighboring ranchers, "not pretty but clean and honest," Gale Lane by name, was visiting the Stewarts at her parents' request while her sister, Sedalia, made preparations for her wedding. Elinore developed a fondness for Gale which contrasted sharply with her feeling for Sedalia—"vain, selfish, shallow and conceited."

One evening, while Gale was at the post office, a Mr. Patterson rode up and went into the bunkhouse to wait until the men would return from the range. "Now, from something Gale had said," Elinore writes, "I fancied that Bob Patterson must be the right man. . .and while I had been given to understand that Patterson was the man Sedalia expected to marry, I didn't think any man would choose her if he could get Gale, so I called him. We had a long chat and he told me frankly he wanted Gale, but that she didn't care for him, and that they kept throwing that 'danged Sedalia' at him."

Within two weeks, Elinore is sewing a wedding dress for Gale and there is a huge feast to celebrate the happy event, climaxed by a sleigh ride in the moonlight through the pine-clad Uintah Mountains.

Her strong feeling for the social bond invests even the death of the first child born to her and Clyde, a boy named Jamie, with communal significance. "I could not bear to let our baby leave the world without leaving any message to a community that sadly needed it. . . . His message to us had been love, so I selected a chapter from John and we had a funeral service at which all our neighbors for thirty miles around were present."

In time, two more children are born, and the letters continue to radiate with pleasure in family and home and satisfaction in her homesteading achievements. "I set out to prove that a woman could ranch if she wanted to. . . . I have tried every kind of work this ranch affords, and I can do any of it. Of course I am extra strong, but those who try know that strength and knowledge come with doing. I just love to experiment, to work and to prove out things, so that ranch life and 'roughing it' just suit me."

Like many other women whose names are not to be found in the history books, she made a small but significant imprint on a particular time and place. And in her letters, she has left a legacy which preserves the living reality of a vanished Western past.

NOTE

[1]*Letters of a Woman Homesteader* was published by Houghton Mifflin Co. in 1914 and reprinted by University of Nebraska Press in 1961.

MARI SANDOZ AND WESTERN BIOGRAPHY

Helen Stauffer
Kearney State College

In her long and prolific career, Mari Sandoz wrote short stories, novels, recollections, articles, essays, juvenile novellas, and histories, always set in the West. Her reputation rests most securely on her nonfiction. Of these, the best representation of her Western point of view are her three biographies, *Old Jules* (1935), *Crazy Horse* (1942), and *Cheyenne Autumn* (1953).

Old Jules, the first to be written, and her first published book, encompasses the period between the 1880s and the 1930s, during the settling of northwest Nebraska. The protagonist is, as the title indicates, Jules Sandoz, a young man of twenty-six at the beginning of the book, running as far away from his problems in his native Switzerland as his money will take him. His money takes him to the sandhills country on the Niobrara River in northwestern Nebraska, south of the present towns of Hay Springs and Rushville; he remains near this vicinity the rest of his life. The book carries us through his turbulent adventures as he becomes an important developer and promoter of the land, until the time of his death in 1928. But the author's purpose encompasses more than the life of her father, as she says in her foreword: "*Old Jules* is the biography of my father, Jules Ami Sandoz: I have also tried in a larger sense to make it the biography of a community, the upper Niobrara country in western Nebraska."[1]

Crazy Horse: The Strange Man of the Oglalas is the life of the man often considered to be the greatest war chief the Sioux ever produced, the young man who rose to leadership after the first encounter of his tribe with the U. S. Army over the Mormon cow killing (the Grattan affair) in 1854 and continued that leadership to the end of the buffalo and his tribe's surrender in

1877.[2] Crazy Horse attracted the author's attention because of his leadership abilities, personal qualities, and tragic death, but she saw him as representing more than just himself. He lived in the nineteenth century, on the plains of the United States, and was an Indian war chief, but his life had in it all the archetypal elements of the classical hero: he was exceptional both in appearance and actions, he had dreams and visions, he was called upon for unusual sacrifice, he led his people well, and he was betrayed and killed. To this day, his people venerate him as someone set apart. In addition, one of the author's purposes was to show what happens when greed causes men to desire something a minority owns—she presents a concrete example of a smaller group who had something the majority wanted, in this case land, especially the Black Hills and their precious metals. The Indians, unprotected by anyone outside, suffered the lot of such minorities anywhere in the world. She called this book a part of her study of man's inhumanity to man.

Cheyenne Autumn, her third biography, traces the lives of Dull Knife and Little Wolf, two "old man" counselor chiefs of the Cheyenne Indian tribe who led their people on an incredible fifteen-hundred-mile journey from Indian Territory (now Oklahoma) back toward their old homeland in Montana, near the Yellowstone River, in the winter of 1878-79. The two chiefs led their little band of about two-hundred-eighty, including only eighty-three fighting men between the ages of thirteen and eighty, back to the North, pursued at times by as many as twelve thousand U. S. Army troops ordered to return the Cheyennes to the hated Oklahoma reservation, where they had been dying from malaria and starvation. The Indians eluded capture until they separated near Fort Robinson, Nebraska. One group followed Little Wolf to eventual safety in the North; the others, under Dull Knife, surrendered to the soldiers and were sent to Fort Robinson, to incarceration, and, for many, to death. Sandoz's book, while portraying the lives of the two Indian chiefs, also illustrates the epic heroism of a people whom the government persecuted and betrayed; she details through the lives of the chiefs and the members of their band what has happened to the Indians of the Plains, "the destruction of a whole way of life and the expropriation of a race from a region of 350,000,000 acres" by the whites.[3]

Although *Crazy Horse* was published seven years after *Old*

Jules, and *Cheyenne Autumn* eleven years after that—a span of eighteen years—the three are remarkably consistent in demonstrating the author's aesthetic treatment of historical facts, indicating her moral values, and revealing her affinity to the Western mythos.

Paul Murray Kendall (*The Art of Biography,* New York: W. W. Norton and Co., 1965), points out that biography is a peculiar genre, lying uneasily between historical writing and belles lettres, "somewhat disdainfully claimed by both." Although it is related to history in that it uses historical facts for its base, it is literature in that the writer must use his imagination and art to create from these facts a believable world for his readers. The three necessary ingredients according to Sir Harold Nicolson (*The Development of English Biography,* London: Hogarth Press, 1959) are history, the individual, and literature. In addition, some insist that biography must do more than create a man and his time; the reader should be able to find a moral lesson by observing the successes or failures in the lives of the great. If one accepts Kendall's definition of biography as "the delicate adjustment between evidence and interpretation" (p. 17), if one expects of it, as André Maurois does, "the scrupulosity of science and the enchantments of art,"[4] it is important to look at Sandoz's use of science—historic fact—as she fused science and imagination to fulfill the biographer's mission, "to perpetuate a man as he was in the days he lived."[5] Sandoz was by nature and training eminently qualified for this kind of writing: she was a meticulous researcher, with access to unique sources, and, as are all good biographers, she was a gossip. Furthermore, as a teacher, an excellent one, she was a moralist. Her purpose in these three biographies is more than simply to present the lives of great men; she wishes to recreate the life of the past as these men knew it, and indicates her strong sympathy for those who are destroyed by the great forces of history.

Sandoz pursued the facts of history diligently through research and interviews. Because she believed no historian has an accurate memory she sought corroboration or authenticity from many sources. Even for *Old Jules* she spent years gathering information, though she herself had been present for many events. The quantity and quality of her research is a major factor in her work. Her material, indexed on thousands of 3x5 cards, came from hundreds of printed sources, from the vast stores of archival material in regional and federal repositories, from scattered private accumulations, and from many personal interviews. In addition she had a large and original collection of maps. From the time she was a tiny child, looking at the maps her father kept for the homeseekers he located in northwest Nebraska, she had been fascinated with them. Many she drew herself, taking them with her on location when she explored the regions she wrote of. Whenever possible she included a map in her books. To her, place was important. She needed to understand it visually and physically.

Her sources went far beyond her written records. Certainly as important were the old storytellers she heard as a child. As she points out in the foreword to *Old Jules* (p. vii), the frontier was a land of storytellers, "and in this respect remains frontier in nature until the last original settler is gone." She spoke repeatedly of having heard such raconteurs as they swapped stories with her father in the smoky kitchen of their farm home, she a silent little listener: "I lived in a storyteller region—all the old traders, the old French trappers, all the old characters who had been around the Black Hills. . .told grand stories of their travels and experiences. . . . The Indians were wonderful storytellers. Many a night I sat in the wood box and listened."[6] She heard her first version of the Plains historical events from them, from the Indians, the half-breeds, traders, government men, and from her father.

These oral tales, heard when she was young enough to absorb them unselfconsciously, gave her a unique insight into the views of those who stopped to "yarn" with her father, for she was thus "inside" their cultures, she understood their allusions, their points of reference. This gave her a sense of authority, for she could judge the accuracy of the various storytellers, could recognize why they told the tales they did in the manner they did. As Richard M. Dorson remarks (in *American Folklore and the Historian*), "A knowledge of the folklore properties of oral tradition can enable the historian—especially the local historian—to separate fiction from fact."[7] Crucially important to her sense of herself as a teller of tales was her belief in the spoken word, both as it was used by the tale spinners she heard as a child and by the Indians and others she interviewed as an adult. (It was also a determinative factor in her style, in the narrower sense of the term. It affected her use of dialogue and contributed to her use of metaphor and other figures of speech characteristic of the storyteller.)

Vital and exclusive information came from Sandoz's interviews "in the field" beginning with a 1930 trip to the Rosebud and Pine Ridge Reservations with her friend, Eleanor Hinman, visiting the aged survivors of the Indian Wars. It was on this trip that the women learned important history not to be found in written records. They recognized that these ancient survivors, He Dog, Short Bull, Little Killer, Red Feather, and White Calf, so soon to be gone, were eye-witnesses to events of the past that whites were not even aware of. They learned a great deal first-hand about the lives of such leaders as Red Cloud, Spotted Tail, and Crazy Horse not known to historians; they learned what the Indians themselves thought about those responsible for events at Fort Robinson that caused the death of Crazy Horse. They also began the process of identifying the complex relationship of various Indian families, tracing the matrilinear lines, the name-giving of various individuals, and the aunt-sister-cousin relationships which eventually resulted in Sioux and Cheyenne genealogical charts Sandoz claimed to be more complete than any other in the world. It was this kinship-loyalty that accounted for several consequential actions of the time. Sandoz learned, for instance, of Crazy Horse's love for Black Buffalo Woman, a woman from Red Cloud's politically ambitious family, and its importance to later events—his injury, his loss of honors, his betrayal, and finally his defeat and death.

Another valuable source was the Ricker Collection at the Nebraska State Historical Society, where Sandoz worked for several years, containing over 200 interviews made by Judge Ricker, of Chadron, Nebraska, with survivors of the Indian Wars, early reservation life, the Ghost Dance, Wounded Knee massacre, etc., notes sometimes so detailed she could later incorporate them into her books almost verbatim. *Crazy Horse,* she said, could not have been written without those pencil tablets.

The truth she sought so diligently, the raw facts of history, was the material out of which she formed her art. The fact that so much information came from such exclusive initial material makes it difficult for those who wish to check her sources. Footnotes and bibliographies in the orthodox sense are not used much in the biographies. To those not grounded in the Great

Plains *gestalt* her worth as a historian might be in doubt, but it is the very uniqueness of her sources and the fidelity to the material she alone had that are the bases for the integrity of her writing.

On one point almost all biographers agree. Kendall, Johnson, Nicolson, Origo, and others stress that the best biographer creates a simulation of the life of his subject by establishing a living bond with him. The best biography is written by one who actually knew his subject, as Boswell knew Johnson. The next-best is written by one who can imagine himself an onlooker and participant in the life he writes of: "The simulation of the life grows out of a liaison with the subject self-consciously cultivated by the biographer as the *primum mobile* of his enterprise" (Kendall, p. 148). Sandoz's works fit well within the standards set by modern biographers who are agreed that a good life-writer must form an empathy with his subject in order to create a simulation of his life. Objectivity and detachment are necessary, but the total impartiality desirable in a historian would show a lack of feeling in a biographer. André Maurois points out the author's obligation to his subject: "The one thing essential is that beneath an objective surface there should be that vivid emotion which gives the book an intensity, a burning passion, which a book written in cold blood can never have."[8] From this aspect of biography, Mari Sandoz is well qualified. She is the daughter of Old Jules and actually appears as Marie, one of the characters in that book; and although she did not know any of the three Indian heroes of her books she did know their friends and relatives and some of the participants in the action she describes, and she had grown up on the very land they had lived in. She knew her characters and their place and time intimately, and thus she presents them to us.

While the author must develop a living bond between himself and his subject, he must at the same time maintain enough detachment, enough distance, to present this life with some perspective, so that events are not too terrible or overwhelming for the reader to contemplate. Sandoz achieves this difficult balance through a dual view in *Old Jules;* she accomplishes this remarkable psychological feat by referring to herself in the third person and by divesting the author of any emotional attachment to characters in the book. Although the reader is told in the foreword that the author is the small girl in the story, nothing in the text itself gives this away. She speaks of a hunting scene, for instance: "Often Jules took the two eldest, seven and eight, small, twin-like, to trail noiselessly behind him when he went on a hunt. . . . When the gun was silent they ran to retrieve the game. . .crushing the backs of the brittle [bird] skulls between their teeth as they had seen Jules do" (*OJ* p. 284). The eight-year-old was Mari. In another, earlier scene, Jules has just proposed marriage to Mary: "She watched the man across the table. He seemed old to her twenty-eight years, graying, nearing forty. His restless hands annoyed her, and the foot he moved a great deal. . . . And sometimes his eyes were pleading as those of an unhappy dog, almost brown, and lost, hungry. Unfortunately Mary didn't like dogs" (*OJ* p. 186). Sandoz is speaking of the two who would later become her parents.

The two Indian books are presented from the Indian point of view, yet because Sandoz uses an external approach, what she calls "over the shoulder" or "front row center," rather than that of an omniscient author, she keeps the reader some distance from her characters. The reader usually knows only what the Indians know, but he is aware that this is not autobiography. In *Crazy Horse,* the hero addresses his followers, " 'These soldiers of the Great Father do not seem to be men like you. . . . They have no homes anywhere, no wives but the pay-woman, no sons that they can know. . . .' " (*CH,* p. 315). And again, "Sometimes it was days before visiting warriors saw the man they had come to follow, for often Crazy Horse kept far from the noise and the drumming, perhaps making a fast, hoping for a vision or a dream to tell him what must be done" (*CH,* p. 312). Furthermore, because Sandoz simulates the language and customs of another race, there is further distance between reader and actor.

Biography presents special problems for the writer in both philosophy and aesthetics, in determining what facts one may present and how they are to be presented. One point of difficulty is the artist's use of "imaginative fill-in." All biographers agree that at some point they simply have no alternative but to use imagination to recreate a situation as it must have been; a certain event is known to have happened, but no documentary proof exists for it. Some writers choose to move as quickly past these events as possible, giving whatever documentary evidence is available. Others "leap" through uncharted history in other ways. Sandoz chose to use dramatic, literary technique, rather than to present a documentary, relying on such devices as direct dialogue and specific action, although not with the license or uncontrolled imagination some critics claim.   Her characters engage in interior monologues or direct conversations she probably could not always prove to have taken place verbatim. However, she was using her material in a way many authorities have accepted, when used properly, from the time of Aristotle: as mythic or poetic truth fused to scientific or historical truth. Sandoz herself spoke of things "that are truer than fact."[9]   But while she felt one could dramatize history, she did not feel he could invent it.   She was adamant that truth is essential to non-fiction, and that the writer must know the difference between reality and his own imagination.

The specifically Western characteristics of Sandoz's biographies reflect the world-view of one imbued with the mythos of the West.   As with other Western writers, Sandoz's close identification with nature and the land is evidenced throughout her books.   One critic said of her love of nature, "Piety is classical and honorable and rare.   Its nature makes her yearn for the old lost golden age of man living atune to nature."[10]   A sense of the physical aspects of the Plains is crucial throughout her work. Listed with the rest of the characters in *Old Jules*, for instance, is "The Region: The upper Niobrara country—and hard-land table, the river, and the hills."   For Sandoz, the Plains are a part of the story which can be said to be a character in her works.   The Plains and the force of nature as manifested through the cycle of years form the unity and activating force in almost all her works.[11]

The land was also her tie with history, for on the Sandoz homestead and nearby were places sacred to the past. East of the house was Indian Hill, where ashes from old signal fires still lay, and near it the spot where the burial scaffold of Conquering Bear, the Sioux Indian treaty chief, killed in 1854, had been. She often played on the hill, finding Indian artifacts, arrows and beads, and when she learned the story of Crazy Horse she envisioned his living at this very place as a boy. "Certain it was that the young Oglala had often walked this favorite camping ground of his people, perhaps thrown plums at the pretty girl for whom the great warrior would one day risk everything he knew of this earth" (*CH,* p. viii). Working within this Western worldview, Sandoz followed mythic tradition and archetypal patterns. She saw the sandhills of Nebraska as a "Jötunheim," an "almost mythical land"; again, she referred to herself as "Antaeus-footed." The mysticism of the Plains Indians attracted her because of its relationship to nature and to the universal. In fact, Sandoz's mythic vision was predominantly that of the Indian rather than that of the white man of "manifest destiny." If she subscribed to the concept of a "new Eden," it would be from the point of view that the white man was the serpent who corrupted the paradise of the Indian.

She sees her heroes as vital forces, often larger-than-life, performing on a vast landscape—actually an epic view which, I believe, is shared by most Western writers. Epic has been defined as, "by common consent a narrative of some length that deals with events which have a certain grandeur and importance and come from a life of action, especially of violent action such as war. It gives a special pleasure because its events and persons enhance our belief in the world of human achievement and in the dignity and nobility of man."[12] Although this definition by C. M. Bowra was meant to apply to Homer, Virgil, and other classical writers, most of the points noted could also apply to both Sandoz's writing and her understanding of life. The Jules she writes of, for instance, is a dirty old man, but he is also a tattered Aeneas, a visionary, settling his people in a new and hostile land, often performing truly heroic feats: killing a monstrous bear; surviving the terrible fall down a sixty-five foot well and the resultant crippling; stunning a courtroom by defending himself in a torrent of four languages; bringing beauty and fertility to a marginal region with his experiments in fruits and crops. The Indians, too, attempting to preserve their culture and their people against aggression, bring innumerable classical images to mind: the Cheyenne, Tall Bull, escaping in the battle of Summit Springs, returning to certain death in order to protect and be with his wife and child; the great warrior Roman Nose, whose magic was broken at the Beecher Island fight, but who rode into battle anyway, knowing he would die; Little Hawk, the brother of Crazy Horse, killed in a fight with the whites while his brother lay sulking in his tent; Woman's Dress, the spy and liar; Spotted Tail and Red Cloud, the men of power, the latter to live surely as long as Nestor; Frank Grouard, the ungrateful guest who repaid his hosts' hospitality with deceit; Little Big Man, who held his friend Crazy Horse's arms while the white soldier stabbed him; Black Buffalo Woman, another man's wife whom Crazy Horse loved—and if you don't believe a war could be fought for a beautiful woman, reread this episode. The Cheyenne chiefs, leading their people home, inevitably recall the biblical exodus, but Little Wolf's feats recall something also of the fabulous Odysseus; Dull Knife reiterates the sorrows of Priam, mourning over his people and his family, his beautiful sons and daughters killed. Sandoz speaks of the Cheyenne fight as "the epic story of the American Indian, and one of the epics of our history" (*CA,* p. vii).

The heroic characteristic of Sandoz's protagonists, the sense of doom for the Indian heroes, the classic battles of man against Fate are apparent. Crazy Horse fits most obviously into the pattern. He is, by Aristotle's definition, a great man and leader, better than most but not perfect, who is caught in a web of circumstances for which there is no right solution. There is no way out. If he had not been killed, his white captors planned to send him to Dry Tortugas, Florida, a banishment that would have been as painful as death to a man who valued freedom in his own land above everything. Sandoz knew the ancient Greek concept of tragedy, including its assertion that the function of tragedy is to purify emotion.[13] The death scene of Crazy Horse is one of the most moving in literature.

Sandoz's use of myth in the biographies, however, is not that of presenting legendary or imaginary adventures in literary form, but rather that of a historian, in the manner defined by Dorson: "The historian cannot 'collect' or record the secular myth of a nation-state, for it exists in no one place or document, but permeates the culture; he must piece it together from a thousand scattered sources, and render it explicitly."[14] It is in this sense that she uses the concepts of myth, symbol, and image, but it is this view that some misunderstand, for they assume that the mythic is opposed to scientific truth, whereas Mari Sandoz, I believe, saw myth as a universal truth or equivalent to truth, not competitive with scientific (historical) truth. Her sense of the mythic was the means by which she presented her creative historical vision, an accepted and necessary aspect of the art of biography according to Kendall, Maurois, and others.[15] The old concept that myth cannot be true may still affect some critics' thinking, with the result that they undervalue Sandoz's work as genuine or authentic history. It seems that the blending of mythic attitude and historical fact is somewhat rare and therefore difficult.

An epic writer is almost forced to point a moral. Bowra states: "Their heroes are examples of what men ought to be or types of human destiny whose very mistakes must be marked and remembered." He further points out that the didactic intention is always there—perhaps not explicitly, perhaps discreetly, but it is there.[16] Sandoz was always aware of this aspect of her writing. In her biographies her message is clear. In *Old Jules* it is the idea that a new country is settled and made habitable by the law-abiding, the steady worker, rather than the outlaw. And in the Indian books it is the loss the white civilization has inflicted upon itself because of its discrimination, her belief that America can never be what it could have been, that it will always carry on its conscience the sin of what it did to the Indians.

Sandoz's perception of the epic quality of Plains history and culture is shared by other writers, historians, anthropologists and philosophers who have noted that nineteenth-century events on the Plains are similar to heroic events in the classics; one writer calls this history "pan-human." John G. Neihardt calls his *Cycle of the West* an American epic because of the heroic deeds it portrays; Hartley Burr Alexander, too, notes the similarity in his preface to *The World's Rim:*

> Indeed, the most direct approach to pre-Hellenic thought may be directly through the study of the forming speculation which the Indian rituals reveal. There is something that is universal in men's modes of thinking, such that, as they move onward in their courses, they repeat in kind if not in instance an identical experience.[17]

Comparisons are made most often to the Greeks because they are most well known, but the similarities exist in the Bible, or tales of Gilgamesh, Cu Chulainn, Beowulf, Siegfried, as well. Charles Brill often referred to the Indian warriors as "red knights,"[18] and George Bird Grinnell spoke of the *gaudium certaminis,* the pure joy of battle, in their society.[19] The epic qualities are obvious to many.

Indeed, Sandoz's understanding and use of myth accords with that of Western realists, as described by Max Westbrook in "Conservative, Liberal, and Western: Three Modes of American

Realism."[20]   He points out that Western writers are concerned about the sacred unity of life. Since this is the major theme of Plains Indian religion, it is to be expected that Sandoz would agree. She often describes both rituals and beliefs with admiration: "The old Cheyennes, even more than their High Plains neighbors, had a rich and mystical perception of all life as a continuous, all-encompassing eventual flow, and of man's complete oneness with this diffused and eternal stream" (*CA,* p. vii).

She would agree with Westbrook too, in the importance of the unconscious, accepting Jung's concept that the archetypes of race memory are inherited by all and that the unconscious, the intuitive, is primary, that conscious reason is unrealistic, "a bifurcation of the human soul." Her Indian heroes direct their lives in response to their dreams and visions. While communication with the unconscious is less obvious with Old Jules, the fact that he survived his many vicissitudes may well be due to his strong intuitive sense of what was right for him, and his following that sense, no matter what happened to himself or others.

Westbrook makes a further point, that for the Western realist determinism and belief in the human spirit can live side by side. This is a paradox that exists in the oldest Greek myths of Oedipus, Phaedra, or Orestes. Sandoz's biographies reveal a similar philosophy. The Cheyenne at Fort Robinson under Dull Knife are defeated by forces they cannot hope to control, but they continue their struggle, knowing they cannot win but fighting because their own integrity, their sense of their own worth as a people, requires it. Crazy Horse is fatally wounded through treachery, malice, and the jealousy of others, but his last words to his father are, "I am bad hurt. Tell the people it is no use to depend on me any more now—" (*CH,* p. 413). Although it would seem all his power has been taken from him, he himself relinquishes it.

Jules's fate, too, came both from the impersonal and from human imperfections. He could not control the elements, but his biographer saw that he was his own most serious enemy: "But in Jules, as in every man, there lurks something ready to destroy the finest in him as the frosts of earth destroy her flowers" (*OJ,* p. 46).

Sandoz's view of life was remarkably consistent throughout

her writing career. She saw man as "larger than life," a creature who could occasionally display nobility. As Walton points out (p. 312), all three of her biographies show men as victims of greed and exploitation but they refuse to be shattered under the blows of fate; she leaves her reader with an affirmative view of man. On her particular landscape, the trans-Missouri basin, certain memorable men appeared from time to time. Her subjects are significant not only because of their own individual qualities as human beings, but because they exhibit in their particular lives universal qualities. Their conflicts are interesting as they respond or react to the force of history as it occurs for them on the Great Plains, as one culture is superseded by another. Some are caught by forces too large for them to control—by a government gigantic and relentless and sometimes apparently mindless. Some earn their fate is controlled by men too small for their responsibilities, too ignorant, or too greedy to value human life. And some fight back. These things have been going on since long before the ancients told of them, and we see them today. The theme of man and his Fate is timeless.

Just as important from the point of view of biography, in *Old Jules, Crazy Horse,* and *Cheyenne Autumn,* Sandoz has combined the "living past" (in terms of an accurate and fascinating picture of the time) with the "living character." She has succeeded in making the human figures compelling on any level by bringing the historical facts into the field of art through the use of her creative imagination. The fact that she knew intimately the protagonists and the landscape on which they struggled makes her work particularly important. Sandoz knew, as does John R. Milton that, "because the area is still young, its writers have the opportunity of taking a position between the Indian and the white man, between primitivism and civilization, between the land and the city, and so on, and examining within a unique time-space complex the essential spiritual problem of a god-like animal."[21] Sandoz hoped to match her subject matter with her art. In these three books she succeeded.

NOTES

[1]Mari Sandoz, *Old Jules* (Boston: Little, Brown, 1935), p. vii. All further references will be to this edition.

[2]—, *Crazy Horse* (New York: Alfred A. Knopf, 1942). All further references will be to this edition.

[3]—, *Cheyenne Autumn* (New York: Avon Books, 1969), pp. v-vi. All further references will be to this edition.

[4]André Maurois, *Aspects of Biography* (Trans. Sydney Castle Roberts. New York: Appleton and Co., 1929), p. 204.

[5]Kendall, p. x.

[6]Mari Sandoz, *Hostiles and Friendlies* (Lincoln: University of Nebraska Press, 1959), pp. xv-xvi.

[7](Chicago: University of Chicago Press, 1971), p. 138.

[8]Maurois, p. 117.

[9]Nebraska Educational Television, "Mari Sandoz Looks at the Old West," Series April-May, 1959.

[10]Robert Knoll, *Nebraska History,* June, 1962, pp. 131-132.

[11]Kathleen O'Donnell Walton, unpublished dissertation, "Mari Sandoz: An Initial Critical Appraisal," University of Delaware, 1970.

[12]C. M. Bowra, *From Virgil to Milton* (London: MacMillan, 1961), p. 1.

[13]University of Nebraska Archives, letter to Mrs. Robert Kryger, March 21, 1939, for example. Sandoz noted that the Greeks saw the

wisdom of tragedy on their stage; from the performances the populace went away happier, rather than saddened. Sandoz studied Ancient History under the classical scholar John Rice at the University and also read classical literature on her own. The Greek concept of tragedy and its katharsis, probably first brought to her attention when she was a mature adult, may well underlie all her writing: many of her works deal with tragedy, the darker side of man, or the grotesque (note "Pieces of a Quilt," "Smart Man with Hogs," "Dumb Cattle," and "The Vine").

[14]Dorson, p. 134.

[15]Sandoz suggested John G. Neihardt as a reviewer of *Crazy Horse*, for example, "because he is a mystic," thus he would be empathetic toward Crazy Horse, who was also a visionary.

[16]Bowra, p. 13, 16.

[17](Lincoln: University of Nebraska Press, 1953), p. xvi.

[18]*Conquest of the Southern Plains* (Oklahoma City: Saga, 1938).

[19]*The Fighting Cheyenne* (Norman: University of Oklahoma Press, 1915, 1956), p. 12.

[20]*South Dakota Review*, Summer, 1966, reprinted in *Literature of the American West*, ed. J. Golden Taylor (Boston: Houghton Mifflin, 1971), pp. 9-22.

[21]John R. Milton. "The Western Attitude: Walter Van Tilburg Clark," *Critique*, II, 3 (1959), 58-59.

WOMEN POETS AND THE "NORTHWEST SCHOOL"

Carol Jane Bangs
Port Townsend, Washington

Two years ago I was on the editorial staff of a literary maga-zine that was planning to publish a special issue devoted to Northwest poets. The poetry editor had asked a number of interested writers to suggest names of poets from whom we might want to solicit work. There were over thirty names on the list; only two names were those of women poets. Yet, when sub-missions for that issue began to pour in, over half the poems sub-mitted were by women.

Soon after this I was involved in a class on "Literature of the Northwest," where students read poems by William Stafford, Richard Hugo, Gary Snyder, and other Northwest poets whose work is commonly available in anthologies and texts. After several class meetings a group of students approached me one day to ask, "Aren't there any *women* poets in the Northwest?" I was familiar with many names but, aside from a few small press publications and limited regional journals, I could not direct students to readily available works by women poets. Further investigation convinced me that available bibliographies of north-west writers are either hopelessly outdated or unprofessionally quixotic. The one recent bibliography of secondary materials I could find[1] listed only one living woman poet from the North-west, and she, Carolyn Kizer, has not lived in this area for years. One could argue, perhaps, that the Northwest has not produced a woman writer of the stature of Stafford or Hugo, but the works I consulted listed many younger poets who have not as yet re-ceived wide national recognition and whose work has never been shown to be superior to that of their female peers. Why, I began to wonder, are the women poets in the Northwest so invisible?

The answer, I have come to believe, lies in the persistent

interest of critics in the historical west, along with a corresponding neglect of more contemporary manifestations of regionalism
in poetry being written in the area. Most attempts to define a
"Northwest School" of poetry have been founded on thematic
similarities among male writers in the region and have attempted
to link these common themes with those often found in the
"Western" novel. Unfortunately, the "Western" novel is almost
entirely dominated by a mythos that is aggressively masculine,
the realm of the cowboy, logger, and trapper. As Gary Snyder
recently described it,

> Out of this society came a great American legend,
> with its own heroic style. It was a male world. Men
> without women, men who had left both mother and
> father behind and were starting from scratch, with noth-
> ing but what they could carry on their backs. The irre-
> sponsibility of it is seen in its exploitation of land and
> people. The charm of it is seen in its adventure and
> humor, in the songs and stories of the cowboy. The
> American West produced one of the great myths of the
> world. Its influence is everywhere: a macho-heroic-Anglo
> image. In Japan youths wear tight imitations of Levis,
> ride around on motorcycles the way cowboys ride horses.
> You can hardly go anywhere people have not seen a cow-
> boy movie.

> This history, this experience of the West, is the con-
> text of my life. Out of it people like myself apparently
> have emerged to become poets of the American West.[2]

This West, Snyder asserts, is a mythic construct. And it is
for the male poets, not just the Gary Snyders but the Joaquin
Millers as well, that this myth of the West can function as a context for poetry. That women poets have been able to see
through this myth, able to see the unmentioned women giving
birth to all those cowboys and mountainmen, we need only turn
to the poems of Gwendolyn Haste, who, on a Montana ranch in
the 1920's, wrote about the West not as an Eden or as a testing
ground for heroes, but as acres of woods, rocks, and sagebrush,
where a woman's life was not made of brave adventures but of
endless toil and privation. .The truth of life in the real West is
captured in her "Montana Wives" sequence, of which this is the
last poem:

Exotic

Her frightened soul shrank
When she saw
The bitter crumbling hills of shale.
And the high cutbank
Gashed and raw,
Struck her eyes like the wall of a jail.

The years ran by
Indifferent
And she never grew used to unfenced land,
Nor dust blown high,
Nor scrub pines bent
In the midst of shuffling wastes of sand.

When she was old
Her voice was sour
And her eyes were as hard as small black beads.
Her mouth was cold
And twisted and dour
For her soul had withered like last year's weeds.[3]

If one were to seek a thematic similarity among modern women poets based on the real western experience, rather than the myth of that experience, one would expect to find many more such expressions of frustration and futility. But one does not. Few, if any, women poets in the Northwest have chosen to follow in Haste's footsteps. And she is not considered part of the "Northwest School."

Last summer, at a Northwest writers' conference attended by over a hundred poets, I asked a number of the participants the following questions: Do you think there is a Northwest "School" of poetry? If so, what characterizes the work of poets in this "school"? Of the men I asked I received many suggestions in response to the second question: A belief in the regenerative powers of nature; a love of the wilderness; a "Frontier" attitude; interest in Native American cultures (on the part of non-Indian poets); use of local place names. Not one answered the first question negatively. Of the women I asked, not one answered positively. The only thing to be said about the Northwest, they told me, was that writers here were friendlier, more like neighbors, than writers in the East and Midwest. It is interesting that this was exactly the response of Carolyn Kizer who, as far as I can tell, originated the term "Northwest School" in an article for the *New Republic* a number of years ago.[4] She was responding to the unusual sense of camaraderie shared by writers in the Seattle area in the mid-fifties.

Kizer did not really attempt to prove a regional *content* to the poetry of the writers she mentions. Rather, she noted the increase in poetic *activity* around the Seattle area, stimulated by the presence of Theodore Roethke and the encouragement of the University of Washington Department of English. What she described was not so much a "School" as a social club, a community of writers bound not by similarities of theme or technique, but by the fact that they shared a love of poetry and a dedication to its craft.

Kizer also pointed out one of the difficulties in evaluating or even discussing Northwest poetry—the almost impossible chore of regional definition among a group of chronically transient writers. Of the poets Kizer singled out for mention, only one, David Wagoner, still lives in the Northwest. The answer to this difficulty, as I see it, is to deal with the contemporary poetry of the region. If there is a "School" of Northwest poetry it should be evident in the work of poets living and writing in the Northwest today.

Reading the work of such established poets as William Stafford, Richard Hugo, and John Haines, one is indeed struck by the number of references to Northwest places and local characters, the influence of Native American traditions, the presence of the wilderness and "nature untamed." But these writers are such distinct individuals one would hesitate to suggest that they are part of some larger regional movement. But these themes are even more readily evident in the work of many younger, less well known writers, such as William Pitt Root, Henry Carlile, Primus St. John, and Duane Niatum. In fact, there seems to be almost an inverse relationship between the reputation of the poet and the importance of such themes in his work. The so-called Northwest themes are most evident in the work of young poets who have not yet published full sized collections, many of whom are students or recent graduates of regional MFA programs. It would seem that those male poets I questioned at the writers' conference had some justification for citing certain themes as typical of Northwest poetry. But why, then, did the women at the conference not agree? Why were they so skeptical of the idea of a "Northwest School"? One has only to turn to the work of women poets in the northwest to find the answer. In the poetry of Beth Bentley, Tess Gallagher, Sandra McPherson, Joan Stone, Joan Swift, Olga Broumas, Vi Gale, Leslie Silko, Madeleine DeFrees, Gwen Head, Eve Triem, Ingrid Wendt, and many others, one finds far fewer place names, far less transposed anthropology, far less pseudo-Indian lore, far less geography and nature sketching than in the poetry of their male counterparts. They do not fit the profile of the "Northwest School" as the male poets defined it. But is this to say that their poetry is not regional? I think not.

Writing in 1933, B. A. Botkin described four types of artistic approaches to regionalism, the Localist, Naturist, Traditionalist, and Culturist.[5] As Rufus Coleman explains these terms,

> The localist [is] concerned chiefly in collection and description, [and] finds his roots in a particular locality; the naturist [has] roots in land and folk, and assumes at times mystical attitudes; the traditionalist, represented by the Southern agrarian interested in a usable past, lays his roots in personal heritage; the culturist, concerned in shaping life as well as literature, but in accordance with interrelated literature, seeks expression in interregional writing, "the combination and culmination of locality, folk, and tradition."[6]

It seems to me that most thematic descriptions of "Northwest poetry" have been based on one or more of the first three types of regional response described here. In particular, they have stressed the elements of folk and tradition, with the latter usually so narrowly defined as to exclude the feminine contributions to local and personal history. At their worst these definitions have, like Snyder's, combined the elements of local familiarity, nature lore, and local tradition to create a definition of Northwest regionalism more true to the fictional world of the pulp novels than to the region as we know it and our grandmothers knew it.

This western mythos makes no place for woman as a creative artist, and the modern women poets in the Northwest know this. This is why they reject the notion of a "Northwest School," preferring to avoid a link with a critical idea based on a myth they know to be false. But it is my contention that this rejection of limited concepts of regionalism has, in fact, given women poets in the Northwest a regional attitude corresponding to Botkin's fourth category, the Culturist, "concerned in shaping life as well as literature." My study of the poetry of women in the Northwest leads me to believe that many of them have indeed found a kind of regional expression that enables them to make use of the local, the folk, and the traditional, and to use these responses in integrated expressions that reach beyond the region to strike much louder chords. By this I do not mean to imply that all male poets hold narrow perspectives, but merely to suggest that the women poets with whose work I am acquainted are, in general, more ambitious than their male counterparts in their pursuit of larger themes, themes less easily categorized as "merely" regional.

One of the best poems I know that illustrates this tendency of women poets in the northwest to look for wider significance even in superficially local subjects is a poem that deals with the role of the external place in the experience of the artist. The poem is Beth Bentley's "Changing a Diaper on Chuckanut Drive":

> We are enclosed by a ring of shadowy cones
> spattered with white.
> Far below, the sand flat's silver glaze
> reflects, a plate
> of no-color, sun already gone.
> The sheer layer
> is sprinkled with dark sandpipers as with seed,
> a random smear.
> Guttural queries creak across the bay;
> all else is mute.
> Receding in a secrecy of blue
> are islands, remote
> as animals; slumbrous, elongated
> ovals, oblongs
> uncertainly outlined, their edges washed gray.
>   (continued, new stanza)

To select then
only the inhuman is the temptation here:
an ideal scene,
the beautiful abstracts unfurled like a peacock's tail
to shimmering grandeur,
the unfragmented sum of all its parts.
Do I take the lure?
I lean down, out, over what can only be
immediate danger,
craving that wholeness. The cold wind urges;
I give ear;
until, temporal, I am recalled by a human cry,
an exact request,
unsparing. I do not linger; but, salute
the ambient Ghost.[7]

Nature, in this poem, is abstract, pure, quiet, whole, but it is not human. The poet, "temporal," does not hesitate to weight the relative pull of natural perfection against the all-too-human need that calls her from the view. She acknowledges the attraction of the scene, but she is also acutely aware of the danger; entering that "ideal scene" of "beautiful abstracts" is never really an option. The Ghost is saluted, not heeded. The natural world, then, is not allowed to become larger than the human, nor is it seen as a source of knowledge or redemption. It is, rather, a temptation, a suggestion that the rather messy realities of human existence could be abandoned for a state of clean, pure, abstract "wholeness." But the poet, though leaning out dangerously far, never leans beyond earshot of that human cry.

Art, too, is abstract, pure, and whole. In another sense this poem stands for the stance of the culturist, "more concerned with life than with literature." Beth Bentley's poems are almost all explorations of basic human experiences. Nature, the external world, is seldom important in itself. Its importance is always relative to its human significance, as in the poem "Wilderness Area" where the individual first accepts the wilderness on its terms and then reasserts her self, her existence in its midst: "You are in the wilderness./You calibrate its messages, all skin, like a plant./Until awareness itself ebbs, and will sends down/its roots; and root strikes heart."[8]

This focus on human values, on human experience in the

natural world, is evident in the work of many women poets in
the Northwest. Sandra McPherson has been building a national
reputation for poetry which combines sophisticated wit with
deep sensitivity and an original style. When she uses a local
scene or story it is seldom the real subject of the poem, but exists
as either a vehicle for the expression of personal philosophy or
as a setting for human drama. The poem "In the Columbia River
Gorge, After a Death" is a good example of this use of regional
materials:

These only wait—

Red apples, thronged
Mouths, whole dumb
Choirs of them—

Tall cliffs, blue,
Shadowy,
Haughty chins.

They are the fathers
Of their own
Feet.

Wading below,
Taking forever
To be carved.

And then
What can they expect?
This is patient country.

Like the river, I should leave here.
I should be home in sorrow with you.
Yet this landscape

Shows me
How he died, how he became suddenly
No more man

But that unseizable
Cleaving
Edge the patient expect.

Even my child,
That first blood shed,
Awake in the hospital nursery,

Born and more
Herself than she will ever be,
Lives only at the mercy

Of cloud and cliff-edge,
Under that weathercock mercy
My little waterfall.

When I come too close,
Earth shuts up its tongues,
But I hear what it means

In the idling motor, in the note
Child-held until the breath runs out,
In the unwinding

Music of the spawning fish,
Playing against the current
Into some longsuffering water.

Land, if I take you
Into my fist,
There

You'll stay, longer than I can hold you,
So patient you are,
Waiting

At the end of the breadline
For your loaf
Of ash,

Of flesh.[9]

   I quote this poem in full because it repeatedly makes use
of the contrasts between things of nature, which are incomprehensible, and human things, which can be comprehended, "the
idling motor," the voice of a child, and, to a degree, the effect of
a death on the still-living. The scenery in this poem, as in Bent-

ley's "Chuckanut Drive," is pure, silent, eternal, providing the contrast to the temporal, not so perfect world of human experience. What the poet learns from nature is not a lesson about the natural world, but a lesson about herself. Nature does not provide renewal. At the best it teaches lessons we'd rather not have to learn.

In McPherson's poems the land is usually alien, something to be seen through a window, from an airplane, or to be read about in someone else's book. In the poem "Trout"[10] it is her husband who goes fishing, while she stays home in a living room painted to mimic the garden outside. The plants she writes about are usually edible; the places are inhabited. It is real feeling she is after, and real feeling is not abstract or clean or whole, but is concrete and messy and often incomplete. So she advises a student poet in "Sonnet for Joe," "the essence of your ocean sentiments is not the ocean," and she tells him to ". . .think of the man/who fell from his fishing boat in the fog off Alaska. He/heard the motor/slowly *trupp*ing away, its cargo of vain fish under its wing./Think of/his widow who detests the sea, who lives beside it,/who writes now to her friend."[11]

The important thing, she tells her student, is not the ocean itself, but what the ocean means to people, how it affects their lives. Nature in itself is not a subject for poetry, but the human experience of nature is.

Beth Bentley and Sandra McPherson are only two of the many women poets now living and writing in the Northwest. The examples I chose from their poems illustrate a tendency among women writers to emphasize at least one theme not commonly considered characteristic of the "Northwest School" of poetry. I have heard editors argue that women poets in the Northwest do not really belong to the region, that their allegiance is to their sex, to the feminine experience rather than the Northwest experience. But it seems to me, reading the poems of Bentley, McPherson, and many others, that there is nothing particularly feminine about being concerned with the human state. I once had a teacher in high school who used to tell her classes that such a concern was what marked the "Universal" in a work of art. While such a generalization may be too simple for the present argument, I still find myself nodding approval. The best poets in any region are those who touch the human heart and that not all male poets in the northwest have held themselves above such concerns is evident in the wide national acceptance found by poets like Stafford and Hugo.

The problem with the "Northwest School" as it is commonly defined is that it not only loses usefulness when applied to most women poets but that it loses usefulness when applied to the best of the male poets.

If I had to make one large generalization about women poets in the Northwest. . .but I would not. Their poetry, like all good poetry, is marked by diversity. Yet this diversity has kept them from being included in regional anthologies and bibliographies which assume that the "Northwest School" is a genuine regional classification. Does this mean that women poets should continue to be slighted by teachers, scholars, and anthologizers? Obviously not. It seems to me that there are two solutions to this problem. First, a new, comprehensive, thematically non-restrictive definition could be devised for the "Northwest School," one which would make the "School" co-educational. This would mean that anthologizers, for instance, could no longer make up a group of poems by "big name" poets and then pad it out with "typical" Northwest poets. Theme would become secondary to quality. Second, the whole idea of a "Northwest School" of poetry could be abandoned, and teachers, scholars, anthologizers, and editors could be relieved of the task of deciding what is and what is not Northwest poetry and could devote their time to serious consideration of the poems themselves, regardless of theme. There are many talented poets in the Northwest, and the prolongation of a misleading regional classification will only hamper the identification and recognition of these writers in their own region. Women writers, in particular, should not have to establish a reputation on the East Coast before being recognized by regional publications and audiences. This is not to say that "Northwestern" is not a useful critical term, but only that it should be applied selectively, to individual authors, as part of a larger evaluation of their work, and not raised to the level of a criterion for critical attention. Once this is common practice the women poets in the Northwest may yet prove to be the most "Northwestern" of all.

NOTES

[1] Richard W. Etulain, *Western American Literature: A Bibliography of Interpretive Books and Articles* (Vermillion, S. D.; Dakota Press, 1972).

[2] Gary Snyder, Lecture at the University of Michigan, Flint College, Febraury 12, 1975. Unpublished transcript.

[3] *The Selected Poems of Gwendolyn Haste* (Boise, Idaho: Ahsahta Press, 1976), p. 23.

[4] Carolyn Kizer, "Poetry: School of the Pacific Northwest," *New Republic,* CXXXV (July 16, 1956), pp. 18-19.

[5] B. A. Botkin, "We Talk about Regionalism—North, East, South and West," *Frontier,* XIII (May, 1933), pp. 286-296.

[6] Rufus A. Coleman, "Literature and the Region," *Pacific Northwest Quarterly,* XXXIX (1948), p. 313.

[7] *Phone Calls from the Dead* (Ohio University Press, 1970), p. 72.

[8] *Ibid.,* p. 77.

[9] *Elegies for the Hot Season* (Bloomington: Indiana University Press, 1970), pp. 39-40.

[10] *Ibid.,* p. 38.

[11] *Radiation* (New York: The Ecco Press, 1973), pp. 67-68.

III

CHANGING IMAGES OF MEN AND WOMEN

HAMLIN GARLAND AND THE
CULT OF TRUE WOMANHOOD

Roger E. Carp
University of North Carolina
at Chapel Hill

"What shall we do about Hamlin Garland?" asks the title of a recent article,[1] succinctly stating the dilemma facing students of American literature and American history who attempt to evaluate Garland's significance. As most scholars agree, only a handful of Garland's many short stories, novels, and autobiographical works have lasting merit. But because he was among the first American naturalists and because he contributed so much to the development of the fiction concerned with rural life, he cannot be completely ignored. The realism he injected into the literary treatment of the farmer, combined with the protests of the Farmers' Alliance and the Populist party and the essay by Frederick Jackson Turner on the historical significance of the American frontier, enhanced a realization of the great influence of the frontier on American life.[2] What made Garland important to the historian, therefore, are the ideas and sentiments about the West and the individualism which he reflected in his writings.[3]

Of Garland's attitudes and beliefs, the ones related to agrarian reform and Henry George's single tax have received the most attention from historians and literary critics. Yet Garland also concerned himself with woman's rights. In some of his early short stories and novels, considering the restrictions on American women, he concluded that women ought to be allowed to acquire education, careers, and culture. When they married they should do so as equals with their husbands. By the turn of the twentieth century, however, Garland appeared to have abandoned these sentiments, for his female characters became submissive and domestic. Attempting to understand why Garland's fictional treatments of women changed not only provides a better perspective on the nature of his interests in woman's rights, but may also reveal a good deal about the contemporary woman's rights movement.

1

A reading of Garland's autobiographies, particularly *A Son of the Middle Border*, confirms that as a boy growing up on the Middle Border frontier he unconsciously accepted the conception of femininity historian Barbara Welter calls "The Cult of True Womanhood."[4] This traditional view described the ideal woman as pure, pious, submissive, and domestic. Garland's grand-mothers' and mother's life demonstrated that a woman's place was very definitely in the home. The only exception to this conviction arose from the years during the Civil War when Garland's mother managed the family's farm while his father served in the army. From his family and the female instructors he had at a small academy in Iowa, Garland saw the inculcation of culture and education were essentially fields for women, whereas labor, business, and politics composed the domain of the male. Further, girls and women were expected to be more innocent than males. The role of men was to protect women from the dangers of the outside world. Reinforcing this general view of women was the sympathy Garland felt for his mother; the desire of his father to go further west and farm new lands brought her great discomfort and loneliness.[5]

In hopes of becoming a teacher of literature, Garland traveled to Boston in 1884. His first years there were spent reading, teaching, and writing. Much of his faith in the tradi-tional conception of femininity was challenged by what he read during these years. Evolutionary thinkers, in particular Herbert Spencer, convinced him that future progress depended on the ex-pansion of individual freedom and development. Interestingly, Garland had no trouble concluding that the individual right to self-improvement applied to women as well as men.[6] The works of William Dean Howells also pointed in this direction, for Howells argued that women should move into the economic and political realms in order to purify these areas with their superior moral and aesthetic senses.[7]

Garland's view of women was also altered by writers on the other side of the Atlantic. He admired Emile Zola's ability to probe the dark and ugly sides of rural life, aspects with which Garland was entirely too familiar. In Zola's books farm women were treated realistically, though compassionately. The false sentimentality that was so common in literary descriptions of country life was conspicuously missing in Zola's works. Garland was critical of Zola's preoccupation with his characters' sexuality, however, feeling greater sympathy and respect or Henrik Ibsen. Garland's own temperament and attitude towards life were similar to the moralism and individualism of the Norwegian dramatist. Female characters, such as Nora in "A Doll's House," especially appealed to Garland, since they possessed the fortitude necessary to rebel and exert their individuality in a male-dominated society. Garland completely agreed that women deserved equal chances to acquire education, culture, and independence.[8]

Through accident and coincidence as well as his own stubborn efforts, Garland managed to meet several authors and editors in his first years in Boston. They encouraged him to write realistically about his experiences on the Middle Border. For Garland, a successful literary career was the means by which to satisfy two goals. First, it would enable him to assist his family financially. In addition, by using his writings to broadcast certain schemes of agrarian reform, Garland might improve the lives of all farmers. He strongly supported Henry George's single tax and joined local and national organizations endorsing that panacea. The amelioration of the poverty and misery suffered by farming families like his own became Garland's primary interest. For the moment, then, expanding the rights and opportunities of women had to take a backseat.[9]

2

Many of the short stories Garland wrote between 1888 and 1891 were designed to show how an environment of ceaseless toil, spiritual and cultural sterility, and economic exploitation was destroying the democratic agrarianism of the West. Female characters were used solely to assist Garland in making his general points about the harshness of farm life and the desperate need for improvement.[10]   Representative of these stories is "A

Common Case," published in 1888. It largely consists of a
dialogue between two frontier women. One is dying and can
only express bitterness for all the hardships she has endured on
the frontier. Her friend's words fail to give her hope.[11]

Three years later Garland published "A Prairie Heroine."
In this story he speaks explicitly about the need for reform and
the ways in which instituting the single tax can solve the farmers'
problems and, by implication, those of farm women. The first
half of the story depicts the ways farm life has brutalized Sim
and Lucretia Burns. They have no hope of improving their
lives or giving their children a better future. The author then
shifts to Douglas Radbourn, a local lawyer and advocate of the
single tax, and Lily Graham, a schoolteacher who personifies
the True Woman. Garland uses Radbourn to express his support
for the single tax while Lily Graham shows the reader what an
unhappy, mistreated farm wife like Lucretia Burns can become
if the proper reforms are instituted.[12]

The technique of placing the "real" woman (Lucretia)
beside the "ideal" woman (Lily) is one which Garland would
employ in several of his short stories and novels. It reveals a
great deal about his conception of femininity. Garland concludes that if life in the West is improved, then farm women like
Lucretia Burns will be able to dress well, speak correctly, and
become educated and cultured. They will assume their natural
role of protectors of moral and spiritual values. In short, they
will become Lily Grahams. What Garland is therefore affirming
as the ideal conception of femininity to which every woman
should have the opportunity to aspire is the innocent, pure,
domestic being celebrated by the Cult of True Womanhood.

Garland had briefly campaigned for the Populists' Presiden-
tial candidate General James B. Weaver in 1892. Although he
soon lost interest in the Populists, Garland did not forget what
he had seen of the farmers' revolt and made it the basis of his
most pronounced political novel, *A Spoil of Office*. Written in
1892, this novel centers on the careers of Ida Wilbur, a fictional
reformer, and Bradley Talcott, the illiterate farm hand whom Ida
inspires to become a lawyer and to enter local politics. Most
of the book is devoted to Bradley's rise and his struggles against
political corruption. He periodically hears Ida deliver speeches
on agrarian reform and woman's rights. Eventually, he falls in

love with her. After first rejecting him, Ida agrees to their marriage.   Soon after they have settled in Washington, she leaves him and returns to the West.   They remain married, but the reform movements will always come first.

The character of Ida Wilbur represents much that is radical and much that is traditional in the nineteenth-century view of women.   She stands out as one of Garland's most memorable female characters, expressing his strongest views on woman's rights.   Garland's readings of Spencer and Ibsen are reflected in Ida's fiery speeches on the right of women to develop their personalities and minds as completely and independently as men. The only instance in Garland's fiction in which he discusses woman suffrage occurs when Ida tells her listeners that the vote is merely a part in the overall movement for equal rights.   She contends emphatically that the root of women's problems is economic and that the extent of their emancipation is based on their ability to earn their own livings.   This oration and others in *A Spoil of Office* stamp Ida as a "free woman" who can think as rationally and act as resolutely as any man.[13]

Garland again utilizes his technique of juxtaposing different sorts of women so that the reader will more fully comprehend which is the ideal.   During Bradley's first years at school, Nettie Russell is infatuated with him.   She is childish and superficial whereas Ida is mature and thoughtful.   Ida's seriousnesss and dedication to what she believes make her far more admirable and worthy of Bradley's and the reader's respect.   In fact, her winning him over to the cause of the Populists saves him from becoming too enamored of the personal benefits his election to Congress bring him.   Nevertheless, there are moments at the close of the book in which Ida loses her calm and detached manner and acts as light-heartedly as Nettie.   Here Garland reverts to the traditional conception of females as subordinate to men and dependent on them to give meaning to their lives.   Once Ida and Bradley are married, however, the woman regains control and reform impulses take precedence.[14]   Theirs does appear to be a marriage of equals, yet Garland not only does not cover their married life in the book, but he separates them less than a month after they are wedded!   It is something of a paradox that Garland's ideal marriage· of equals is not presented as an enduring relationship.

The weaknesses in this last portion of *A Spoil of Office* reveal the inconsistency in Garland's ideas about women and their rights. On the whole, Ida and other women are portrayed as more moral and reform-minded than men, thus perpetuating much of the prevailing Cult of True Womanhood in the West. Yet Ida Wilbur is emancipated from many of the sanctions bearing on women. Her energetic participation in various agrarian movements sets her apart from the stereotyped helpless females ignorant of the outside world; in those respects she represents the highest degree to which Garland affirmed the right of women to live as fully and freely as men.[15]

Three years after *A Spoil of Office* was published, the right of women to develop their personalities and minds was treated even more fully by Garland in *The Rose of Dutcher's Coolly.* The story opens in the hills and meadows of Wisconsin where young Rose plays and explores. Her carefree and independent nature is coupled with a devotion to her studies which enables her to attend the state university. There she chooses a career as a writer. Once she graduates she moves to Chicago. She is introduced to Warren Mason, a journalist whose criticism and assistance improve her poetry. Although Mason believes that most women hide their intelligence in coquettish behavior, he realizes how different Rose is. Finally, he proposes to her in a long letter in which he confesses his faults and reveals his fear that he will make a poor husband. However, he promises that their marriage will be one of equals. The book closes as Rose accepts his offer.

The Rose of Dutcher's Coolly is similar to *A Spoil of Office* in vacillating between radical and traditional conceptions of femininity. In assessing the radical aspect of the novel, one must begin with the figure of Rose Dutcher. She is no ordinary heroine of late nineteenth-century literature. A youth spent on the Middle Border leaves her free-spirited, independent, and self-confident. Reared predominantly by her indulgent father, she possessed the liberty to explore and enjoy her world. The "feminine" qualities of submission, domesticity, and piety have little meaning or merit for her. At college and later in Chicago she follows her interests and goals, refusing to be sidetracked by social values dictating marriage and maternity. To accentuate the uniqueness of Rose's personality, Garland used the technique of juxtaposing Rose against more typical young women who are flirtatious, silly, and bored by higher education and serious careers.

Rose served Garland as a vehicle by which to express his firm belief that women should have the freedom to acquire an education and to enjoy the culture of society at large. He emphasized the importance of their pursuing careers and included among his characters female physicians, lawyers, and artists. Moreover, there are frequent passages in which Rose is warned against marrying at too young an age. Only when she has graduated from college and worked for a few years should she wed. And then, of course, only as an equal.[16]

Nevertheless, while these characteristics of Rose diverged from many of the common attitudes towards women and matrimony, an essentially traditional conception of femininity underlay the novel. The male as well as the female characters who pontificate on the importance of equal rights for the sexes at other times appear to restrict the liberty of women. This is primarily done through the prevailing attitude towards marriage. A woman has the right to seek higher education, acquire culture, and pursue a career. But accompanying that right is the responsibility to marry and bear children. Furthermore, matrimony and motherhood provide a woman with greater joys and satisfactions than can any college degree or profession. The reasoning behind this conviction is explained when another man tells Warren Mason that a woman is only happy for a few years in the realms of education and art. Then she moves " 'into the pain and responsibility of marriage not merely willingly, but eagerly.' "[17] Finally, the fact that this novel, like *A Spoil of Office,* ends at the time the leading characters wed testifies to Garland's inability to conceive realistically what a "marriage of equals" would be like. What seems apparent is that while Garland could grant women the opportunities to become educated and cultured, in the end no other roles could be seen for them except those of wife and mother.

The novels Garland wrote between 1900 and 1914 differ from earlier works in several significant ways. Although romance and sentimentality had never been lacking in his fiction, romantic love thoroughly dominated these new works. The setting was moved from the drab flatness of the Middle Border to the majestic heights and forests of the Rocky Mountains. Garland filled

these works with the stock characters of contemporary frontier
literature: violent game poachers and miners; brave, upstanding
forest rangers and sheriffs; and dainty, sensitive ladies. Nearly
alike in their plots, these conventional tales exhibited good
triumphing over evil and love conquering all in the end.[18]

Representative of this phase of Garland's career is *Her
Mountain Lover,* a novel published in 1901. Jim Matteson, a shy
but proud miner from Colorado, is sent to England to acquire
financial backing for the mine he and a friend own. Jim's primitive western ways contrast sharply, and often humorously, with
the refined traditions of London. Of the people he meets, only
Mary Brien, an Irish authoress, appreciates him and his language,
ideas, and way of life. Attracted to her, Jim cannot help feeling
uncomfortable because of her independent and open nature. At
the same time, he thinks of Bessie Blake, a quiet, genteel, innocent young girl to whom his mining partner had recently introduced him. When Jim leaves England and meets his partner in
Chicago, he finds Bessie—usually reserved—playing the coquette
and making him doubt that she cares for him. Once he departs
for Colorado, however, Bessie realizes how much she loves and
needs him. She follows him to the Rockies and they decide to
marry. She has no trouble giving up the concerts and museums
of Chicago and accepting the roles of wife and housekeeper.[19]

Just as he did in previous novels, especially *A Spoil of Office,* Garland juxtaposed two very different types of women in
Her Mountain Lover. Bessie is the quintessential True Woman.
She is pure, dependent, submissive, flirtatious at times, refined,
and domestic. With no sense of loss she forsakes the cosmopolitan atmosphere of Chicago to be with the man she loves in the
far reaches of Colorado. There she will rely on him completely
for her safety, security, and happiness. But Mary Brien represents something altogether different. Although she also is educated and cultured, she finds little to admire in English upper-
class society. She wishes to adopt the ways of the West and
prove to Jim that she can be hardy and self-reliant—that is,
demonstrate that she is his equal, a "man wearing skirts." Jim
may occasionally find her appealing, but in the end, he does not
want this kind of woman. Thus, he is anxious to return to Bessie
with whom he can assume a superior place. They have no intention of marrying as equals. The outside world will be his sphere,
the home hers. In writing this book, Garland has quite obviously

moved far away from the ideals of Spencer and Ibsen and earlier characters such as Ida Wilbur and Rose Dutcher.

3

As nearly every literary critic that has dealt with Garland has realized, a central question is why, after *A Spoil of Office* and *The Rose of Dutcher's Coolly,* he loses interest in reform— feminist as well as agrarian. In *Roadside Meetings,* a collection of reminiscences of famous people he had known, Garland says that his interest in reform gave way to a concern with more popular "artistic" themes.[20] Attracting a wide audience had always been important to him, especially after he assumed responsibility for the well-being of his parents in the 1890's. Garland's responsibilities increased after he married Zulime Taft in 1899. The births of two daughters, one in 1903 and the other in 1908, apparently made him decide to write the romantic fiction which contemporary editors and readers wanted.[21]

Besides making Garland anxious to sell more books, being married certainly influenced his attitudes towards women and matrimony. Once he encountered the difficulties inherent in marriage, Garland probably realized how unmanageable the idea of a "marriage of equals" was for him. One way to solve his intellectual problem was to embrace the traditional conception of femininity. Fortunately for Garland, his wife abandoned her plans to be an artist and devoted herself to caring for the family. Zulime cheerfully followed Garland on his trips to the Rockies and Southwest, though she was not accustomed to the hardships of traveling and camping in the West. She provided her ailing mother-in-law with solace and love. Still, despite the assistance Garland gave her with the children, Zulime naturally bore the brunt of their care. Not until the 1920's is she found expressing any distaste with being a housewife and mother. By then, Garland can only sympathize and attempt to improve things by taking her to England. Just as his mother had subordinated her wishes and comforts to the desire of her husband to farm and prosper on the prairies, Garland's wife similarly adopted willingly the roles of wife and mother and allowed her husband's literary career to shape much of their marital relationship.[22]

While studying Garland's wish to be a successful writer as

well as his marriage may give us some indication why his female characters changed so drastically, even more fundamental is the question of how much Garland truly changed. How committed was he to woman's rights and how radical were his views of feminine emancipation in the first place? As I have already shown, Garland was reared with the True Woman as his feminine ideal. Chastity, morality, piety, and domesticity were the traits a woman was supposed to possess. From the memories of his grandmothers and his experiences with his mother, he associated women with love, culture, compassion, and suffering. They could not escape the awful life on the frontier as he could. Once he had fled east, however, emotions of guilt and responsibility compelled him to do all he could to alleviate the pain endured by his mother. He devoted himself to her, building her a new home, limiting his travels to be with her, and perhaps postponing his own desire to marry until he was certain she would approve.[23]

Garland continued to uphold this traditional conception of femininity in his fiction of the early 1890's. Even Ida Wilbur and Rose Dutcher shared some of the characteristics of the True Woman. Yet around the turn of the twentieth century, when this view of the female was so widespread, newer and more radical ideas were emerging. The "New Woman" was being born. Housewives found industry and government usurping many of their economic and welfare functions. The external controls over morality which perpetuated the Cult of True Womanhood were being undermined by the growing individualization of the modern city. Many women, possessing the liberty to make significant choices about how they would live, found themselves searching for an identity. Illustrations of this rising independence of women were seen in the increasing numbers of working women and the spreading support given to birth control as a woman's right. While many of these New Women were simply restless middle- and upper-class wives with more wealth and leisure than they knew what to do with, others were young, self-sufficient laboring women intent upon establishing new roles for themselves.[24]

The most radical ideas at this time concerning the social and economic roles of women were perhaps those of Charlotte Perkins Gilman. While most advocates of woman's rights concentrated on winning the right to vote or expanding educational opportunities, Gilman looked at the status of women throughout history in order to determine how real equality for women might be attained. In *Women and Economics,* written in 1898, she observed that for centuries women had been using their physical beauty to attract men who would protect and provide for them. This had conditioned women to think of themselves and be seen as weak, timid, emotional, and capable only of domestic chores. Gilman concluded by encouraging women to leave the home and work as equals to men. To solve the problem of who was to run the home and rear the children, she proposed in *The Home* (1903) that large housing units be created, staffed by professionals to manage nurseries and kitchens and to provide cleaning services. Gilman was, in effect, calling for a domestic revolution in social and cultural values.[25]

The notion of the New Woman and the theories of Gilman can serve as a means to understand and evaluate Garland's own late views of women. There is no evidence, of course, that he ever read or was familiar with the writings of Gilman. Considering the extent to which he glorified the traditional family structure and the female roles of wife and mother, it can be assumed that he would have found Gilman's ideas preposterous. As for the New Woman, entries in his diaries and passages from his autobiographies confirm that he was adamantly opposed to such a conception of femininity. According to Garland, all that the New Woman and the woman's rights movement showed was that women could be as vulgar and profane as men. He believed that marriage, chastity, and home life were the victims of the drive for women to have their so-called rights. In particular, he found the literature of the day pornographic and disgusting in its depictions of women smoking, drinking, and engaging in sexual activities. That his daughters were maturing in such an age greatly distressed him.[26]

More acceptable to participants in the woman's rights movement of the late nineteenth and early twentieth centuries than the ideas of Gilman was woman suffrage. For, as Aileen S. Kraditor has noted, most of the support for woman suffrage was founded on the idea that women should be allowed to vote because their moral superiority would enable them to clean up the American political system.[27] Although Garland never commented on woman suffrage or the passage of the Nineteenth Amendment in his autobiographies or in the published selections from his diaries, the essentially conservative nature of this reform would probably have elicited his support as it did that of his friend and mentor William Dean Howells.[28]

As for expanding the opportunities for women to become educated and cultured, Garland's short stories and novels testify to his firm endorsement of this change. In his own life, his paternal grandmother had exemplified the woman who dedicated herself to her home and family yet still knew how to read and write and was familiar with the culture of her native New England. His mother, on the other hand, had led a stultifying existence on the barren prairies. By protesting against the conditions of the West and creating characters such as Rose Dutcher who were able to study and appreciate art and literature, Garland may have tried to ease his feelings of guilt for leaving his mother and to improve the lives of countless other women suffering on the frontier. Yet what remains clear is that acquiring education and culture and pursuing careers were not ends in themselves but only means for producing better wives and mothers.

Disgusted, then, by the wild, "masculine" qualities he saw women adopting, Garland produced his own type of "New Woman." That image was identical to the "educated consumer" and "modern mother" that women's magazines such as *Good Housekeeping* and the *Ladies' Home Journal* were extolling in the first years of the twentieth century.[29] Polite, pious, loving, educated, and competent in the kitchen and nursery, that New Woman was the True Woman brought up to date. For Garland, she was in fictional terms Rose Dutcher. In real life, she was his wife. Zulime Garland had been able to study art and pursue a career. When she had married she had voluntarily abandoned that career and devoted herself to her home, husband, and children. Garland hoped that his two daughters would follow that same path and was pleased with their artistic endeavors. Eventually, however, they also gave up their dreams of becoming artists and actresses and married. Garland saw nothing wrong with their sacrificing themselves so that their husbands could progress. Until his death in 1940, Garland clung to this basically traditional conception of femininity, convinced that the women in the world around him were losing all of their charm and virtue.[30]

4

The nonradical core of Garland's views on woman's rights and his conception of femininity mirrored that of the woman suffrage movement and most other aspects of the campaign for increased freedoms and opportunities for women. Genuine radicalism, as expressed by Charlotte Perkins Gilman's schemes for a transformation of the social and sexual roles of men and women, was spurned by the genteel middle- and upper-class women who joined and supported the General Federation of Women's Clubs, the National American Woman Suffrage Association, and other contemporary organizations of women. Garland stands in the conservative mainstream of the woman's rights movement of the late nineteenth and early twentieth centuries. He represents not only the limitations of feminist reform in this era, but also those which colored the entire Progressive period. As a feminist and an agrarian reformer, Garland reflected the tendencies of the Progressives to look backward and to romanticize the individual, believing that if only the free and equal conditions of the mythic past could be resurrected the United States would prosper. The result of romantic fantasy, such views failed to deal with the realities and problems of modern America; problems which, as a few intellectuals and activists were coming to realize, demanded more far-reaching change.

NOTES

[1]Warren French, "What Shall We do about Hamlin Garland?," *American Literary Realism: 1870-1910,* 3 (Fall, 1970), pp. 283-289.

[2]Henry Nash Smith, *Virgin Land: The American West as Symbol and Myth* (Cambridge, Massachusetts: Harvard University Press, 1950), pp. 247-260.

[3]Donald Pizer, *Hamlin Garland's Early Work and Career,* University of California Publications: English Studies, no. 22 (Berkeley and Los Angeles: University of California Press, 1960), pp. 1-2.

[4]"The Cult of True Womanhood: 1820-1860," *American Quarterly,* 18 (Summer, 1966), pp. 151-174. Throughout this paper the terms "Cult of True Womanhood" and "True Woman" will be used to signify this conception of femininity.

[5]Hamlin Garland, *A Son of the Middle Border,* edited and with an Introduction by Henry M. Christman (New York: Macmillan, Co., 1962), pp. 3-6, 14-15, 22-3, 148, and 157; Hamlin Garland, "My Grandmother of Pioneer Days," *Ladies' Home Journal,* April 1895, p. 10; and Hamlin Garland, "The Wife of a Pioneer: A Tribute," *Ladies' Home Journal,* September, 1903, p. 8.

[6]Garland, *A Son of the Middle Border,* pp. 272-274. See also: Pizer, *Hamlin Garland's Early Work and Career,* pp. 6, 72, and 152.

[7]Donald Pizer, "Romantic Individualism in Garland, Norris and Crane," *American Quarterly,* 10 (Winter, 1958), pp. 463-468; and Gail Thain Parker, "William Dean Howells: Realism and Feminism," in *Uses of Literature,* edited by Monroe Engel, Harvard English Studies, no. 4 (Cambridge, Massachusetts: Harvard University Press, 1973), pp. 133-134 and 144.

[8]Lars Ahnebrink, *The Beginnings of Naturalism in American Fic-*

tion: A Study of the Works of Hamlin Garland, Stephen Crane, and Frank Norris with Special Reference to Some European Influences, 1891-1903, Essays and Studies on American Language and Literature, no. 9 (New York: Russell & Russell, 1961), pp. 233-235, 363-366, and 408.

[9]Garland, *A Son of the Middle Border,* pp. 264-265, 269-281, 309, 313, and 317-319.

[10]Stanley R. Harrison, "Hamlin Garland and the Double Vision of Naturalism," *Studies in Short Fiction,* 6 (Fall, 1969), pp. 549-552 and 554.

[11]Under the title, "Before the Low Green Door," this story was added to *Other Main-Travelled Roads* (New York and London: Harper & Brothers, 1910), pp. 293-301.

[12]Under the title, "Lucretia Burns," this story was added to the second edition of *Prairie Folks* (New York: Macmillan Co., 1899), pp. 83-117.

[13]Hamlin Garland, *A Spoil of Office: A Story of the Modern West,* new and revised edition (New York: D. Appleton and Co., 1897), pp. 142-144, 227, 248, and 251.

[14]*Ibid.,* pp. 367-375. See also: Jean Holloway, *Hamlin Garland: A Biography* (Austin, Texas: University of Texas Press, 1960), pp. 64-65; and Eberhard Alsen, "Hamlin Garland's First Novel: *A Spoil of Office,"* *Western American Literature,* 4 (Summer, 1969), p. 98.

[15]Recollecting this early phase of his literary career, Garland wrote:
"Ida Wilbur was in advance of her time. As I look back on her, I see that she was a lovely forerunner of the well-dressed and wholly competent leaders who followed Susan Anthony's austere generation. I find her not altogether despicable. I knew her type as well as I did that of Bradley Talcott, but I failed to make her lovable."
(*Roadside Meetings* [New York: Macmillan Co., 1930] , p. 186).

[16]Joseph L. Carter, "Hamlin Garland's Liberated Woman," *American Literary Realism: 1870-1910,* 6 (Summer, 1973), pp. 255-256; and Ahnebrink, *The Beginnings of Naturalism in American Fiction,* pp. 87 and 377.

[17]Hamlin Garland, *The Rose of Dutcher's Coolly* (New York and London: Harper & Brothers, 1899), p. 275. See also: pp. 286-288.

[18]In a study of frontier fiction, Nicholas J. Karolides notes an overwhelming trend towards romantic sentimental love stories between 1900 and 1910. He provides a good description of the heroines of these novels, one that includes Garland's female characters of that period, in *The Pioneer in the American Novel, 1900-1950* (Norman, Oklahoma: University of Oklahoma Press, 1967), pp. 83-88. See also: William Wasserstrom, *Heiress of All the Ages: Sex and Sentiment in the Genteel Tradition* (Minneapolis: University of Minnesota Press, 1959), pp. 45-46.

[19]Hamlin Garland, *Her Mountain Lover* (New York and London: D. Appleton-Century Co., 1939), pp. 382-394.

[20]Garland, *Roadside Meetings,* pp. 187-188.

[21]Hamlin Garland, *A Daughter of the Middle Border* (New York: Macmillan Co., 1921), pp. 17, 19, 22-23, and 139-140.

[22]Various episodes in the married life of Zulime and Hamlin Garland are described in: *Ibid.,* pp. 146, 157, 168, 172-173, 192-193, 199-203, 207, 223, 237, 286, 290, 322, 324, 330-331, and 369. See also: Diary entry for April 23, 1922, quoted in Donald Pizer, editor, *Hamlin Garland's Diaries* (San Marino, California: Huntington Libraries, 1968), p. 81.

[23]Garland, *A Daughter of the Middle Border,* pp. 17, 62-63, 67, 71, 82, and 84.

[24]David M. Kennedy, *Birth Control in America: The Career of Margaret Sanger* (New Haven, Connecticut: Yale University Press, 1970), pp. 36-40, 50, and 56-57; James R. McGovern, "The American Woman's Pre-World War I Freedom in Manners and Morals," *Journal of American History* 55 (September, 1968), pp. 318-319; and Carroll Smith-Rosenberg and Charles Rosenberg, "The Female Animal: Medical and Biological Views of Woman and Her Role in Nineteenth-Century America," *Journal of American History,* 60 (September, 1977), pp. 347-348.

[25]Carl M. Degler, "Charlotte Perkins Gilman on the Theory and Practice of Feminism," *American Quarterly,* 8 (Spring, 1956), pp. 22-36; and William L. O'Neill, *Everyone Was Brave: The Rise and Fall of Feminism in America* (Chicago: Quadrangle Books, 1969), pp. 39-44 and 48.

[26]Pizer, editor, *Hamlin Garland's Diaries,* pp. 240 and 242; Hamlin Garland, *Back-Trailers from the Middle Border* (New York: Macmillan Co., 1928), p. 156; Hamlin Garland, *Companions on the Trail: A Literary*

Chronicle (New York: Macmillan Co., 1931), pp. 532-533; and Hamlin Garland, *Afternoon Neighbors: Further Excerpts from a Literary Log* (New York: Macmillan Co., 1934), p. 108.

[27]Aileen S. Kraditor, *The Ideas of the Woman Suffrage Movement, 1890-1920* (Garden City, New York: Doubleday & Co., 1971), pp. 43-45.

[28]Parker, "William Dean Howells," pp. 134 and 144.

[29]Christopher Lasch, *The New Radicalism in America (1889-1963): The Intellectual as a Social Type* (New York: Alfred A. Knopf, 1966), pp. 47-50.   Garland's diary entry of October 27, 1913, records a conversation he had about the "woman's movement" with Edward Bok, the editor of the *Ladies' Home Journal*. Pizer, editor, *Hamlin Garland's Diaries*, pp. 241-242.

[30]Garland, *Back-Trailers from the Middle Border*, pp. 337-340.

GERTRUDE ATHERTON'S CALIFORNIA WOMAN: FROM LOVE STORY TO PSYCHOLOGICAL DRAMA

Charlotte S. McClure
Georgia State University

Readers and critics have long identified literary California with images of miners, gold-hearted prostitutes, ranchers, and common folk in the works of Mark Twain, Bret Harte, Frank Norris, Jack London, and John Steinbeck. Some readers may recall the pathos of Helen Hunt Jackson's California Indians and the evocation of California's natural endowment in the poetry of Ina Coolbrith and in the prose of Mary Austin. But only recently has the more complex fiction of a once very popular California-born novelist, Gertrude Atherton, been recovered. Born in San Francisco in 1857, Atherton combined California history, San Francisco society, and a new type of California woman and created a fictional "motive" that extended throughout her sixty-year-long career. From her first California story in *The Argonaut* in 1883 to her last in 1946, *My San Francisco*, a chronicle of a wayward city, Atherton wove these three elements into a paradigm of a new stage in western civilization. While she lived in and around San Francisco and in such diverse places as New York, London, Munich, Chicago, and Butte, Montana, she published eighteen novels, three collections of short stories, and three histories, all reflecting her California material. Always she was interested in telling a good story about unchanging human nature as she saw it and in extending her readers' knowledge of the great world that, she thought, was obscured by their genteel existence.

Although Atherton used the historic conflict between Spain and Mexico for possession of California, the customs of the early Californians, and the evolution of San Francisco from a raw frontier town to a corrupt and cosmopolitan city, she is more than a member of a school of local colorists. Atherton always resisted being associated with any literary school or with any region. Her ambition was to be a "correct historian" of her times[1] wherever she lived. Her California material provided a romantic-realistic milieu on which she could project a new and ironic western figure who would embody American values as the nation struggled to become more democratic without sacrificing its aristocratic origins. This new figure was the California woman, a type different from the New York girl of Henry James and of Edith Wharton and from the domestic heroine of the "Howellsian garden."

This type of woman reflected Atherton's view of the effects on women and on the American novel of the social, economic, and psychological pressures of western civilization. Women had few choices in regard to their life purposes beyond romantic love, marriage, and motherhood. Hence Atherton believed that romantic love had remained the major motive of American novelists because writers could be no more original than the world in which they lived.[2] However, observing that both the American woman and the American man possessed an individual will and self-reliance,[3] she predicted that the combination would produce a new race and a new civilization—or chaos. Thus the new fate that she imagined for her independent, self-knowing California woman served as a measure of the evolution of western civilization from an aristocracy of birth to an aristocracy marked by the development of individual talent and achievement. And her fictional theme of a woman attempting to know herself and to develop common interests with a man before choosing to marry him provided the novel with a different motive without entirely sacrificing the traditional sentimental one.

Atherton derived from Hippolyte Taine her fictional technique of selecting types of real people and of placing them in extraordinary circumstances that developed their latent potentialities.[4] This realistic-romantic synthesis was her own original and imaginative version of realism in the novel, which one of her characters in *The Sisters-in-Law* (1921) defined as "a memoir of contemporary life in the form of fiction" (p. 340). Moreover, Atherton took seriously Taine's contention that studying the external aspects of man enables one to understand man's inner nature; hence like him, she unveiled a psychology, the inner life of woman. Then she added the psychology as well as Taine's race, surroundings, and epoch to a study of human nature as she saw it and created a series of novels featuring a California woman as a fictional transcript of contemporary manners in successive decades.

It is important to place Atherton's California novels and woman in the context both of San Francisco's turbulent history and of the cultural milieu in which she was working. Her heroine reflects, as well as is a part of, the wayward growth of San Francisco from a frontier town in a jewel-like setting to a wealthy and corrupt, bohemian, and cosmopolitan, city. In 1914, Atherton wrote an "intimate history" of California,[5] romantically commencing with the "geological drama" of its birth and realistically carrying it through its periods of revolution, gold fever, southern aristocracy, politics and vigilance committees, and the civilizing efforts of honest men. Her last two books, *Golden Gate Country* (1945) and *My San Francisco, A Wayward Biography* (1946), inimitably retell this saga.

Her novels revealing the inner life of a new woman may be seen as part of a general reaction which was developing in the 1890's against the restrictions, the confinements, the proprieties, and the dullness of middle-class culture in California as well as in the East.[6] Evidence of a new vigorous spirit appeared in the enthusiasm for sports, the outdoors, and adventure stories, a spirit fostered by California's sunny climate, its natural beauty of ocean and forests, and its space to move in. Atherton's heroines expressed the woman's side of this general change in spirit and the revolt against the genteel conception of woman's nature and role. They refused to see home as their place and frequently adopted careers considered the place of men, such as journalism, politics, diplomacy, or business. Some of them chose to marry, but none thought of marriage and motherhood as the end of their fate. Vigorously healthy and given to outdoor exercise, they denied the validity of the nineteenth-century woman's acceptable invalidism. They typically identified with their fathers rather than with their mothers. They early recognized the evils of the world and their own capacity for wrongdoing. As women, they claimed no spiritual or moral superiority over men, and through their knowledge of Darwin and Spencer, they rejected traditional religious beliefs and looked instead for guidance in personal and social conduct to their own intelligence and instincts.

These heroines were not feminine in the traditional sense, yet their creator insisted upon their essential womanliness. They were intelligent and devoted to developing their minds, even when ruefully acknowledging that the awakening of their womanhood—their sexuality—make their brains appear merely as annexes to their bodies. Hence Atherton's heroines sought a clearer understanding of their sexuality and desired a companionable and sexual relationship with a man. Both her homely and her beautiful heroines possessed erotic feelings and an active intelligence and combined their sexuality with strong character and a capacity for the most exalted kind of love. But it is easy to understand that these active, intelligent, and erotic heroines experienced a high degree of self-conflict when they were expected by their middle-class culture to be pious, moralistic, passive, and sentimental.

With this type of highly romanticized heroine, Atherton's novel could not be a mere love story. It would have to follow Atherton's conception that the novel, like life itself, is a succession of reactions and incidents, peculiar to the people portrayed.[7] The reactions of her heroines composed the plot pattern of a journey or a quest taken by a woman. It must be understood that Atherton was attempting to create the image of a new type of woman—one who would be able to deal triumphantly with the problems peculiar to woman's experience as Atherton saw it and one who would expand her contribution to civilization by knowing herself, by seeking a companionable and loving relationship with a man, and by participation in her society beyond marriage. Hence Atherton's novels are composed of incidents that show her heroines' intense craving for a varied life and their trying to overcome parental restrictions, their discontent under the bonds of an unhappy marriage, or the despair that assails them as older women who see life slipping away from them. In several novels she explored various new courses which women might take, imagining their struggles, frustrations and satisfactions. Among the most difficult problems they would meet was a type of dragon for a woman to slay—the idea of romantic love which would tie their emotions and intellect to the old images of femininity and perpetuate the ennui that resulted when their self-identity and interests were defined solely by their culture. Yet when they solved their practical battles of self-identity and self-support, they found themselves still hoping for and half expecting the ideal lover who would bring them fulfillment. Only after intensely disillusioning experiences did they separate the romantic myth from the human reality of love. And only after they had freed themselves of a woman's "fool's paradise" of false dreams were they able to explore other interests, create new dreams, and discover a new man who would match their new expectations. In Atherton's novels, the real decision about love usually occurred at the end of the psychological drama of a woman's quest.

Only briefly can I introduce you to four of Atherton's California women. Their psychological dramas are related respectively in *The Californians* (1898), *Ancestors* (1907), *The Sisters in Law* (1921), and *The House of Lee* (1940). In each of these novels, the heroine has a distinguished old world or American ancestry; this is a conventional note in an epoch obsessed with heredity and environment, but Atherton linked ancestry to racial development and civilized progress. Such an ancestry either defines her heroine's fulfilling life purpose or it is a "fool's paradise" of ennui and complacency against which she must struggle if she is to fulfill her own inner desire.

In *The Californians*, Magdalena Yorba represents a type of old world aristocratic woman inhabiting an arcadian setting near San Francisco in the 1880's, an unusually tranquil decade. Magdalena's name suggests the sources of her self-identity—worship of the Virgin, filial duty, a sentimental view of romantic love, a life purpose restricted to marriage and motherhood. She is plain of speech and face and eager to develop her intellect, but her narrow self-image and environment inhibit her yearning to become a writer and to emulate the glib tongue and seductive behavior of her "pagan" friend, Helena Belmont. A series of crises in Magdalena's inner life initiates her into knowledge of her self. Her religion vanishes after her study of Darwin and science, and she writes in secret because of her parents' censure of women authors. When she finds an intellectual companion in world-weary Jack Trennahan, she romantically idealizes him rather than passionately loves him, and then sentimentally releases him from their engagement when she discovers that he and Helena think they are passionately in love.

Deprived of faith in a woman's friendship, in a man's love, and in her ability to become a writer, Magdalena despairs as she squarely faces the question—What am I to do with my life? The initiation of her disintegrating will into experience occurs in a Jungian night journey through the underworld of San Francisco. On a night of fierce trade winds that howl off the Pacific, she leaves her father's house, "that ill-ventilated prison." She walks down to San Francisco, through the street of prostitution where she guesses that the women, knowing their purpose, might be happier than she is in her Nob Hill world. She travels through a street of crime and lawlessness where the sexual desire for her in the eyes of a blond-bearded Russian unlocks her "starved affections and implacably controlled passions." Finally she arrives at Spanish town, which heretofore she has pictured as gay with young people but which she discovers to be sordid and aged. Her passion simultaneously awakened and purged and then capable of being joined with thinking rationally about her life, Magdalena achieves her initiation into experience. She accepts her future of "interminable years" with only two points of hope—her father's death, which would free her from dependence on him, and the return of Trennahan from his self-imposed exile after Helena rejected him. The two hopes are fulfilled, and a mature love story is suggested only in the last five pages of the novel. The suicide of her father, Don Roberto, by hanging himself with the American flag symbolizes the emptiness that gold lust brought to many Californians. The return of Trennahan from his own journey of self-discovery and the renewal of the engagement suggests the possibility that individuals and a civilization might mature if new understandings of the relationship between nature and human beings and between man and woman could prevail.

While Magdalena at first accepts a woman's dependency on a man in a patriarchal society, Isabel Otis in *Ancestors* inherits the liberty to choose her fate. Two strong-willed ancestors—one Spanish Californian and one American—have bequeathed to her an independent mind and will, and her father has passed on to her a ranch by which she can support herself. Despite her financial freedom and in spite of her activity in proving "the whole game of woman a sham, a fool's paradise," Isabel, like Magdalena, must ask herself what is the real purpose of her life. Perceiving that her inherited freedom might be a "fool's paradise" because she has not earned it by her own efforts, the willful, independent Isabel actively searches for that purpose in San Francisco in the years of graft and corruption just before the earthquake of 1906.

In the first part of this three-part novel, Isabel meets her third cousin, Jack Gwynne, in England. By his aristocratic birth, he has inherited a seat in Parliament, a responsibility that he rebelliously rejects because as a member of the Liberal Party he desires to reform the English government in regard to its policies toward the working class. Isabel discovers her life purpose by her decision to aid her cousin's intention to shift his life purpose to building a political career in California.

The proximity of these two attractive, ambitious, and rebellious young people suggests that a typical love story would ensue. But Isabel and Jack do not fall in love at first sight; they disagree on political and economic issues, social attitudes, and personal goals. Only gradually through friendship and a sharing of intellectual interests and political activities in San Francisco, where political and social leadership are needed, do they lose their fear of becoming dependent upon and dominated by the other. It is significant that their love story begins in the last 100 pages of this 700-page novel when Isabel admits that though she prefers her private idealization of a man, she cannot help loving Jack and wanting to share his life.

Aristocratic Alexina Groome and middle-class Gora Dwight, the sisters-in-law of the novel, *The Sisters-in-Law,* represent the human dilemma that peculiarly affects women. Each asks herself whether to accept the traditional womanly role according to the expectations that her birth in a certain family or class provides or to work out her destiny based on her self-knowledge and on the varied experiences open to an energetic, talented, and intelligent woman. Their choices are acted out in San Francisco after the 1906 earthquake and through the war years when in France Gora sees combat as a battlefield nurse and Alexina does hospital work. Their hidden love of the same man becomes crucial only in the last pages of the novel, when the young man chooses Alexina, the sheltered society woman who has matured into a socially responsible and self-supporting woman, rather than Gora, who having lived deeply through her experiences of war and death, is destined to continue to write the novel, "the memoir of contemporary life in the form of fiction" (p. 340). By approving the growth to maturity of her heroines, Atherton criticized the outmoded social code of aristocratic San Francisco Society that in part kept women unaware victims of vanity and sex instinct (p. 181) and delayed or even prevented their maturation.

A "new aristocracy of intellect, talent, and ability" in America (p. 223) and the opportunities for individuals to develop themselves throughout their lives are the themes of *The House of Lee,* written when the real world was again at war. In this novel on the "changing and moving times" of the late 1930's in San Francisco, three generations of the Lee family—grandmother, daughter, and granddaughter all named Lucy—adapt their lives to the fact that because of their diminished inherited income, they must discover their abilities and find creative work to support themselves. Through the three Lucys, Atherton seems to suggest that women financially and emotionally self-reliant as men would help to mould a civilization which truly values and enacts the full development of the individual. Hence they perpetuate aristocracy in a new and ironic dimension.

In the characterization of the three Lucys, Atherton telescoped the evolution of the California heroine from dependency on vanity and family position as determiners of self-identity and life purpose to a California woman as hero, romantic in searching for a self-defined personal as well as a social purpose but also realistic in adapting to the social, economic, and aesthetic needs of the evolving western civilization.

NOTES

[1]*New York Times,* October 6, 1900, p. 660.

[2]"The Woman in Love," *Harper's Bazar,* 43 (December, 1909), p. 1179.

[3]Epigraph, *Patience Sparhawk and Her Times* (London, New York: John Lane, The Bodley Head, 1897).

[4]"Wanted: Imagination" in *What Is a Book? Thoughts About Writing,* ed. Dale Warren (Boston: Houghton Mifflin Company, 1935), pp. 47-48.

[5]*California: An Intimate History* (New York, London: Harper, 1914).

[6]John Higham, "The Reorientation of American Culture in the 1890's," in *The Origins of Modern Consciousness,* ed. John Weiss (Detroit: Wayne State University Press, 1965), pp. 25-48.

[7]"What the Day's Work Means to Me," *The Bookman,* 42 (February, 1916), pp. 691-695.

MADNESS AND PERSONIFICATION IN
GIANTS IN THE EARTH

Sylvia Grider
Texas A & M University

Settling the Great American Desert required people with vision, strength of purpose, and sometimes almost superhuman endurance. But what of those who failed? What can be said on behalf of those who could not cope? History is usually mute about the forgotten souls, usually women, who lie in unmarked graves along the road west. But literature has crystallized the traditions about them passed from family to family, generation to generation. Consider two twentieth century novels, my example *Giants in the Earth* by O. E. Rølvaag, and *The Wind* by Dorothy Scarborough, both of which chronicle the suffering and defeat of their respective heroines—these two fictional women are literary symbols of all those other unnamed but very real women who suffered and were broken by the West.

Both novels were written by authors only one generation removed from the events they were fictionally re-creating. Rølvaag was himself an immigrant from Norway, born in 1876, a year in the period about which he wrote. Dorothy Scarborough's parents homesteaded a claim near Sweetwater, Texas, and although her book was published before the great Dust Bowl of the 1930's, she had nevertheless seen the fury of the wind-driven sands of Texas first hand. The books have almost contemporary publication dates, 1927 and 1925; here the external similarities end. *Giants in the Earth* has become a classic of immigrant literature, first in Norwegian and then in English translation. And ensuing generations of Plains dwellers of Scandinavian descent recognize and identify with the harsh truths which this powerful novel examines. The book is a reaffirmation for each of them of the suffering that many of their real ancestors endured. *The Wind,* on the other hand, even though it too deals with the basic unpleasant realities of homesteading the frontier, is read by very few today. The truths it exposed caused the book to be suppressed soon after it was published because so many Texans resented the negative image of the land and the people which it depicted.

Madness on the Plains

Settling the Plains was regarded by many men as the ultimate in excitement and adventure, but for women the experience was generally much more of an ordeal. Beret, the Norwegian fisherman's wife who is the tragic heroine of *Giants in the Earth*, epitomizes the women unable to cope with the rigors of the frontier. She is driven mad by the alien quality of the Plains environment in which she was expected to raise her family and create a home. She is a helpless victim of fate, or, as the author says in his preface, a literary symbol of "the human cost of empire building." Throughout the course of the novel, Beret is entangled in a constantly deepening depression brought on by a combination of forces: the Indians, the plague of grasshoppers, the Plain itself. Furthermore, her religious upbringing and Old World training combine to convince her that she as well as the other inhabitants of the little settlement are sinners beyond the reach of God because they have chosen to live in a place so far removed from civilization and reason. She is not only gradually alienated from her husband but she begins to shun contact with the other settlers around her as well. The Plain becomes her constant adversary; she is crushed by her vision of Nature as a supernatural villain gnawing away at all that was familiar and turning her husband into a pagan who consorts with Indians and foreigners.

In her home village in Norway, Beret had all of the qualities which were valued in a woman. Physically beautiful, she had a very loving and gentle disposition. She was devoted to her husband and children but at the same time maintained loyalty to her aging parents. But on the Dakota plains these very virtues become her chief liabilities. She chastizes herself bitterly for leaving her parents behind in order to come to America with her husband. She broods over having married Per Hansa in the first place, although her parents disapproved of him, primarily because she had conceived their first child out of wedlock. The harsh Dakota climate and rigorous living conditions as well as the traumatic birth of a fourth child erode her beauty. The mysticism and devotion surrounding this child born on Christmas with a caul bewilders Beret and she regards the name Per Hansa gave him, Peder Victorious, as an affront to God himself.

Because of her gentleness and lack of self confidence, then, Beret cannot adjust to the emptiness and hostility of this new environment. Nothing in her background has prepared her for the ordeals of day to day living on the Great Plains without any comforts or hope of ever escaping. All she has known was protection and dependency, and pioneering therefore threatens her very existence because it demands constant self-sufficiency and ingenuity. Her dilemma is intensified because the same environment provides amusement, challenge, and adventure for her husband and sons. When she begins to fear and distrust nature itself her whole world falls into chaos.

The other women in the settlement are not as disturbed by the alien environment as Beret is. They are physically stronger and lack the agonizing guilt feelings that haunt her. They are determined to help their husbands create a new and better life, regardless of the obstacles they face. But nevertheless they are sympathetic to Beret throughout her deepening depression and emotional disorientation. By contrast, in Scarborough's *The Wind* the other women only increase the heroine's distress because they are openly contemptuous of her weakness and dependency. Beret would not have survived at all, nor would she have eventually recovered from her illness, had she been subjected to such ridicule.

In an apparent attempt to remind us that Beret's affliction was not unique in the westering experience, Rølvaag presents a vignette of another woman driven totally and violently insane by the shock of having to bury her child in an unmarked grave and leave him behind while they wandered pitifully in search of their travelling companions who had gone on ahead. This poor women is so deranged that her husband has to tie her in the wagon to keep her from running back across the Plain in search of her dead child. In their brief encounter it is Beret who comes closest of all the settlers to comforting the pitiful woman and understanding what has happened to her. Beret recognizes her own suffering and alienation mirrored in the other mad woman and the recognition temporarily enables Beret to hold onto her own sanity for a while longer. She feeds the woman, soothes her, and puts her to bed as though she were a child. But Beret's very compassion almost backfires tragically when the woman takes Beret's young daughter in the night and tries to run away with her. But regardless of how the other women are presented in the novel, Beret continues to stand out from them in stark contrast. It is as though the fears and inadequacies of the whole settlement are focused on the martyred Beret and expressed for all of them through her sickness.

The Personification of Nature

"Personified" is hardly adequate to describe fully the characterization of nature in this novel. Nature itself functions as a character throughout, a character who surpasses the men and women in strength and cunning. Nature is envisioned as a primal force, a sentient being from another realm of consciousness. It is a supernatural, formless being, a demon bent on the destruction of the puny humans who have invaded its realm. The Plain, then, is a constant, lurking presence throughout the novel, always waiting, always watching:

> . . .the Great Prairie stretched herself voluptuously; giantlike and full of cunning, she laughed softly into the reddish moon. "Now we will see what human might may avail against us. . . . Now we'll see!"

And still again:

> Monsterlike the Plain lay there—sucked in her breath one week and the next week blew it out again. Man she scorned; his works she would not brook. . . . She would know, when the time came, how to guard herself and her own against him.

Beret, because of her weakness and emotional instability, is the logical focus of the demon's wrath. Her sensitivity makes her more vulnerable than her more prosaic companions.

The Great Plains are, in fact, so different ecologically from the rest of the United States that a radically new lifestyle was necessary for the early settlers to even survive, let alone prosper, there. The lack of trees and the prevailing winds create a hostile landscape totally unlike what the settlers had been accustomed to, either in Europe or the eastern United States. Houses had to be dug out of the ground and blocks of sod were stacked to form walls. The women in particular usually hated the dank dirtiness of such dwellings. The land itself visually defies logic because of its unbroken expanse. In response, it is not surprising that both Rølvaag and Scarborough chose to depict the Plain as some*body,* as a supernatural force, rather than as an inert stage or backdrop for the human drama. Rølvaag carefully developed this literary device in his personification or "demonification" of the Great Plains; Scarborough used the same imagery to explore the causes of the madness of her heroine, Letty Mason. Both authors acknowledged man's helplessness in the confrontation between civilization and the pan-animistic forces of nature.

Homesickness for a more gentle and recognizable landscape of trees, flowers, water, and familiar buildings is at the root of Beret's sickness. She simply cannot adapt because the new environment of the Great Plains is so alien and hostile that it is beyond her comprehension. Above all, Beret cannot stand the emptiness:

> But more to be dreaded. . .was the strange spell of sadness which the unbroken solitude cast upon the minds of some. Many took their own lives; asylum after asylum was filled with disordered beings who had once been human. It is hard for the eye to wander from sky line to sky line, year in and year out, without finding a resting place!

Her recurring thought, "There's no place to hide!" becomes a poignant litany throughout the book. The visual disorientation and deceptive distances of the Plain permeate and distort her whole perspective toward herself, her family, and all that they experienced together; her very senses betray her. Not only does she have to contend with the Indians and their burial ground, the enforced loneliness of her husband's trips to town, and the grasshopper plague, but she is also haunted by the supernatural emanations which surround her:

> Beret was gazing at the western sky as the twilight

fast gathered around her; her eyes were riveted on a certain cloud that had taken on the shape of a face, awful of mien and giantlike in proportions; the shape seemed to swell out of the prairie and filled half the heavens.

She gazed a long time; now she could see the monster clearer. The face was unmistakable! There were the outlines of the nose and mouth. The eyes—deep, dark caves in the cloud—were closed. The mouth, if it were to open, would be a yawning abyss. The chin rested on the prairie.

Black and lean the whole face, but of such gigantic menacing proportions! Wasn't there something like a leer upon it? And the terrible creature was spreading everywhere; she trembled so desperately that she had to take hold of the grass.

Such a menacing creature in the clouds is part of the extraordinary worldview which was commonplace among Norwegian folk from traditional village backgrounds, and Rølvaag of course was familiar with this Nordic mythology. The devastating plague of the fourteenth century, for example, was depicted in oral tradition as a hag wandering through the countryside with a broom and a rake. This folk belief network was filled with superstitions and supernatural creatures which the settlers brought with them to the New World. Per Hansa, for example, is constantly bedeviled by his belief in trolls, those inimical ogres in folk belief who molest humans and are just as much at home on the sea as in the hills. Beret is terrified when Per Hansa flouts the boundary spirits by digging up and burning the Irish section marker stakes because this act is a sin which folk belief said would be punished by divine or supernatural retribution involving forces far beyond human control. She blames Per Hansa's foolishness on bewitchment. She is terrified of the Indian burial ground on the hillside because ghosts and wandering corpses are very real threats in the traditional worldview. And because of the supernatural belief network to which she ascribed, she sees demons everywhere as her mind deteriorates. At last Nature itself becomes such a real and threatening creature to her that she resorts to hanging curtains over the windows of the sod hut to keep the demon from watching her.

But even though Beret experiences such symptoms of madness as clairvoyance, hallucinations, and premonitions of death, she ultimately recovers enough to function relatively normally except for a religious fanaticism and self-righteousness which is almost unbearable to the other settlers. Beret's mental health is restored after an itinerant minister from the homeland finds his way to the isolated settlement and conducts service there, including the christening of the child, Peder Victorious. But ironically it is Beret's recovery which precipitates the concluding tragedy of the novel: human sacrifice to placate the vengeful demon. Nature triumphs in spite of Beret's recovery. The final section in *Giants of the Earth* is entitled, "The Great Plain Drinks the Blood of Christian Men and Is Satisfied," a reference to Per Hansa's death after Beret so irritates him that he embarks on a hopeless journey through the frozen countryside to get help for his dying friend, Hans Olsa. Per Hansa and Hans Olsa were physically the strongest and most resourceful of the settlers and ironically it is they who die as a direct result of the fury of a Plains blizzard. It is as though Beret through her recovery becomes the means by which the demonic Plain finally destroys its most capable adversaries. In that sense her recovery indicates that she is demon-possessed at last.

CONRAD RICHTER'S SOUTHWESTERN LADIES

Barbara Meldrum
University of Idaho

Roy Male, in *Hawthorne's Tragic Vision,* wrote that America has been "from its beginning. . .a predominantly masculine venture. . .a gamble that movement westward might assure not only prosperity but also some kind of moral purification. . . . In this predominantly masculine enterprise, the role of woman has always been anomalous."[1] Male's statement suggests both an idealistic and a materialistic goal in the western movement, a duality that is also present in Frederick Jackson Turner's discussion of the significance of the frontier. Turner spoke of a "perennial rebirth" on the frontier as the pioneer at first returns to "primitive conditions," then "little by little. . .transforms the wilderness." In this process certain character traits develop and American democracy is fostered.[2] Although Turner emphasizes the idealistic aspects of this process, his thesis is, as Robin Winks points out, "materialistic, emphasizing an economic determination which dwells upon land, upon size, upon space and upon its relative value in terms of the population."[3]

The role of woman in westward development is, indeed, both anomalous and ambiguous. She is linked with the more idealistic aspects in the sense that woman is regarded as a civilizing force, promoting the values of community life, family relationships, and social refinement.[4] However, she is also closely related to the materialistic aspects. The word "materialism" derives etymologically from roots which suggest both "mother" and "matter" or substance.[5] Classical mythology associates materialism with Demeter, the Greek goddess of corn, who is both matriarchal and agricultural. Woman is associated with productivity of the earth, and also with sorrow and death (suggested by the tale of Persephone, Demeter's daughter, who is claimed by the underworld for four winter months each year).

The matriarchal tie is a visible, material one. In contrast, the patriarchal tie is invisible, seemingly nonmaterial and, in this sense, spiritual.[6] In western terms the man is "idealistic" in the value he places on individualism and freedom; these ideals are associated with masculinity in the conquest of nature or of other people (Indians, nesters, etc.). This masculine idealism is more closely associated with the frontiersman than with the agrarian settler—frontiersman not only in the early sense of Crevecoeur's "ferocious, gloomy, and unsociable [back settlers] "[7] and the mountain men of fact and fiction, but frontiersman in the later manifestation of rugged cattleman, gambler, and gunfighter. The agrarian settler, however, is more closely associated with the feminine values of home, family, and the productivity of nature. Moreover, the male agrarian seems to be a blend of the freedom-loving, individualistic frontiersman and the home-loving, productive agrarian.

The role of neither the man nor woman in western development is a simple one. A distinction between masculine and feminine seems to be more appropriate than a distinction between man and woman: the distinction is one of gender rather than of sex. The psychologist David Holbrook provides, I believe, a key to the masculine-feminine dichotomy as it relates to the western experience: according to Holbrook, "Our society attaches the problem of identity to *doing* and *becoming:* to acquisitiveness, prowess, having and making"—all modes of " 'false male doing.' " What we need are "opportunities for us to complete our processes of growth, in terms of *being* by human contact, by love and sympathy, by creativity and modes of the 'feminine element.' "[8] In applying Holbrook's definitions to the western experience we can say that the movement westward has been a predominantly masculine venture characterized by acquisitiveness, prowess, having and making; to the extent that women have worked together with men in exploiting the opportunities of the western environment, the role of woman has been a part of the myth of western achievement through conquest. But the feminine element has also exercised a continual self-criticism of that myth by suggesting that true achievement of self comes through human contact, love and sympathy—that self-realization is not an external achievement gained by "doing," but is an internal state of being.

Conrad Richter's three novels of the Southwest provide us

with provocative portraits of women on the frontier and at the
same time suggest a feminine perspective on western achievement.[9] Each novel focuses on a central female character whose
story is told by a male narrator recalling the experiences of his
boyhood and youth. The boy is in each instance a family relation of the man who is married to or closely associated with the
leading female character. The boy thus provides a sympathetic
but essentially external view of the woman: characterization is
limited to what the boy knew, nuances of motivation remain
mysteries, and the women emerge as essentially idealized portraits shaped by a man's nostalgia for a lost youth. Though such
an approach may be frustrating for a reader interested in psychological probing of character, Richter's mode is eminently
suited to portrayal of an essentially symbolic perception of
Southwestern life.

The first of these novels, *Sea of Grass* (1937), is actually a
double story: a tale of family relationships and a tale of the
transition from open range country to an agrarian economy in
New Mexico. But Richter has interwoven these two stories
through the symbolic associations of the leading characters:
Jim Brewton personifies the old pioneer spirit, the aggressive,
conquering male who thrives in the open though harsh realities
of the sea of grass; his wife Lutie is associated with the taming of
that pioneer spirit by her instinctive hate for the sea of grass, her
ties with Brice Chamberlain (the eastern lawyer who champions
the nesters), and her femininity. Though there is no intrinsic
tie between the domestic tale and the historical theme (for what
happens to the sea of grass would likely have occurred whether
Lutie left her husband or not), the symbolic associations in the
story are so strong that the domestic and historical themes seem
to be interdependent. In this way, I believe Richter suggests a
perspective on the historical theme through his handling of the
Brewton family fortunes.

Colonel Brewton is the pioneer who has opened up the land
and made it safe from Indian attack; then the farmers come, but
they are not the happy farmers of Crevecoeur's idealized pro-
phecy. Though the nesters would seem to be the harbingers of
progress as a civilized, agrarian society takes hold, they are
actually unwitting villains who transform what was once a comparative garden of lush growth into a wasteland of plowed,
dusty, barren fields; for the limited rainfall of this region simply

cannot sustain the homesteads of these farmers. Brewton fore-
sees the inevitable destruction wrought by these people and tries
to resist them; a hard man not afraid to use a gun when necessary, he nonetheless is disciplined and "civilized," for he will
not fight his own country's troops no matter how much he
despises those who get others (that is, the army) to fight their
battles for them. " 'You can keep the nesters from being blown
away,' " he says to the commanding officer, " 'but God Himself
can't the prairie!' " (p. 80).

In stark contrast to Brewton, Brice Chamberlain epitomizes
the worst in the new civilization overtaking the region. He
mouths the cant phrases of progress and rights of individual
families to make a living off the land; but he hides behind the
emigrant canvas which he uses as a shield between himself and
Brewton (pp. 56-62), even as a weapon to get at that which is
closest to Brewton, his wife Lutie (pp. 40-41). For Chamberlain has apparently fathered Lutie's son Brock, and Lutie's decision to leave Brewton seems to stem from Chamberlain's
promise to join her in Denver—a promise he fails to keep when
Brewton, gun under his coat, waits for him at the railroad depot.
Chamberlain fails because he is a feminized man who cannot
cope directly with the masculine Brewton. Brock also fails
because he lacks Brewton's character: Brock cheats at cards, an
act Brewton finds far more reprehensible than Brock's fight
which ends in the death of his opponent. Both Brock and Chamberlain manipulate others to their own ends. Chamberlain within
the guise of the law and Brock outside the law. As Brock lies
dying, Chamberlain fails to appear (just as he had earlier failed
Lutie); but Brock reveals that side of himself which has en-
deared him to Brewton—that suggestion of his mother's character. And, ironically, his death becomes the catalyst for bringing
Lutie back to Brewton and restoring peace to the household.[16]

What, then, is it in Lutie which enables her to emerge as a
flawed but still eminently admirable character, in spite of her
associations with the despicable Chamberlain? It is, I believe, her
essential femininity—a femininity which in men is weakness or
even duplicity, but in woman is a source of strength. Lutie is
both fragile and delicate, and yet strong enough to overpower
even Brewton so that this towering, pagan, godlike creature, a
Jove from whose eyes shoot thunderbolts, becomes a merciful
God-the-Father who proclaims that Brock is his beloved son in

spite of all that has happened.[11] Here, the symbolism of characterization blends with the historical theme, for the pioneering spirit of Brewton wants and needs the civilized, humanizing influence of Lutie and seeks to bring her into his world; but the initial transition is too sharp, and though Lutie tries to transform the desert by planting trees, beautifying the house, and hosting social gatherings, she longs for the life she has left in the city and leaves, returning only when Brock's fate brings her back. The narrator Hal notes, as Lutie worships in church the day after Brock's death, that "the click of her beads was strangely like the click of six-shooters, and the sibilants of her lips like those of the wind drawing through rusty barbed wire and yerba de vibora" (p. 133).[12] Lutie forges a tenuous balance between violence and civilization, masculinity and femininity, in her turbulent union with Brewton. For them, the two worlds converge but are never one; for the narrator Hal, the union is complete as he, an androgynous character, achieves the best of both worlds. Imagery is internalized as we see that the wasteland of the nesters has become the wasteland of Brewton's inner life at the low point of his trauma, for his furrowed face was "like a worn-out field" and the "inward drouth had dried up the last few water-holes of life and power" (p. 122). The narrator, who earlier had learned that underneath the "thin veneer of Eastern schools" he "was only a savage young Brewton from an untamed sea of grass" (p. 100), becomes a doctor and takes up his practice in the region of his youth where he learns to face "the winds that in my profession usually blow in the night" (p. 124). His education, his eastern civilization, blend with his Brewton heritage, and he is further humanized by Lutie's influence so that the ethereal blending of Lutie's aroma of violets and Brewton's cigar smoke (p. 147) becomes for him a living, enduring unity which undergirds his life.

Richter's second Southwestern novel, *Tacey Cromwell* (1942), focuses on the inherent materialism of western life, for the central female character, Tacey, is both matriarchal and materialistic. Tacey is a madam in a sporting house in Socorro, New Mexico, who is living with Gaye Oldaker, half-brother of the narrator, Nugget. When the young boy Nugget runs away from his uncle in Kansas to join his brother, Tacey at first resents his presence; but then her maternal instincts are aroused, and she and Gaye take Nugget with them to Bisbee, Arizona, a mining town hopefully far enough away from Socorro so that they can begin a new life together. Tacey is shown to be ambitious, eager to achieve success for Gaye and herself in spite of the stigma of her past. But when her past catches up with her, she is condemned by the community and stripped of her loved ones: though presumably in the West a person's identity can be established by merit, regardless of social class, rather than be determined by one's past, Tacey discovers that social class and prejudice overrule merit, and she is defeated. But she continues to direct the lives of her loved ones, primarily through her influence over Gaye, who is weaker than she and always yields to her direction. In an unlikely but intriguing series of events, Tacey severs her outward relationship with Gaye, urges him to rise in the world by becoming a real banker rather than a faro banker and later by entering politics, promotes his marriage to the daughter of the town's leading citizen, rises in the town herself by establishing a successful seamstress business, and finally is reunited with Gaye and Nugget after the death of Gaye's wife. It is a rags-to-riches story with a peculiar western twist as this one-time prostitute achieves success in a reputable career as seamstress, proves herself to be an ideal mother, and succeeds finally in joining the mainstream of respectable western society. For Tacey, western development is a material-social ideal not easily achieved and at times belied by prejudice, a double standard social morality, and an inconsistent regard for a person's individual background; but it is an ideal that can be achieved through persistence and good luck.

The materialistic-matriarchal theme of this work is developed by Richter through imagery and incident. Both Tacey and Gaye have established themselves in business, through prostitution and gambling, vocations financially rewarding and apparently suited to the western environment, though prostitution carries with it a stigma not associated with Gaye's gambling even though Tacey has achieved the management position of madam. Tacey's materialism further expresses itself in her ability to transform a house into a home which expresses her personality, through careful use of material possessions (pp. 87, 174-75). Her uncanny ability to copy the lines of fashion through observation and sewing skill leads to her success as a seamstress when the attractiveness of her product finally breaks down the barriers of prejudice; for when she can offer something the leading citizens want, they promptly forget their prejudices to the extent that they accept her product, if not herself. In her

influence on Gaye's career her feminine materialism is most
evident, for she urges Gaye to take a job in a real bank in lieu
of his position as a faro banker. But Nugget and many of the
miners believe Gaye has actually "gone down in the world"
by taking a job with a bank which has a less stable financial
reputation than the faro tables, and Gaye complains that he has
become simply a clerk with less respect than he commanded
at faro (p. 129). However, Tacey is proven right in her sense of
ultimate financial and social gain, for as the town becomes more
"civilized," the people forego faro and follow Wall Street as
stock market speculation, with bigger stakes than ever crossed
the faro table, becomes the gambling pastime (p. 206).

The image of a "golden West" links the matriarchal-materi-
alistic motifs with the narrator's own experience, for as an orphaned boy in Kansas he had been drawn by the light in the
Western sky, "golden like the house had been when my mother
was here, and it lay toward the West where I thought her spirit
would like to be" (p. 5). When he arrives at his brother's town,
he believes this "must be the golden West at last where people
had more money than they could spend in the day-time" (p. 12).
But when Tacey's initial reception is cold and forbidding, Nugget
decides that the "golden Western light. . .was false as a gypsy.
It might look bright enough back in Kansas. But once you were
close, it came through the window gray and mocking." However, when he awakens, the light looks "golden again streaming
through the red curtains," and Tacey has instinctively placed her
maternal arm around him (p. 23). From that time on, Tacey's
maternal traits dominate, and the golden West becomes identified
with maternal fulfillment. She becomes surrogate mother for
an orphaned neighbor girl, Seely; when she opens the bedroom
door to let her friend look inside, all the narrator sees is Seely
and her brother asleep; but to Tacey's friend (also a reformed
prostitute), it is "as if Tacey had showed her a vein of gold in the
blasted rock" (p. 88). And of course, Nugget's name suggests
that he too is a nugget of gold. The real treasure to be claimed
in the West is the gold of family relationships, even though
adoptive rather than blood relation. Tacey is the suffering
mother, separated from her would-be children Nugget and Seely
by the petty jealousies of the townswomen, suffering especially
for Seely as she sees her own self in that girl and longs to give
her the direction she needs, but vindicated at last when Gaye's
wife, who fails as Seely's adoptive mother, recognizes the validity

of Tacey's love for Seely. Tacey's suffering has come from long experience, and it prepares her to help Seely; whereas Gaye's wife, for whom life was always easy until she found she could not cope with Seely, suffers too late and is destroyed by her own suffering. In this western tale Tacey becomes the New World Demeter, ironic though she be, as this one-time madam achieves a surrogate family, suffers as a mother, and inspires the material productivity of her loved ones.

Richter's third Southwestern novel, *The Lady* (1957), provides a more complex view of the masculine-feminine dichotomy in western experience. The lady, Ellen, is the daughter of a Mexican mother and an English father, heiress of a large sheep ranch first established by a Spanish grant. In the central plot of the novel she is involved in a power struggle with her brother-in-law Snell Beasley, a land-hungry shyster American lawyer. Thus she represents a blend of Old World and New in the clash of cultures which took place during the transition from a Spanish past to an Anglo-American dominated present.

In portraying this complex woman, Richter suggests parallels between the dualities of the racial heritage, the masculine-feminine traits Ellen embodies within herself, and the basic masculine vs. feminine conflict between Beasley and Ellen. As was true in the earlier novels, Richter focuses on the strength possible to the feminine character, a strength he seems to identify with the female principle and, in an historical sense, with an advanced stage of civilization. Ellen's "complex femininity" is a blend of "English abruptness" and "feminine Mexican wile," a strong willed capability and an "appealing helplessness" that invariably inspires men to rescue her and, in so doing, to bring "masculine pleasure" to themselves (pp. 16-17). Her complex character manifests itself in seemingly conflicting roles, for not only is she a lady who must be waited on, but she can manage the large family sheepranch; her beauty and delicacy are offset by her propensity for violence, her skill with a gun, and her expert horsemanship. The imbalance of her masculine-feminine traits provides the germ of the story, for it is her masculine reliance on violence made effectual by her marksmanship which precipitates the long train of events that eventually claim the lives of her husband and son; and it is her feminine expectation that she will be rescued from her difficulties by the men in her life which draws her loved ones into the enveloping destruction. Her salvation eventually comes when, ironically, no men remain to help her and an accident brings about the death of the villainous Beasley. Her sister then inherits Beasley's fortune, and the two sisters are reunited in love and material prosperity. The ultimate victory of the feminine is indicated by the fact that Ellen cries for the first time when reunited with her sister (see pp. 119, 191) and by the irony that Ellen's deliverer is a woman rather than a man (see pp. 17, 180-81, 191).

Shortly before the climactic ending, Ellen obviously struggles with her propensity to violence as she paces the floor at night with gun at hand while Beasley sits, an easy target, in his lamplit study next door. But her Spanish catholicism urges her toward longsuffering love, and though no direct connection is drawn between that love and her fortuitous rescue, Richter seems to suggest that evil will destroy itself if love will restrain any tendency toward violence.[13] The more feminine virtue of love proves to be stronger than the masculine aggressive evil of Beasley.

Thus in Richter's Southwestern novels western development is portrayed in part in its more easily recognizable material forms, identified with the land and material possessions. But Richter's peculiar accomplishment is that he has internalized the achievement of western goals and has attributed both power and fulfillment to the female principle. To Richter, the real land of promise lies within the individual (though inward fulfillment may be matched by outward prosperity), and the real achievers are the women. The old myth of conquest remains, but only in the nostalgia of the narrator, whose recreation of a by-gone era is a silent recognition of the closing of the frontier and the anachronism of the myth. It is Richter's women who endure and prevail, and their femininity is the key to their success.

NOTES

[1](Austin: University of Texas Press, 1957), pp. 3-4.

[2]Frederick Jackson Turner, "The Significance of the Frontier in American History" (1893), in *The Frontier in American History,* ed. Ray A. Billington (New York: Holt, Rinehart and Winston, 1962), pp. 2-4, 37.

[3]*The Myth of the American Frontier: Its Relevance to America, Canada and Australia* (Leicester: Leicester University Press, 1971), pp. 10-11.

[4]Ray Allen Billington stresses women's function as "harbingers of civilization" in *America's Frontier Heritage* (New York: Holt, Rinehart and Winston, 1966), pp. 216-217.

[5]*"māter-,"* in *American Heritage Dictionary of the English Language* (1969), p. 1527.

[6]For a discussion of Johann J. Bachofen's theories of matriarchal-patriarchal historical development, see Lisa Appignanesi, *Femininity and the Creative Imagination: A Study of Henry James, Robert Musil and Marcel Proust* (London: Vision Press, 1973), p. 7, and Carolyn G. Heilbrun, *Toward a Recognition of Androgyny* (New York: Harper & Row, 1973), pp. xiii-xiv.

[7]J. Hector St. John de Crèvecoeur, *Letters from an American Farmer,* ed. W. P. Trent and Ludwig Lewisohn (New York: Albert & Charles Boni, 1925), pp. 66-67 (Letter III).

[8]"R. D. Laing and the Death Circuit," *Encounter,* 31, no. 2 (1968), p. 39.

[9]Page references are indicated in the text and are to the following editions: *The Sea of Grass* (New York: Alfred A. Knopf, 1937); *Tacey Cromwell* (New York: Alfred A. Knopf, 1942); *The Lady* (New York:

Alfred A. Knopf, 1957).

[10]The imagery is religious as Brock becomes a Christ figure. See pp. 138, 148.

[11]See pp. 91, 117-118, 121-122, 136 for pagan, godlike character of Brewton; p. 148 for merciful father.

[12]The literal meaning of yerba de vibora—snakeweed—underscores the duality suggested in this passage. The plant is associated with the emigrants and with Lutie's sense of the fatality associated with the nester movement on pp. 13, 24-25.

[13]See pages 155 to 158, and 162 to 168. (Ellen's niece, Felicitas, plays an important role when she offers flowers—an expression of love—which Ellen accepts.)

WESTERING AND WOMAN:
A THEMATIC STUDY OF KESEY'S
ONE FLEW OVER THE CUCKOO'S NEST
AND FISHER'S *MOUNTAIN MAN*

Joseph M. Flora
University of North Carolina
at Chapel Hill

The fact of the West, the fact of the frontier, has been the distinctive shaping factor in the American experience. And, as we all know, our literature from the first has wrestled with the American male's conflict about the compatibility of the female with the promise of the frontier, or at least her compatibility with the frontier as symbol of male fulfillment. James Fenimore Cooper, in giving us Natty Bumppo, gave us the archetypal frontiersman, attracted to but frightened, eventually, from woman. The theme has persisted. Huckleberry Finn wants to light out to the territory because Aunt Sally is about to civilize him. The freedom that Huck found on the raft is anathema to the likes of Aunt Sally, a Widow Douglas, or a Miss Watson. In our own century Faulkner has comically and seriously treated the role of woman on the frontier in *Go Down, Moses.* In "Was," Uncle Buck and Uncle Buddy want to retrieve Tomey's Turl to prevent Miss Sophonsiba's encroaching on their land. And those two go for months without ever seeing a white woman. They convey Natty Bumppo's dilemma nicely. Uncle Buddy is absolutely determined that no female will ever ruin the place or catch him. Uncle Buck intellectualizes the same position, but because he wears the red tie we know that he wants Miss Sophonsiba, or some female, to catch him eventually. And Faulkner makes it clear that roan-toothed Miss Sophonsiba is a very clever hunter. In the ante-bellum years she helps domesticate the male dominated Yoknapatawpha frontier. In "Delta Autumn," near the end of the novel, Ike McCaslin, Buck and Sophonsiba's son, is still having trouble coping with the female, in the decaying Eden in which he has lived his long life. And surely Faulkner convinces us that through miscegenation old Carothers McCaslin brought a curse on the Mississippi land in a context that was essentially frontier. Old Carothers operated on the promise that on his frontier land new codes of conduct towards women, black though they be, were in order. *Go Down, Moses* is Western as well as Southern.

But my point here is to remind us of the pervasive problem. I wish to emphasize the continuing dilemma by focusing on two more recent novels by unmistakably Western novelists, Ken Kesey's *One Flew Over the Cuckoo's Nest* and Vardis Fisher's *Mountain Man*. These two novels invite comparison on many counts. They were published in a short span, Kesey's in 1962 and Fisher's in 1965. Kesey's novel was a first novel, Fisher's the last of many novels. Kesey's work was a young man's novel. Fisher was the "dean" of Western novelists. Kesey's novel was immediately taken up by the young and was widely read and re-read on college campuses. Here was a book that exposed the establishment for what it was. Fisher's novel did not become widely known to the same young readers, but in its paperback editions *Mountain Man* in the past ten years has probably rivalled Fisher's *Children of God* as his most familiar title. In both *Cuckoo's Nest* and *Mountain Man* we respond to other than the realistic tale. The realism of both books has been questioned. Both books, in fact, have been charged with sentimentality. Both books deal with myth, particularly Western myth.

Furthermore, both novels were made into popular motion pictures in the 1970's, motion pictures with critical as well as popular approval. Symbolic of the success of *Cuckoo's Nest* is its dominance in the 1976 Academy Awards. *Jeremiah Johnson* (the title of the adaptation of Fisher's novel) did not win an Oscar for 1972, but it was in 1976 one of the recent film successes chosen for special Sunday Night movies on television. Among film critics Pauline Kael did not like *Jeremiah Johnson*,[1] but American audiences were more in tune with Jonathan Yardley, who reviewed the movie in the *Greensboro* (N.C.) *Daily News* on February 5, 1973. Yardley wrote: "In every regard 'Jeremiah Johnson' is an exemplary movie. . . . The photography is lovely without being arty, fully conveying the beauty and danger of the mountains. Sydney Pollack's direction is firm and un-obtrusive. The secondary performances are all excellent. But this is Redford's movie. He is, indeed, becoming one of those rare actors who dominate each film they make. . . . Now, in 'Jeremiah Johnson' he has created a character who is wholly realized and believable, a complex man whose depth is at once surprising and persuasive. It is one of the memorable performances of recent years, and one that must be seen."

Both movies and both books are one in glorifying the spirit of the free man. Kesey's novel may be taken as the ultimate horror the mountain man might have imagined as he saw the settlers coming into the Western territories. *Jeremiah Johnson,* with hardly an indoor scene, is one of the great outdoor films we have had. Movie, like book, conveys the love for a magnificent land. The Kesey movie, like the book, takes place almost totally indoors. Its Jeremiah Johnsons and Sam Minards have been emasculated, or rendered impotent, and hardly think of the outside. Chief Bromden looks out of the window from time to time and sometimes has reveries about a great land—to remind us of what has been lost. There is one "escape" to the sea for the inmates of the asylum when they experience something of the freedom of the mountain man. But the name of the boat, *The Lark,* makes clear just what that escape is. It is only a lark. After that, McMurphy is reduced to bringing Candy Starr and her friend *in* to the asylum. It is noticeably easier to get the girls in than to get the men out.

But even as Candy and Sandy seem to be on McMurphy's side, they underscore one of the major dimensions of Kesey's novel—the basically negative effect of the female on the male drive towards freedom and fulfillment. In fact, the novel is as vehement as "Hansel and Gretel" in portraying the female in an unflattering light. Kesey shows us only two kinds of women: the maternal emasculator and the whore—both fascinated with the same feature of the male anatomy.

I have mentioned "Hansel and Gretel" because when we as adults read this story to our children we can sense it as a harmless manifestation of the child's hostilities toward the mother, with whom he spends most of his time and who frequently tells him "no." In the fairy tale we change mother to stepmother, for it has always been justifiable to feel resentful towards a stepmother. She is the one who *makes* father treat the children so badly. Of course, he doesn't want to, and we recognize that he's perfectly helpless before her. Undoubtedly she is the real witch! At story's end we will wish her dead, and the children will get to live with father without any mother figure. The old witch with the gingerbread house is only a replay with variation, but a bit more fun since Gretel gets to push her into the oven. (It seems that witches wish to devour little boys more than they do little girls.) Then it is only a matter of time before brother and sister can live together, with father, in primal innocence. It's a great story—particularly for Gretel.

Kesey's novel does not allow the total wish-fulfillment of the old fairy tale. The Chief escapes, and in the book the Nurse's power is broken—but McMurphy is dead. Still, what movie-goer will forget the scene when McMurphy assaults the Nurse? A lot of wish fulfillment there! But book and movie are for an older audience than is "Hansel and Gretel," and we cannot push our witch into an oven. The movie gives even less triumph than the novel, for Big Nurse goes on, her power hardly checked.

The nurse is traditionally the mother of mercy. We might be reminded of the war front in Hemingway's *A Farewell to Arms.* There, too, we find mainly nurses and whores. In a sense (a good sense) Catherine Barclay combines both roles. Particularly when we compare her with Kesey's Big Nurse we can sense the injustice of much of the prejudice against Hemingway's treatment of women. Surely Catherine is a growing, sensitive person— an important tutor for Frederic Henry—the most important tutor in the book. As the novel ends, Frederic seems to have only intimations of what she tried to teach him, but the reader is supposed to see more. Kesey's world has darkened all that Catherine represents; it vehemently cries out that Huck Finn did well to strive to escape Aunt Sally and her kind.

Kesey's very title underscores the maternal threat. Note that word *nest.* Hasn't the Western hero always felt a shudder at the notion of the sweet little nest, out there in the West? Kesey's novel brings home the ultimate nightmare: Big Mama is Big Nurse—her big breasts give no comfort. She wants nothing more and nothing less than to keep her little boys forever in her efficiently managed nest. She is so powerful that her boys "choose" to be where they are—a fact that McMurphy, the modern mountain man, finds totally shocking.

Big Nurse has a name: Nurse Ratched. For the more sophisticated, there is the play on the *ratchet* wheel—but there is also the little boy's naughty "rat shit." Calling the nurse by that name gives him a false sense of power. He *knows* what she is, even if he can't do anything about her. The name conveys the novel's truth about the Mother of Mercy.

Let us quickly survey some of the other indictments of "female" in the novel. We should start with Chief Bromden's mother since, after McMurphy, the Chief is the most important male in the novel. He is institutionalized because his white mother "did in" his Papa, insuring the victory of the Combine, the great white real estate interests. The Chief is Kesey's narrator, and he consistently presents the mental hospital as the creation of women. The visitors who come to the wards—teachers or whatever—are women. Public Relations only seems to be a man, and his public is female: "Oh, when I think back on the old days, on the filth, the bad food, even, yes the brutality, oh, I realize, ladies, that we have come a long way in our campaign."[2] Harding, the most intellectual patient in the ward, is under Nurse Ratched's care because of his inability to relate to women; the Chief reports that Harding complains that his wife is "the sexiest woman in the world" who "can't get enough of him nights" (p. 23). He is terrified. And poor Billy Bibbitt! His mother is a declared ally of the Nurse, dedicated to keeping Billy just that: *Billy.* Sexual initiation, McMurphy feels, might launch this lad of thirty into manhood. Billy stops stuttering only once, in the climactic scene of the novel after McMurphy has procured his sexual initiation with Candy Starr. But Nurse Ratched can undo it all in a moment as she utters the most frightening word in the ward: "What worries me, Billy. . .is how your poor mother is going to take this" (p. 264). Mother, as Hansel and Gretel knew, never did want us to have any fun.

It is significant that McMurphy, though thirty-five, has never married. In cowboy legends, he should not be married. This cowboy has gone a bit beyond: he has found only one redeemable feature in women, and to obtain that he has not found it necessary to marry. The whole tenor of McMurphy's life view is illustrated by his youthful initiation into sex, which had taken place when he was about ten and the girl less. Yet she "drug" him to bed. McMurphy had wondered if they ought to announce their "engagement," his own instinct being that the sexual event should symbolize something important: "But this little whore—at the most eight or nine—reached down and got her dress off the floor and said it was mine, said 'You can hang this up someplace, I'll go home in my drawers, announce it that way—they'll get the idea' " (pp. 217-18). So much for McMurphy's idealism. With such limited views toward women McMurphy could never defeat a force as formidable as Big Nurse.

While Fisher's *Mountain Man* shares with Kesey's novel anguish over the invading hordes of the "civilized" and the loss of freedom to the individual man, it could hardly be more different in its portrayal of women. Western writers have not always viewed women with the vitriolic distrust we find in Kesey. We will do well to keep in mind the subtitle of Fisher's book: "A Novel of Male and Female in the Early American West." In fact, the title *Mountain Man* is not the one Fisher wanted for his novel, but is a compromise he worked out with his publisher. Fisher's original title was *Male and Female,* and it is useful for coming to terms with the kind of book *Mountan Man* is, for the novel is a departure in many respects from the traditional Fisher approach. We recognize the matter and the style as his surely, but many readers were so accustomed to thinking of Fisher as the hard-boiled realist or naturalist that they were puzzled by his last novel. It is as if the great debunker of the romantic novel had at last bared his own romantic soul, as if the great proponent of the rational would give the emotional its full due. Incredibly, in Fisher's novel, we find a mountain man breaking forth into noble song as he makes his way through perilous terrain. Had Fisher written a novel or an opera?

Fisher knew what he was about, and probably the risks he was taking. He did think of his work as a symphony to the West that he loved. Furthermore, he used the imagery of the Biblical story of creation in a sustained way, joining the ranks of other American writers who had seen the American story as paralleling the account in Genesis. And he emphasized the female as much as the male, which is one reason the title *Mountain Man* is not quite adequate and why we have the subtitle. "Male and Female created he them," we read in Genesis. Fisher's intention of balancing Male and Female, while focusing on the story of Sam Minard, is seen in his division of the novel into three sections: Lotus, Kate, Sam.

In fact, only these three characters receive much attention. Unlike Kesey, Fisher was not much interested in many characterizations, though we meet many mountain men. We remember their stories rather than their characters. Fisher keeps the focus on Lotus, Kate, and Sam through frequent use of indirect discourse and by treating the other mountain men in a catalogue manner. The script writers of *Jeremiah Johnson* had to invent their supporting characters, for while the catalogue technique might work in a novel, a movie does not have the leisure wherewith to stress the sense Fisher builds of the mountain men as a group.

In fact, we come to realize that not even the major characters are to be taken finally as individuals. Fisher's original title is valuable for emphasizing the representativeness, the mythic dimension of his major characters. Sam is *the* mountain man, representative in something like Emerson's sense. He is not the average, but embodies the finest qualities of his kind: he sums them up. Fisher has purposely made him bigger than life. He is named Samson John Minard. The Samson is another Biblical reference that keys us into the heroic dimensions of Fisher's character. Sam is six foot four, and he towers over the other mountain men physically as well as intellectually, artistically, and every other way. He is both strong and gentle. He is a man of great faith—and as Fisher's original title makes clear—he is Adam in the brief moment when Eden was to be found in the American West. He is living life as his Creator intended life to be lived. No other character in Fisher has so keen a sense of a Creator.

But at age twenty-seven, after eight years as a mountain man, Sam Minard feels that something is missing from his life. He is an Adam whose Eden is not yet complete—so he seeks the lovely Indian girl he saw first a year ago. We are reminded of Genesis 2:18: "And the Lord God said, It is not good that a man should be alone, I will make him an help meet for him." The maiden has been much on Sam's mind. Fisher begins with Sam's journeying to find his bride—she is no accidental thing as she is in *Jeremiah Johnson*. The movie is closer to the Western stereotype in making Johnson reluctant to take a wife. Fisher lets us know that many mountain men did fear alliance with a woman. Windy Bill warns Sam:

"I tell ye, Sam, if she be female, no matter if red-
skin, blackskin, or whiteskin, she will torment the life
outta ye fer foofarraw. Day and night she will. I know
mountain men has tried them all, even the Diggers, even
the Snakes, even the niggers; and I been tole the nigger
she is as sweet as Hank Cady's honey. But I swear by the
ole hoss that carried me safe twenty mile with fifty blackfeet runnin outta their skins to lift my hair that wolf is
wolf and female is female, and this ole coon can't stand
no more. . . . A woman's breast it's the hardest rock the
Almighty made on this ole earth, and I can see no sign on
it. I could track even a piece of thistledown but I never
could see no tracks in a woman's heart."[3]

But Fisher shares instances with us of mountain men who lived
happily with their Indian wives, and Sam's marriage proves to
be that ingredient that makes his cup run to overflowing.

For his Indian maiden, Lotus, is beautiful and all that Eve
could ever be. The Edenic quality of Sam's relationship with his
new bride is suggested in several ways. Sam must teach Lotus
many things, importantly the English language. So he names and
points out to her, allowing Fisher to poetize repeatedly on the
magnificence of the natural world they live in. Fisher's Adam
and Eve discover each other's bodies and the delights thereof in
a similarly pastoral manner. Eve responds to her man's gentleness. "And they were both naked, the man and his wife, and
were not ashamed." Repeatedly in the Lotus section we sense
the quality of the shared experiences of Adam and Eve. He is
older, not superior. And he looks for children as the natural
fulfillment of their love. After Lotus becomes pregnant, Sam is
eager to accept responsibility for the child as he has for the wife.
Lotus does not threaten Sam's manhood, but she allows him to
express aspects of it hitherto subdued. Fisher tells us: "In the
vacuum where for seven years he had known only eating and
killing and dodging his enemies he now enthroned her and she
began to fill him; and his emotions enfolded her as she enfolded
him, until on awaking she would be the first thing he would
think of, and the last thing before falling asleep" (p. 69). All of
this is, of course, worlds away from McMurphy's experience.
We know, however, that brevity is part of the essence of any
Edens we have ever read about. Thus, it happens that Sam loses
Lotus, but he will never forget the bliss of that married fulfill-

ment.

While the given of *Mountain Man* is Sam's decision to marry, the opening dramatic scene of the novel has to do with another woman, Kate Bowden. Sam happens upon the Bowden wagon just after Kate has killed with an axe four Blackfeet who have murdered her three children. Kate becomes a legend to all of the mountain men, but she becomes most significant of all to Sam, who has marvelled at her strength in crisis and at the mother love that keeps her the guardian of the graves Sam helps her make and consecrate. To the rational view she is mad, but in the spirit of Fisher's novel, Kate is transported into a sacred world. As Sam is the representative mountain man and Lotus the representative young maiden, Kate becomes the highest representative of motherhood: Thus, it is that Sam, bent on vengeance after his loss of Lotus, turns more and more to Kate. It is his vision of Kate, the representative mother, that enables him to give up his path of vengeance, to attain to a higher degree of manhood.

In the Lotus section, Sam is the teacher. In the second and third sections of the novel, Kate is the needed balm and inspiration that teaches Sam. Fisher's novel celebrates both sexual love and mother love. Father love is made possible only because of the female qualities, and even though Sam loses his biological child, Fisher gives strong emphasis to the deepening concept of fatherhood in Sam. Significantly, exactly in the middle of *Mountain Man,* Sam kills a young Indian. Chapter 15 ends with Sam looking down "a full five minutes" at the brave youth. He does not take the scalp and cut off the ear, as he has been doing, but gives the youth as noble a grave as he can. This is the first check to what Fisher presents as male aggressions— Kate also killed, but in the instinctive moment, not programatically as Sam is doing. Sam's zeal for killing lessens, and mid-novel he is on his way back to Kate. Later in the novel, after his escape from the Blackfeet, he again returns to the mother— for healing, for comfort, for insight. Part II ends with Sam's resting his head on the lap of Kate, who has been the inspiration that has saved his life and his soul.

In the final section of the novel there is yet the rendezvous of the mountain men and their collective vengeance for the insult put on Sam, but it is clear that Sam sees things differently from the other mountain men because of his experience with Kate.

Sam's fatherhood needs time to grow, and it does in the final movement—which progresses from recovery and vengeance to forgiveness and peace. The importance of the mother to the process is emphasized at the end of the novel through Kate's death. Sam is shocked and humbled by the Indians' response to Kate's death: they buried Kate by her children and placed a monument of stones over her. Sensing the beauty of Kate's devotion that crosses racial and cultural lines, Sam decides it is time to make peace with the Indians.

Positive accounts of women in the novel are not dependent upon Kate and Lotus. Sam has good memories of his own mother and sister. He has not gone to the wilderness, as did many mountain men, because he had turned his back on the idea of home and family. Sam's past has nourished his experience in the great West. He has been singularly blessed. His own father is also a positive memory. Sam's background facilitates the growth of his concept of fatherhood.

Fisher is supportive of the female and the concept of family in other ways. The novel finds mother love strong in the Indian culture, and Sam can read it everywhere in the world of nature.

Thus, while Ken Kesey's *One Flew Over the Cuckoo's Nest* is filled with frightening female images, not every Western writer has found the female so threatening—certainly not Vardis Fisher, whom Alfred Kazin described as our last authentic novelist of the frontier.[4] There is undoubted force in Kesey's novel, but his vision is like that of "Hansel and Gretel"—distorted, incomplete, and—in its treatment of women—amoral if not immoral. Fisher's conception and treatment of women is, by contrast, moral, responsible, and (to use a key Fisher concept) adult.[5] And it should be noted that while *Mountain Man* is Fisher's most poetic tribute to wifely and motherly love, that novel is not unique in Fisher's canon. From his first novel, *Toilers of the Hills*, onward, Vardis Fisher has turned a sensitive eye to the problems and contributions of women. If American novelists have pondered most often about the American Adam, Vardis Fisher has sought to understand and to portray the American Eve as well.

NOTES

[1] See *The New Yorker,* December 30, 1972, pp. 50-51.

[2] *One Flew Over the Cuckoo's Nest* (New York: New American Library, 1962), p. 14. Hereafter references to the novel will be given in parentheses and will refer to this edition.

[3] *Mountain Man* (New York: William Morrow & Co., 1965), p. 51. Hereafter references to the novel will be given in parentheses and will refer to this edition.

[4] Alfred Kazin, "Our Last Authentic Frontier Novelist," *New York Herald Tribune Book Review,* August 27, 1939, p. 3.

[5] It is true that the archetypal dimensions of *Mountain Man* have disturbing implications concerning the role of woman in America. The American Eve as wife is destroyed, and the American Eve as mother is cut off from her family. Fisher's novel leaves open the possibility that Sam may remarry, but it is far from a certainty. The Eden of the American West emerges as much more congenial to Adam than to his helpmeet. Nevertheless, Fisher is unequivocal about the necessity of the female virtues for the West.

HEROES VS. WOMEN:
CONFLICT AND DUPLICITY IN STEGNER

Kerry Ahearn
Oregon State University

Wallace Stegner said in his essay "Born a Square" that he had no choice but to write about the West, for he knows it better than anything else. But thinking of his novels in relation to the region reminds me of the homilies of our Puritan divines: be in the world, but not of it. In the deepest sense, Stegner's fiction is in the West but not of it. By West, I mean of course the regional characteristics invented rather than discovered: Stegner has made his way among the faded props of the Wild West myth, as disgusted with the spectacle as Bruce Mason was with his father Bo. But even the disgust has not been given overt expression. The West is not the primary issue in his writing, not even the primary interest; what has fascinated Stegner from the beginning is the most earnest theme of all, the way to live—how shall a good man conduct himself. The evidence suggests that "man" here should not be taken in its most general sense. Men are the trouble in Stegner's fiction.

We are probably all painfully aware of the narrow way implied by the term "Western Hero," that mobile American bully, however well-intentioned, who in the center of his soul remains untouched by women and other of life's complexities, who resents authority, lives for principles that don't quite cohere in a social context, and never recognizes the destructive impulses of his worship of wandering (psychic and physical). In his youth, Stegner knew lots of men who defined competence by what he in *Wolf Willow* called this "masculine and semi-barbarous" standard. The juxtaposition of those adjectives tells a good deal about Stegner's vision; masculinity has always been defined in his fiction as a savage impulse, always prone to extreme positions. Women provide spoken or unspoken challenges to those positions, and tend to suffer as a result. Consider Paul Condon in Stegner's early novel, *Fire and Ice* (1941), an angry young man whose every thought is couched in Young Communist League rhetoric; or Edwin Vickers of *On a Darkling Plain* (1940), a young World War I veteran who gives himself to a melancholy misanthropy and who views society as "a jungle of animals, slavering after the blood of their enemies, hot for mean pleasures, riddled with hypocrisies and rotten with lies." Consider Bo Mason from *The Big Rock Candy Mountain*, who is given to almost every masculine excess that could in 1943 be described in print. And to eliminate the suspicion that this is merely an early phase, think for a moment of Oliver Ward in *Angle of Repose* (1971). By the end of that fine novel, Oliver's mulishness seems more important to his grandson than any other trait. Finally, we have Joe Allston of *All the Little Live Things* (1967) and *The Spectator Bird* (1976), a curmudgeon many believe beyond salvation. Stegner returns instinctively to the spectacle of the man who is confused about where to give his faith or who has given it and perhaps his energy to a dubious cause. Furthermore, his definition of good is not the achievement of the opposite—no man ever turns out "good" in his fiction: the best Stegner can allow is to leave an open-ended situation where a man comes to recognize his fallibility and desires to guide himself henceforth with that knowledge of weakness. His best books, those which explore the problem most fully, end with those resolutions untried. We leave Bruce Mason, Lyman Ward, and Joe Allston on thresholds, with their new paradigms of the self untested by experience. Once the reader understands that Stegner's optimism is conditional, and that always, always, men prepare themselves for "salvation" through some kind of self-renunciation, the relationships between Stegner and the West and between men and women in his fiction become clearer.

Those conceptions of the "good man" (what might be called the optimism of defectiveness), so far from the conventional ideas of the brave hombre, the Western hero, provide the destination, but not the enlivening stuff, of Stegner's fiction. He is fascinated by the brute strength of self-reliance's delusions. Consider the scene in *Wolf Willow* where Alfie Carpenter takes a foul tip square in the mouth, spits out two teeth, and calls for play to resume. Stegner's dual response is telling: he discounts the bravado as an obvious act, but marvels that though the ball hit Alfie at least four times as hard as he had so often dreamed of smashing that face, the fellow was still standing. That kind of bravery could never be the absolute center of a Stegner novel because it lacks sensitivity to recognize its limitations. It does figure prominently in the fiction, though, because of its destructiveness and because Stegner like the rest of us is trying to discover how far it is motivated by the beauties of the tough-guy myth and how far it is really tough.

Stegner has chosen to test that conception of heroism with complexity rather than allegorical simplicity. He elevates those whose toughness is enduring rather than brute and fitful. In the archetypal Wild West versions of human conduct, that is female toughness. Hemingway, to his eternal credit, recognized and prized that quality, though many of his readers have not. Stegner believes civilization depends on it, though he cannot avoid the faintly apologetic way he defends the virtue. He knows well what Henry Nash Smith noted in *Virgin Land,* that violent myths may have little to do with reality and yet still move masses of people. The characters who for him embody virtue stand against that movement, but they are not exciting people. The kind of identity they represent would never lead to the White House or the Cotton Bowl, and Stegner feels that too.

Women tend to be the embodiment of virtue in his work, and he has habitually used them to make living unavoidably complex for his male protagonists. They are the prophetesses of reduced expectations, of objectivity, of the desire of live by controls, and like all bearers of bad tidings, they suffer. In this, Stegner does not reinforce the sexist myths of feminine weakness and subordination; he reflects their existence, and by implication attacks them. When Blake wrote that "Prudence is an ugly old maid courted by Incapacity," he anticipated the neo-Romantic creed of the epic West: the man without a grandiose plan or an exaggerated sense of his own individuality is a man without talent or worth. Men cannot equivocate in their plans or value moderation without casting doubt upon themselves. One has only to read *Wolf Willow* to know how much this problem preoccupies Stegner; his goal is to take the narrow world of the Alfie Carpenters and bring a more complex norm to bear on it. He emphasizes that a grand plan and developed talent are the only means for an individual to transcend such limitations as he knew during a childhood in various parts of the West, but he illustrates nowhere a belief that men instinctively know the limits of that

impulse. Stegner's distrust of "breaking loose" (no character in
his fiction ever gets away with such an audacious course) is
to be traced to misgivings with men and the way they use the
mobility society gives them, often at the expense of women.
He's saying more than that men are unfortunately shaped by the
"tough guy" myth; he implies that the myth derives something
from men themselves.   Thus the simultaneous bias against and
fascination with spontaneous masculine agressiveness.   There are
two exceptions.   The first is Alec Stuart, in the first novel *Remembering Laughter* (1937), who fathers a child by his sister-in-
law and who escapes detailed analysis only because the novel is
short and because Stegner has chosen to look instead at the
blight resulting from the wronged wife's cold, unremitting
Calvinism.   The second is Sabrina Castro, who attempts in *A
Shooting Star* (1961) to break loose from a social confinement
Patricia Hearst might recognize.   She belongs to a group I would
like to speak of later.

In sum, Stegner's men (except for secondary roles) are not
so likeable as the women, though they seem more vital.   They
are either plagued by guilt and self-loathing, or incapable of guilt
and therefore pitied by their creator.   The men move plots, but
the effort characteristically adds up to futility; in his fiction
women are the only ones who endure with grace and good temper.   I cannot recall having encountered in Stegner's work a female he gives no sympathy.

Such absolutes bring us ever closer to clichés, however,
and lest Stegner seem guilty of creating a species of long-suffer-
ing, weak-chinned and vacant-faced women, let me add that just
as the men have become more complex—haunted now by the
past as well as the present—the women have grown stronger, too,
a good index of Stegner's growth as a writer.   Since Stegner has
defined human conflicts to a great degree in terms of men and
women, and since the couples have got older as he has, it is help-
ful to examine the women in three successive categories: young
victims, rebels, and old partners.

The women-as-victim was a preoccupation difficult for Stegner to modify.   It is a constant theme in the early works, sometimes developed, sometimes there like a reflex: Ina Sundstrom
in *On a Darkling Plain,* the coed Paul Condon tries to rape in
Fire and Ice, and most extensively, Elsa Norgaard Mason in

The Big Rock Candy Mountain. Overstatement is a constant danger, though sometimes the theme works well when the fiction concerns itself less with the victimization than its consequences, as in "The Blue-Wing Teal." The weakness is Stegner's vagueness about motives; it is never clear why the women continue to suffer so acutely, and prolonged suffering, sometimes for decades, strains credulity and patience. Writers often relieve us, as we might ourselves, with dark humor; that has seldom been Stegner's interest. Others investigate the perversity and self-delusion inherent in stalemated suffering; *Of Human Bondage* comes immediately to mind. But Stegner was preoccupied with the male's desire to dominate; to introduce such variables might weaken his charge. To avoid them prevents the early fiction from being as good as it should have been. As I have tried to show elsewhere,[2] Stegner's desire to attack Bo Mason brings inconsistency to the narrative structure of *The Big Rock Candy Mountain* and finally makes Elsa seem weak and pitiable, which is not his intention. Later novels show that he learned something from such overkill.

The Big Rock Candy Mountain also gave Stegner the terms by which he would explore the man-woman relationship; earlier novels tended to avoid the issue of marriage, but Stegner's best fiction uses it to illustrate the best and worst of man-woman confrontation. The best illustration of Stegner's unease with questions of what motivates the man to dominate and the young wife to accept or perhaps even seek subordination is the story of frontier Saskatchewan, "Carrion Spring," a finely structured narrative of a young rancher and his wife leaving their spread, defeated by a winter that killed three-fourths of the cattle on the range and redefined the frontier's line. Ray is typical of many men found in Stegner; he is possessed by a dream of wrestling the land into submission and made only more adamant by defeat. Molly, "a tough and competent little body," is "determined to take her man and her marriage back where there was a chance for both." The battle of wills takes just a short buckboard ride to enact; despite having lived through a blizzardy winter without seeing another woman, despite watching a filthy bit of local color named Schultz slaughter and scalp some coyote pups, despite the stench of rotting cattle and the sight of rivers dotted with their bloated bodies, this tough and competent little body succumbs to what can only be described as petulance on the part of her husband. We must weigh her desperation at the

"matted filthy, lifeless, littered. . .place of her imprisonment,"
against "this antagonism between them like a snarl of barbed
wire," and Ray's taunting her for showing weakness. And yet
there must be something more in this relationship to explain
why a tough woman matured further by months of neglect in a
cultural vacuum should give in so easily to her husband's next
and even madder scheme. The lavender crocus she lays against
his cheek and all the other symbols so carefully evoked in the
story do not answer all the questions. In all fairness to Stegner,
it should be noted that the story assumes our knowing that the
frontier wife's first duty was as helpmeet, and that Molly's returning with a peevish husband would have been received back
home with mixed emotions. But these notions are only part of
the complex frontier situation, and no story can lean very
heavily upon them. "Carrion Spring" surely reflects part of the
reality of early Saskatchewan, but I think Stegner neglects the
most interesting reality his own story uncovers.

Molly could, of course, have turned rebellious, cutting
herself off from traditions and seeking a new, isolated way.
Stegner has dealt with such cases, always presenting isolation as
the primary risk, for in his world isolation is the worst of all
conditions—a character left alone, seeking no remedy, is a character damned.

Sabrina Castro, protagonist of *A Shooting Star,* caught in a
malaise that seems all the worse because it is Californian, challenges the traditions of both her present and her past because neither will sustain her. She is Stegner's first strong and rebellious
woman, and though the novel is not among Stegner's very best, it
deserves attention because the nature of the past and present
Stegner creates for her reveals a good deal about how much he
values control and how much flexibility can coexist with it. The
story shows his freedom from dogma and narrow certainty.

Sabrina is "homo-duplex." On her father's side was
Hutchens' vitality, good looks, and a taint of vulgarity; he left
long ago, and is not talked about in her mother's house. The
Wolcotts, on the other hand, embody New England gentility,
the caution of those who inherit wealth, and a reticence and
sterility of attenuated Puritanism. Sabrina's present provides her
with money, Pasadena society, a remote husband, an affair with
a businessman who wants home and mistress too, and, most

abundantly, guilt. Every wish to break out of the pattern is suspect, the Hutchens' sensuousness. The Wolcott creed, summarized by grandmother Emily's diary, provides only the empty
precepts of self-reliance without warmth for the self: "I will ask
few questions. . . . I will ask hlep only when it is clear I cannot
get on without it. . . . I will never borrow from the servants
. . . . I will not be too eager to oblige." The past, in other words,
chokes the present, and the family chokes the individual.

The situation provides a good corrective for those who have
memorized Stegner's pronouncements about the importance of
history and the need for individuals to set themselves in a continuum, accepting the lessons and limitations it provides, and
thus avoiding the kind of arrogance Jim Peck in *All the Little
Live Things* and Rodman Ward in *Angle of Repose* are supposed
to represent. It is good to remember the crotchety narrators of
those novels and their tendency to overstate. Stegner is more
directly in control of *A Shooting Star,* and his moderation on
the subject is unmistakable. Sabrina has cut loose, and no scene
better illustrates how completely she has let go than the backseat tryst with her businessman/amour. But Stegner criticizes
her not for her renunciation. The pity is that she has temporarily lost that sixth,esthetic sense which all Stegner's good
people possess—she regains it, however, learning from her lover's
touch rather than from Emily's list that her present course will
bring spiritual destruction. She recognizes that both her marriage
and affair are over, and without consciously willing it, she is
receptive to new ideas from outside her experience. In this
instinctive hope from a hopeless situation, she best embodies
Stegner's notion of optimism.

In one important way, this novel reverses the customary sex
roles of Stegner's earlier fiction: Sabrina, who can find no peace
because she cannot rid herself of notions of absolute formulas
for happiness, receives insights from Leonard MacDonald, a Levi-
clad schoolteacher who has no money, no status, no genealogy.
Leonard is a low-key, faintly sarcastic Socrates, and although
Stegner presents his role in oversimplified terms, the point is
effective: you can be yourself and live love even in a California
tract development. But there are no signposts to follow, no way
to be sure you are doing well, and even in the end, when Sabrina
decides to bear the illegitimate child of her affair and begin life
again, she finds herself longing for a formula to give final assur-

ance. Leonard, with the instinctive sharpness of recent Stegner males, calls hers "a sound, aggressive, do-good-and-love program," cautioning her that there are

> "many different kinds of things you can make a halfway decent life out of if you believe in them and work at them. Likewise it's funny how no combination really turns out to be exactly the Kingdom of Heaven, you know? I think you'll do some of those things, sure. But I don't think you're going to emerge out the other end clothed in white samite. . ."

> "You don't believe in conversion," she said. "You don't believe there's anything a person can do."

> "I believe in repairs."

Leonard MacDonald stands as the only male in Stegner's novels to separate the barbarous from the masculine and put the philosophy to use (Bruce Mason is similar, but we are not privileged to watch him apply his lessons). But even his example leaves lingering doubts: first, we do not see him among other men; second, Stegner makes sure that this primary man-woman relationship in the novel remains uncomplicated by sexual desire— the tension between Leonard and Sabrina is intellectual and philosophical, and characterized by a detachment unknown to Stegner's married couples. No marriage could survive Leonard's condescension. As such, the book has an unreal quality about it —Leonard lives in an untested calm, yet is presented as the true teacher. If the situation has to be arranged this way, we should be curious to know why. The portrayal of Leonard at home with his pregnant wife does not explain how they resolve their tensions; her apparent lack of an intellectual dimension makes him an even more dubious Socrates. Likewise, Sabrina's naiveté before him seems excessive. Some themes justify overstatement— such as her night walk into the desert near Carson City, for Stegner a ritualized attack on the ritual (popularized and simplified by the Wild West) promising that you can find yourself only by losing yourself, preferably in an arid setting—but those in a social context do not, and there, characters representing vice seem overdone.

But Sabrina has one saving grace for Stegner: when confronted with disintegration, she responds with self-hatred, whereas Stegner's men in the same situation follow their first instinct to blame someone else.   Bo Mason might be the best example, but not the last, as Stegner's three most recent novels feature narrators depressed by modern America and convinced they see society destroying itself.   Although their aggressiveness is largely verbal, as befits old men, they retain the instinct.

All the Little Live Things introduces Joe Allston, an aging California literary agent full of barely suppressed anger and guilt at the death of his son years before and also at some horrifying trends in contemporary California, where he moved, he admits, to live by the Garden myth.   He is a little guilty of his own prosperity, too, referring to his home in the hills above San Francisco Bay as a domain for Prospero; his guilt, in fact, is the catalyst for much of what happens to him in the novel, a strange romance wherein what characters stand for seems more important than the characters themselves.   It probably should not have been narrated in the first person, not just because Richard Chase made a good case against it for any romance,[3] but also because Allston's stubbornness and guilt are not enough to sustain the significance implied for them.

Moreover, *All the Little Live Things* can be grouped with *A Shooting Star* in that its man-woman problem is not for Stegner the ultimate one: the central relationship here is father-daughter, Allston and his neighbor Marian Catlin, thirtyish, energetic, totally Romantic and optimistic, also pregnant and recovering from a cancer operation.   She awakens joy in him with precisely the same strength that Jim Peck, a hippy squatter on Allston's land, destroys it.   At one point, Allston says, "It's only the literary, hot for novelty, who fear cliché," but the irreconcilable differences among the trio, the tendency of each to exaggerate his position, the concurrent growth of cancer and fetus, the earnest guilt of Allston that blooms dark at the melodramatic climax, bring the novel too close to cliché.   The immense energies of the participants do not lend enough life to the story, proving, I think, that Stegner's imagination is moved to sustain fictional flights only by the ultimate man-woman question that is answered in his fiction only by marriage: does the man seek a total relationship with a woman, and does he make it work?

From this point of reference, Stegner culminated his fiction with *Angle of Repose.* That this novel is his most ambitiously and perfectly crafted only hints at how fully it grew from the thinking and experience most moving to him over the years. The story of the Ward family has the scope of an epic and the control of a lyric because it draws together all the threads of Stegner's thinking about the West and about that final man-woman judgment. In that sense, the questions of his earlier fiction have only been preludes.

The masterful portrait of the novel, the wandering marriage of Oliver and Susan Ward, allows Stegner to explore a changing relationship, and even if that were the only level in the narrative it would have been a major work. Susan Burling Ward passes through all three stages Stegner's females have seen, while Oliver progresses through the ages of previous male protagonists, allowing the novel to replay and reassess marriage in all seasons.

Though Susan Burling's intellect and character are stronger than Elsa Norgaard's, their situations are similar in that marriage provides a choice more attractive than any other before them, but one made more attractive than it is by the severe limitations single life offers. Susan's intimate triangle with Augusta Drake and Thomas Hudson has been broken by their marriage, and Susan becomes a tentative young woman who without quite knowing why is captivated by Oliver's "protective male" aura and the possibility that temporary Western adventure will be better than permanent Eastern disappointment. Stegner provides a classic portrayal of the joys and misunderstandings of early marriage, and though Oliver's failure to communicate candidly with his wife reminds the reader of other Stegner males, Susan's Victorian stiffness in the West and her impatient wish for a quick financial breakthrough to send them East to stay also contribute to the deterioration of the union. Susan is never really the victim Elsa proves to be; her greater strength allows Stegner to make this stage of the marriage a transition rather than an end.

It is praiseworthy that the novel doesn't show its "seams," that the reader cannot point to any particular event as signalling Susan's movement from tentative to rebellious. Certainly her dissatisfaction with Oliver increases sharply after his refusal (out of principle) to take the mining job in Michoacán, for here she begins to feel like a captive. But she has consistently underestimated her husband's talents because of her tendency to discount all achievement that cannot be measured from her humanist-artist perspective, so the narrative has long been foreshadowing the flare-up. She asks Augusta in New York, "What kind of a wife is it who half wants her husband's bad luck to continue so that she can stay longer near someone else?" And though Lyman Ward wonders about the possibility of lesbianism, it is more likely an intimation Stegner has dealt with before—the potentially destructive sexual tension existing in all marriages.

In a nice touch, Stegner places their breakup in Vardis Fisher country, and though the themes are similar to *Toilers of the Hills* and *Dark Bridwell*, Stegner carefully avoids the overstated pathos Fisher gave to women in that situation. Lyman cautions, "This is not a story of frontier hardships, nor of pioneer hardihood." In the end, we are able to measure Susan's rebellion in retrospect, in terms of her relationship with Frank Sergeant, a vague test, but as Lyman notes, it is certain "that passion and guilt happened." When, after Agnes drowns and Frank kills himself in Susan and Oliver's old bedroom, Susan accepts her exile in Boise, the reality of rebellion is as clear as the guilt and punishment.

Here, however, Stegner changes pace, and in doing so makes the novel the superb work it is: Oliver and Susan are at the same point in their marriage that Lyman is in his, and although Lyman has reached the point in his grandparents' lives when he can for the first time relate his narrative first hand, Stegner "reveals" him, as it were, by exposing the possibility of bias: Lyman might, even subconsciously, be distorting memory to ensure that he finds justification in his grandparents' story for his own refusal to take his wife back from adultery. Although Lyman agrees Susan was guilty and that the "extenuating circumstances" of loneliness and cultural deprivation did not excuse her, his interpretation of Oliver's response becomes even more important than Susan's guilt. Based upon his own somewhat dubious observations, he concludes that Oliver never forgave her though they lived together fifty more years: "Through all the changes, but not a change in them." Their angle of repose was horizontal, in death. Thus Oliver becomes a kind of Chillingworth, whose refusal to bend is ultimately worse than his wife's sin of the flesh.

This union of histories opens up a multitude of ambiguous

possibilities. The reader can take the story as Lyman asks: he
is bored with his own life, and during his researches into his
grandparents' finds a remarkable parallel to his own broken
marriage. He has gone to the past, to the grandfather whose
standards he most admires, for self-justification. He finds a lesson in that history he is reluctant to accept; he has "pontificat-
ed" at young Shelley Rasmussen, herself in a confused marriage,
about the decline of morality, all the while blind to his own and
Oliver's sins of pride. By his reckoning, if he can repair his marriage he will prove himself "a bigger man than [his] grandfather."
According to this theory, Stegner, implacably hopeful, is in control of the novel and determined that it will illustrate his theories
of history as a vital check on emotion and blindness. On the
other hand, there is sufficient evidence in the narrative that
Lyman does not judge his grandfather justly: he perhaps mis-
interprets the rose named Agnes, the fact that he did not see or
does not recall having seen his grandparents touch. He clearly
ignores the beautiful house Oliver built for Susan in Grass Valley
to replace the Idaho home. The reader should wonder, too, how
it is that Lyman has so completely misjudged Oliver for a life-
time. Or has he just now judged his grandfather so harshly out of
a sense of his own guilt in a failed marriage he is afraid to resume
because it will force him to come to terms with the same ultimate man-woman question Stegner places at the center of the
novel? There is, in the end, no way to tell for sure: the first
version does confirm Stegner's interest in the individual coming
to terms with history and his own limitations, but it does not
reconcile the presence of evidence that Lyman misjudges.

The Oliver-Susan marriage presents a wide variety of dilemmas, and the fact that the union suvived is remarkable. That it
seems to have survived on better terms than Lyman admits raises
the possibility that Stegner has used a kind of melodrama to escape from what have seemed to be throughout his work irreconcilable dilemmas between men and women. Lyman must judge
his grandfather worse than he was to ensure that his own
thoughts about a reunion with Ellen will seem more courageous
than they are. But courage is not the point: to make it so blinds
the reader to the problem of what kind of marriage they can rescue. Better than a truce? He dreams of achieving as his angle of
repose the false arch, two lines propped together, but his pretending to know that his grandparents failed to achieve as much
bothers me. To examine someone else's marriage and claim such

conclusions implies a vision I have never known in anyone. To reach such conclusions through admittedly soft research, guesses, and the observations of childhood makes them seem even more suspect. Does this measure Lyman's self-delusion, or does it signal in Stegner the "duplicity" Lawrence found in many American literary minds, "a tight mental allegiance to a morality which all their passion goes to destroy"?[4]

The energy of *Angle of Repose* lies in the historical account of the marriage of two good human beings who have problems because, though they come from the same culture, they are of different needs. They try to hold things together while pursuing separate dreams; they seem to accept the irreconcilable tensions between them with an unspoken agreement to keep those tensions under control. In contrast, Lyman's level of the novel, as skillfully integrated as it is, nevertheless contains infinitely less energy than his grandparents'; if the petulant outbursts are excluded, it contains hardly any. And because Lyman resembles Joe Allston so much in his manners and attitudes, I wonder if he doesn't represent what D. H. Lawrence called the unconscious "duplicity." What sparks Stegner's genius is the historical level of the novel. Susan and Oliver have spunk and the willingness to take chances, qualities their grandson aspires to but does not possess. His characterization is strained and his message given to grouchy overstatement, implying that Stegner regards Lyman's function in the novel with ambiguous feelings: he doesn't totally believe what Lyman says; but for reasons outside the inevitabilities of the novel, he cannot leave it unsaid, either. His recent captivation with the Lyman/Allston personality makes me wonder if he isn't overselling the ethic they represent by underestimating the values of energy.

Stegner's later novel, *The Spectator Bird* (1976), brings his history of marriage as far as it can go short of death. The narrative illustrates some of the same problems of execution and intention as *Angle of Repose* in that personal history is narrated skillfully and with a rush of energy and humor while Joe Allston constricts much of the rest with complaints about the world in chaos. What is most interesting about the novel, and what binds the concerns of personal past and present, is the marriage, for Ruth Allston has been put on center stage, and as a picture of an old marriage partner, she is one of Stegner's best characters.

The examination of the past, Allston's reading of his European journal, reflects on the present, which for him has been narrowed to his marriage and the aches of advanced age. The marriage is a verbal battlefield. A Stegner reader will find familiar lines, though more sexual terms have crept into Allston's vocabulary. He assaults Ruth, the embodiment of gentle resiliency always found in Stegner women, with a practiced style and a knowledge of precisely what will irritate her. He loves to be taken care of, but turns on vulgarity if he needs to fend her off. The spectacle is similar to my picture of Lyman and Ellen Ward back together, with one major change: the guilt for the affair (in Allston's case there was only the desire) rests with the man.

But in this combativeness there is a new sense of acceptance I have not noticed in Stegner's fiction before. In one sense, Joe and Ruth are easier with one another because they have been through it all together; the sexual tension Joe can evoke is really a remembered tension, now a matter of words. The real source of uneasiness now is death: a good friend is dying, and even their doctor is older than they. Though Joe makes frequent jokes about how little time they have left together, Stegner makes it clear that death is a subject that brings them closer together. The novel's final scene is, after all, a transition from the remembered almost-affair to talk of death and a symbolic embrace of a man and woman that suggests a new meaning. The end of Allston's journal tells of a moment of love with Astrid Wredel-Krarup, a kiss with a countess twenty years before. He had offered to save her from a life of shame; reading his account of that night reminds him of the ambiguity of his affection and the self-renunciation of her refusal. He rushes from the house in tears.

> I would hate to have a recording of that conversation I
> held with myself, lurching up and down the moonlit drive.
> It would sound like the lecture of a scared graduate assis-
> tant, taking over the philosophy class in the professor's
> absence.

Part of the self-deprecating impulse here can be attributed to the recent habit of Stegner males to loosen up in their final chapter, but Joe Allston goes beyond this.

> The truest vision of life I know is that bird in the Vener-

able Bede that flutters from the dark into the lighted hall,
and after a while flutters back again into the dark. But
Ruth is right. It is something—it can be everything—to
have found a fellow bird with whom you can sit among
the rafters while the drinking and boasting and fighting
go on below...

It is the lesson Stegner's male characters have long been faced
with, and only the woman can teach it. Age seems to be the crucial fact enabling the man to perceive even the substance of the
woman's calm message; to accept it, as Allston does, requires at
least a ritual of humility. It is he, after all, who approaches Ruth
at the end and shows affection to break the spell his reading has
put over them. No previous Stegner male has done more than
contemplate such an act.

But more important than the reconciliation, which may or
may not convince all readers, is the timing. Why must it come
so late? Why must Allston see himself and his fellow bird as
spectators, and the energetic life as "drinking and boasting and
fighting"? Why should the only young male in the novel, an
Italian novelist, be a sexual predator? Are there not other al-
ternatives?

An overview of Stegner's fiction implies there are not. The
"honestly offered spirit" Stegner has presented has long been
concerned with the irreconcilables between men and women.
It is good to remember that in the last two novels reconciliation
between the sexes is possible only because the male has somehow
been robbed of his physical aggressiveness, Lyman Ward by
amputation, Joe Allston by an old man's general deterioration.
I am reminded of the horrible scarring Charlotte Brontë had to
inflict upon proud Rochester before she could allow him to
marry Jane Eyre, and it seems to me that *The Spectator Bird*
and *Angle of Repose* only reconfirm the idea that Stegner is
fascinated by and makes his most moving fiction from the battle
of the sexes, and imperils his novels with an overlay of morality
whose source is renunciation of that energy, as though all energy
must tend towards evil. Clearly then, his optimism is of a curious
kind. Stegner has that "partly feminine sensibility" Richard
Chase perceived in Hawthorne and James, that "sense of the
complexities of the psychological life"[5] that men in a *Wolf
Willow* world are not comfortable with. His women have always

been complex in their vulnerability, while his men want to deny complexity because it restricts them. Yet Stegner remains fascinated with the aggressiveness and the opportunity for tests of will that characterize the male-dominated world of his fiction. His novels use women, but are inevitably about men, and to read them is to see restatements of free will, of optimism, of men hoping to remake themselves, but the overwhelming weight of evidence points to stasis and confusion where the guilt-inspired wishes of the head meet the implacable heart. A kind of pre-destination by hormones. Those who dismiss Stegner because he is merely optimistic do not read the real Stegner and do not see that the "honestly offered spirit" is also the consciously offered spirit, and not necessarily the whole or true one.

NOTES

[1] "Fiction: A Lens on Life," *Saturday Review,* 21 (April 22, 1950), p. 9.

[2] "*The Big Rock Candy Mountain* and *Angle of Repose:* Trial and Culmination," *Western American Literature,* X (May, 1975), pp. 11-27.

[3] *The American Novel and Its Tradition* (Anchor Books, 1957), p. 23.

[4] *Studies in Classic American Literature* (Viking Press, 1971), p. 51.

[5] *The American Novel and Its Tradition,* p. 71.

IV

THE WOMAN AS WRITER

WILLA CATHER AND THE SENSE OF HISTORY

Bernice Slote
University of Nebraska-Lincoln

In the years before she was a well-known novelist, Willa Cather once said to her family that she could tell the writers of current popular Western fiction things about the Old West they had never heard of—but, she added, "because I wear skirts and don't shave they wouldn't believe me." Eventually she did tell about her West. More than half of her dozen novels and much of her short fiction are set, at least in part, in the Nebraska-Kansas region of the Great Plains, or in Wyoming, Colorado, New Mexico, and Arizona. This whole region, she once said, seemed like one great state to her—the West. Still, I would not call her a Western or a regional writer in the sense that the interpretation of that area was a primary intention of her art. She used the materials of the West more subtly; they were deeply the substance of her own experience, and were natural to her. Though Willa Cather's fiction often deals with the past in juxtaposition with the present—the lively past, one might call it—she was not a historian nor even a historical novelist. She was not writing to record events, places, or periods, but to create out of herself moments of imagination that might become realities. This is the truth of feeling, of belief, of conviction, of possession; it resides in the person who perceives rather than in events or chronologies themselves. It is time which passes but never passes away. How well Willa Cather succeeded in creating such realities is suggested in a comment by Marcus Cunliffe, English historian and scholar in American literature, when he spoke at the Seminar on the Art of Willa Cather held in Lincoln in October 1973: Imaginatively, he said, she brought much of the fragmentary and discontinuous American past "into a continuum. Figuratively, it could be said that she was the discoverer of the cliff dwellings at Mesa Verde and the pueblo on the plateau at Acoma. She restored them to the American historical consciousness, and thereby enriched it." Professor Cunliffe adds that he himself, "as a wandering student of American history, went to see them a quarter of a century ago, having read about them in Willa Cather, and know that they enlarged the meaning of that history for me."[1]

The reality any fiction writer creates is, of course, shaped by the writer's own perspective—how he sees the world and what sense he makes of the things that happen to him. Even though Willa Cather did not write history, she wrote with a strong feeling for the reality and the significance of the past as it blends into the present and the future—what one might call the sense of history. She was strongly motivated in her choice of themes and subjects by the need to show how things began, how they turned out; to trace patterns of human lives and their import; to show the changing countenance of the land she knew as "West." (There is one distinction to make about her use of the land: In her best known Nebraska novels—*O Pioneers!* [1913], *My Antonia* [1918], *A Lost Lady* [1923]—the land itself changes through man's use; in the accounts of the Southwest—in portions of *The Song of the Lark* [1915] and *The Professor's House* [1925], and in *Death Comes for the Archbishop* [1927]—the land is fairly immutable, little touched by man, though man himself changes in the encounter.)[2] The sense of history includes one strong recurring theme in her fiction—the effort to realize a lengthened past, individual or social. This and other elements of historical time and the patterns of human change can be traced through Willa Cather's own experience.

What affected Willa Cather most strongly in the West was the sharp change, even shock, of her coming from Virginia in 1883, when she was nine, to the new, largely uncultivated, region in Webster County, Nebraska, called the Divide. There were other settlers besides the Cathers, but the land was mostly wild prairie, grass covered and treeless. The effect on her was vivid, indelible. Though lesser in degree, her experience had enough of that of the pioneer-immigrant to place her inside, not on the outside as an observer. She was a personal witness to the changes brought about eventually in the Nebraska countryside through settlement and cultivation. A second influence was the impact of the landscape itself. In the part of southern Nebraska she knew best, the land stretches high and resolute in some parts; in other parts it is rough, clawed and banked in hills and draws by streams running down to the Republican River; elsewhere the land may flow smoothly with the river in bottomlands through cottonwoods and willows, near sandy islands and bluffs. In later years this world blends with the mesas and deserts of the Southwest. A third influence was her knowledge of the immigrant pioneers who also settled in Webster and adjoining Franklin Counties. The 1885 census shows the varied pattern of European immigrants to be exactly as she described them in *O Pioneers!* and *My Antonia*—families (and loners, too) from Sweden, Norway, Denmark, Germany, and Bohemia. There were also settlements of German-Russians and French-Canadians. This mingling of languages and cultures and Old-World memories gave what many see as Willa Cather's strongest individuality; nobody before her had used the immigrant melting-pot of the Great Plains so fully and sympathetically in fiction. The three influences of change, landscape, and people might be called primary sources in Willa Cather's rather special encounter with the early West. But any mention of her usable experience must include the other cultural forces which worked strongly in her imagination. The young Willa Cather lived in a time when the classics were necessary to an education; one grew up reading the *Aeneid* and playing at being Odysseus out on the wine-dark prairie. In one of her early poems, "Dedicatory," she recalls the "vanished kingdom" she had created with her brothers—"our days of war and ocean venture,/Brave with brigandage and sack of cities;/. . .the Odysseys of summer mornings."[3] She also grew up with the Bible. If Rome was just around the corner, so was the world of Job and Isaiah and Jacob.

That Willa Cather had a rather down-to-earth understanding of history—Biblical and otherwise—is shown in one of my favorite Cather essays. In 1895, as a young journalist just out of the University of Nebraska and working on a Lincoln newspaper, she contributed to a symposium answering the question, "Does not the Bible teach that God created woman subject to and subordinate to man?" Most of the contributors, including Mary Bryan, the wife of William Jennings Bryan, said yes. Willa Cather's comment begins, "The Bible undoubtedly teaches that woman should be subservient to man, but does it say that she was, is, or ever will be?" And after citing case studies of women like Eve, Rachel, Delilah, and others, who somehow got the better of their men, Willa Cather concludes: "These are only a few of the hundred Biblical instances in which the women who were

undoubtedly created subservient turned the tables. In theory the
Jews maintained the superiority of man but in practice it did
not always follow. Woman may be man's inferior but she makes
him pay for it."[4]

Willa Cather used her personal material to recreate a world—
combining, choosing, shaping. She takes Red Cloud and the
Webster County region in Nebraska but alters its geography,
changes the dates of real happenings, places events in different
contexts. The town of Hanover in *O Pioneers!* is located where
Bladen now is, but its description fits the town of Campbell,
and its store is most like the Miner store she knew well in Red
Cloud. *My Antonia* is generally based on Willa Cather's own early
experience in coming to Nebraska, and some of the characters
have real life prototypes, but it cannot be taken as strictly autobiographical; too many details have been changed. In real life
the Bohemian family, the Sadileks, for example, did not arrive
with the Cathers by train in Red Cloud, as the Shimerdas arrive
with Jim Burden in *My Antonia,* and the two families were not
close neighbors. It is unlikely that Willa Cather roamed over the
prairie with Annie Sadilek, as Jim did with Antonia. The story
of the suicide of Mr. Shimerda in *My Antonia* (and two versions
of it in earlier short stories) is based on fact, but the actual
tragedy happened in 1881, two years before the Cathers came to
Nebraska. When Jim is a student at the University of Nebraska
in Lincoln, he and Lena Lingard see a performance of the play
Camille. Though crudely performed, for the first time the play
draws them in to the wonders of the theatre and evokes visions
of another world, richer and more exotic than anything they
had known. It is a window opening on a wider landscape. The
time is spring, a lilac-perfumed April. One showing of *Camille*
(with Clara Morris) in Lincoln in November 1893 (not in April,
as the novel has it) was important to Willa Cather, but it was not
a first revelation of the theatre. She was then far more sophisticated in the arts than Jim Burden seems to be. But this performance of *Camille* in 1893 was special, the subject of Willa
Cather's first long review of a play, one published in the *Nebraska State Journal* at the beginning of her successful journalistic
career of nearly twenty years. The feeling of genesis was true,
though the facts were altered. Another example of the changing of literal history is in *Death Comes for the Archbishop.* The
lives of real persons—Archbishop Lamy and Father Machebeuf
as French missionaries in the Southwest—are used as a basis, but

enough details are altered so that one has the sense of biography tilted to a fictional world. It was exactly what Willa Cather intended. She said that she had always wanted to do something "in the style of legend,"[5] and *Death Comes for the Archbishop* is of that genre. Legends are not accurate or verifiable histories but tales of the heroic or spiritual imagination in which fact is reshaped in the retelling, refocused in time.

Willa Cather's works do not emphasize what is usual in the fantasies or myths of the West—cowboys, immigrant trains, explorers and heroes, or the Plains Indians. These did not have an immediate emotional impact on her. Her central subject was historical, but it was history in a low key. She wrote of the understated West—settlement, the process of acculturation, the passing of lives. Still, as modest as the subject may sound, it is one of empires and great distances of the past. The story of Nebraska took its place in the cycles of history as the rise of a civilization was reenacted. Within that historical view Willa Cather found an emphasis for her fiction—the evocation of a lengthened past which would support a strong sense of identity. Such an impulse is from her own experience. She had come early into a place without an apparent past, where human identity was nearly obliterated by space. In a 1913 interview she remembered that sense of isolation in her coming to Nebraska as being "thrown out into a country as bare as a piece of sheet iron." And, she said, "I felt a good deal as if we had come to the end of everything—it was a kind of erasure of personality."[6]

Jim Burden's reaction in *My Antonia* is that "the world was left behind, that we had got over the edge of it, and were outside man's jurisdiction. . . . Between that earth and that sky I felt erased, blotted out" (pp. 7-8). Human habitation on the plains seemed tentative, precarious. The town of Hanover, Cather writes in *O Pioneers!*, was "anchored on a windy Nebraska tableland,. . . trying not to be blown away." The buildings looked haphazard, "as if they had been moved in overnight," or "as if they were straying off by themselves, headed straight for the open plain. None of them had any appearance of permanence, and the howling wind blew under them as well as over them" (p. 3). As Willa Cather observed the world of her youth, even cites and universities seemed young and raw. It was a commonplace in Lincoln newspapers of the 1890s to remark with a kind of satisfaction that by now some houses were old enough to be falling into ruin.

There was always exultation over the changing landscape of fields and trees and houses that reshaped the open prairie. This country had had no past—it was looking for one. In the beginning, as Willa Cather observes in *My Antonia*, it was "not a country at all, but the material out of which countries are made" (p. 7). Thus there was the need to lengthen the past, to seize on every element that would suggest a more complete identity—Old World origins, memory, remains of a mythical or mysterious past (Coronado, the cliff dwellers, fossil hunters), evidences of change in the present, the continuity of art. This is true of books that deal with a personally remembered life (like *My Antonia*, or even *O Pioneers!* and *A Lost Lady*) or those which evoke a deeper historical past (like *The Song of the Lark, The Professor's House, Death Comes for the Archbishop*, and, from other regions, *Shadows on the Rock* and *Sapphira and the Slave Girl*). If one can see a bare landscape as the beginning of civilization, its heroic women like Antonia to be "a rich mine of life, like the founders of early races" (p. 353), or the mingling of nations on the prairie like the varied peoples of central Europe or Russia, then time and space have been extended. One is not buffeted alone on a windy plain.

Although the idea of a lengthened history in new lands emerges in many ways in Willa Cather's fiction, one might look at four of her major characters as examples: the singer Thea Kronborg in *The Song of the Lark*, Jim Burden in *My Antonia*, Niel Herbert in *A Lost Lady*, and *Tom Outland in The Professor's House*.

Thea Kronborg's discovery of identity through history is a personal fulfillment, for it is in the quiet, sun-lit, eagle-flown air of Panther Canyon (in real life, Walnut Canyon in Arizona) and not in the drawing rooms or studies of Chicago that Thea finds her direction as an artist. As she spends time alone in the places where ancient cliff dwellers had lived and worked and created, she gains an understanding of the artist's commitment through a physical realization of the past and in an almost mystical sense of the unity of man's effort. From this place she senses "a voice of the past, not very loud, that went on saying a few simple things to the solitude eternally" (p. 375). She identifies with the people who walked those paths:

> It seemed to Thea that a certain understanding of those
> old people came up to her out of the rock-shelf on which

she lay; that certain feelings were transmitted to her, suggestions that were simple, insistent, and monotonous, like the beating of Indian drums. They were not expressible in words, but seemed rather to translate themselves into attitudes of body, into degrees of muscular tension or relaxation; the naked strength of youth, sharp as the sun-shafts; the crouching timorousness of age, the sullenness of women who waited for their captors. (p. 376)

All living drama had been played out in that canyon so many years ago, and there were left only the houses cut in the rock, bits of pottery, and the stream: "In the rapid, restless heart of it, flowing swifter than the rest, there was a continuity of life that reached back into the old time." And Thea herself, her perceptions enlarged and extended, begins to understand the union of life and art:

The stream and the broken pottery: what was any art but an effort to make a sheath, a mould in which to imprison for a moment the shining, elusive element which is life itself—life hurrying past us and running away, too strong to stop, too sweet to lose? The Indian women had held it in their jars. In the sculpture she had seen in the Art Institute, it had been caught in a flash of arrested motion. In singing, one made a vessel of one's throat and nostrils and held it on one's breath, caught the stream in a scale of natural intervals. (p. 378)

She feels a commitment to the past and to all who had created before her. When she becomes a great Wagnerian opera star, her performance is described in similar living terms—of spring and flowering growth. Such completeness of body and mind and memory she had first learned in Panther Canyon.

In *My Antonia* Jim Burden extends the limits of his own life as he studies the classics with a teacher who "could bring the drama of antique life before one out of the shadows—white figures against blue backgrounds" (p. 261). But even as he yearned toward those new forms, he writes—"my mind plunged away from me, and I suddenly found myself thinking of the places and people of my own infinitesimal past. They stood out strengthened and simplified now, like the image of the plough

against the sun" (p. 262).   In a sense reality and imagination
blend, and the persons in Jim's life take on some of the vivid,
chosen outlines of art.   These figures from his "infinitesimal
past," he says, "were so much alive *in me* [italics mine] that I
scarcely stopped to wonder whether they were alive anywhere
else, or how" (p. 262). By the end of his story (which is indeed a
book of memory), Jim Burden has heard Antonia say, " 'I guess
everybody thinks about old times, even the happiest people' "
(p. 321), and he concludes with that final affirmation of memory
and the reality of his own particular life: "Whatever we had
missed, we possessed together the precious, the incommunicable
past" (p. 372).   The old roads are only traces circling through a
pasture, but what Jim Burden remembers has become art, a book
called *My Antonia.*

In *A Lost Lady* we see things through the consciousness of
Niel Herbert, though he is not actually the narrator.   Niel is a
studious young man, imaginative, romantic, idealistic.   Through
books Niel extends his world beyond small-town Sweet Water:
"He was eavesdropping upon the past, being let into the great
world that had plunged and glittered and sumptuously sinned
long before little Western towns were dreamed of."   Thus he
gained "a long perspective" (p. 81-82).   Niel becomes disillu-
sioned both with his idealized lady, Mrs. Forrester, and with a
present reality less beautiful than an idealized past, which he
thinks of as the glory of the pioneer.   To understand *A Lost
Lady* fully, I believe we must hold the vision of that pioneer
world closer to Niel's consciousness than to the author's theme.
Though Willa Cather no doubt had moods of such nostaglia,
Niel's lament cannot be taken as a full and reasoned statement of
her view of life.   It is important, however, to reveal Niel's attitude as part of his mistaken view of Mrs. Forrester.   Of the past
he says,

> This was the very end of the road making West: the men
> who had put plains and mountains under the iron harness
> were old; some were poor, and even the successful ones
> were hunting for rest and a brief reprieve from death.
> It was already gone, that age; nothing could ever bring it
> back. The taste and smell and song of it, the visions those
> men had seen in the air and followed,—these he had
> caught in a kind of afterglow in their own faces,—and this
> would always be his. (pp. 168-69)

Niel is only partly right. His next thought is tragic, that Mrs. Forrester should have gone out with the pioneer and the buffalo. Here he is at odds with the book's thematic vision of the life-giving, life-holding, Mrs. Forrester.   Few readers would want her burned away, yet Niel held it against her "that she was not willing to immolate herself, like the widow of all these great men, and die with the pioneer period to which she belonged; that she preferred life on any terms" (p. 169). I am insisting a little on this view of the past as something organic to the novel and to Niel's characterization, not as a programmatic statement on history by Willa Cather, for I feel too many readers of *A Lost Lady* have ignored its final pages, in which Niel at last sees his life, and Mrs. Forrester's intensity and beauty, more clearly in the full light of day. In maturity, "he came to be very glad that he had known her, and that she had had a hand in breaking him in to life" (p. 171).

With Tom Outland in *The Professor's House* the lengthened past becomes a discovery of ancient America, the sense of this nation's history as something that extends far beyond the May-flower, something deep and rooted and irradicable to those who are captured by its reality. Tom Outland finds relics and bones of ancient Indians in the cliff-dweller ruins of the Blue Mesa (modeled on Colorado's Mesa Verde); he tries but fails to make them part of an American heritage. Still, in the story of his achievement of wholeness on the mesa Willa Cather has made his effort significant and real. As he spends some time alone on the mesa, Tom says that at last "all of me was there. . . . Something had happened in me that made it possible for me to co-ordinate and simplify. . . . For me the mesa was no longer an adventure, but a religious emotion. I had read of filial piety in the Latin poets, and I knew that was what I felt for this place" (pp. 250-51). Tom Outland was a cowboy who memorized and recited the *Aeneid* on the mesa, in the presence of ancient Indian America. He is a fitting symbol for an American identity.

Willa Cather's books are very quotable. There is the comment about Alexandra Bergson in *O Pioneers!*: "The history of every country begins in the heart of a man or a woman" (p. 65). And, of Alexandra and her belief in the land: "Under the long shaggy ridges, she felt the future stirring" (p. 71). History is also traced with infinite fascination in human lives. " 'How strangely things work out,' " says Carl Linstrum to Alexandra.

Again, " 'There are only two or three human stories,' " he says, " 'and they go on repeating themselves as fiercely as if they had never happened before' " (p. 119). If Willa Cather wrote of the understated West as she saw it in history, it was with an emphasis on what happened to people, what lives were like; on the course of events that make or break humanity; on the passing hours from birth to death. I have often heard her friend Carrie Miner Sherwood say that from her childhood Willa had wanted to know all about people. She would ask questions about everybody. To friends Willa Cather said that she liked to follow the lives of persons and families she knew, as if they were characters in a Russian novel. So the two or three human stories became the important histories of human endeavor and defeat, caught in a mould, a sheath, as Thea Kronborg saw the form of art.

Willa Cather was interested in the juxtaposition of desire and defeat, of triumph and sorrow, of death and love in ordinary lives. These contrasts are at the heart of her fiction from *O Pioneers!* (1913) to "Neighbour Rosicky" (1930), or even from her first story, "Peter" (1892), about defeat in the new land of pioneers, to her last novel, *Sapphira and the Slave Girl* (1940), about evil under the cloak of civility and comfort. I see *Death Comes for the Archbishop* not as primarily the history of the Catholic Church in the Southwest, nor a poem of its landscape (though it is that), but the gathering together of the consciousness of a man, Father Latour. He comes from France, a young priest, to re-establish the Church in the great diocese of New Mexico and Arizona. He mingles with the Spanish, the Mexicans, the Indians, the Anglos; he adjusts and changes, and is changed, so that when it is time to return to France to spend his old age he chooses instead to stay in the Southwest with its bright, young air and the world he had helped to create. The story is really what Jean Latour, the Archbishop, has become; in his last days he "sat in the middle of his own consciousness" (p. 293). Willa Cather's sense of history—both in the course of a life and in the concept of America—is symbolized in the scene where the Archbishop goes into Santa Fe for the last time. At sunset, at the edge of town, he looks at the golden cathedral he has built. And he sits, says Cather, "wrapped in his Indian blankets" (p. 272). It is the Old World and the New World made one.

NOTES

[1]"The Two or More Worlds of Willa Cather," *The Art of Willa Cather*, ed. Bernice Slote and Virginia Faulkner (Lincoln: University of Nebraska Press, 1974), p. 41.

[2]Citations in my text are to the following editions: *O Pioneers!* (Boston: Houghton Mifflin Company, Sentry Edition, 1962); *My Antonia* (Boston: Houghton Mifflin Company, Sentry Edition, © 1954); *The Song of the Lark* (Boston: Houghton Mifflin Company, Sentry Edition, 1963); *A Lost Lady* (New York: Alfred A. Knopf, 1923); *The Professor's House* (New York: Alfred A. Knopf, 1925); *Death Comes for the Archbishop* (New York: Alfred A. Knopf, 1927). Page references are in parentheses in the text.

[3]*April Twilights* (1903), ed. Bernice Slote (Lincoln and London: University of Nebraska Press, 1968), p. 3.

[4](Lincoln) *Courier*, September 28, 1895, p. 10; reprinted in *The World and the Parish: Willa Cather's Articles and Reviews, 1893-1902*, ed. William M. Curtin (Lincoln: University of Nebraska Press, 1970), p. 127.

[5]"On *Death Comes for the Archbishop*," *Willa Cather On Writing* (New York: Alfred A. Knopf, 1962), p. 9.

[6]"Willa Cather Talks of Work," [Philadelphia] *Record* (dateline New York, August 9, [1913]), reprinted in *The Kingdom of Art: Willa Cather's First Principles and Critical Statements, 1893-1896*, ed. Bernice Slote (Lincoln: University of Nebraska Press, 1966), p. 448.

DOROTHY SCARBOROUGH'S CRITIQUE
OF THE FRONTIER EXPERIENCE IN *THE WIND*

Barbara Quissell
Idaho State University

When Dorothy Scarborough published *The Wind* in 1925, there was an immediate, unfavorable reaction from Sweetwater, Texas, the locale of her novel. Members of the West Texas Chamber of Commerce accused the author of maligning Sweetwater and deliberately exaggerating the dry climate of the region.[1] In her replies Scarborough explained that, although she was a loyal Texan, she was also a novelist, not committed to be a booster for the climate of West Texas.[2] The controversy was a brief skirmish in what is a recurrent critical battle in the literature of the American West: as Scarborough summarized the local newspaper discussion of *The Wind*, she had been "convicted of realism in the first degree."

The Chamber of Commerce and its most vocal champion, Judge Crane, demanded that *The Wind* satisfy their version of historical accuracy in order to be a true novel of the West. Scarborough, enjoying a good fight, responded:

> Has the West Texas wind got on your nerves, Mr. Crane, and the sand blinded you to the difference between a novel and an historical treatise? You complain that you can't find any old-timrs near Sweetwater that recall the plot of my recent novel, *The Wind,* and you haven't dug up the murdered man's body from any sand drift there. Hence the book is fiction. Why, bless your historical heart, that's all it was ever meant to be! If story-tellers weren't allowed to invent characters and situations, fiction would be even duller than it is. . . . A novelist writes impressionistically, and fiction need conform only to the essential truth of time and place.[3]

Since the novel had been favorably reviewed in other parts of Texas as well as nationwide, Scarborough was not worried by what she labelled the "sandstorm of controversy." "I'm sorry you dislike my book [Mr. Crane], but I console myself with thinking of others who say they do, among them Irvin Cobb, Edna Ferber, Ellen Glasgow, Vachel Lindsay, etc. . ." Then, after quoting from reviews praising her novel, she concluded, "Conceited, you'll say? Yes, of course! But if Texas dislikes my book, no other praise can quite make up to me for that!"[4] The furor was good for the novel's sales; and there is, in fact, evidence in her unpublished papers that she had been attempting to stir up just such a reaction in order to publicize her novel.[5] Scarborough did suggest that she was not upset by the heated rhetoric of her critics: "We Texans understand each other. What may seem like violence to an ignorant Easterner, I recognize as only friendly enthusiasm."[6]

But, as the letters from readers later showed, Texans felt that Scarborough had attacked more than just one small community. Her interpretation of Western life contradicted the persistent optimism in their own attitudes toward their region. A letter from an Abilene investment banker to Scarborough's publisher best illustrates this point:

> I have personally witnessed the hopeless desparation [sic] that Drought Wind and Dust with its resultant disasters can cause.

> I have seen the same country yield magically to the ingenuity endurance enterprise and patriotic efforts of those who envisioned its possibilities and accepted seriously from fate no defeats disappointments nor rebuffs.[7]

In essence, this Texan protested that the West had been won. In his evaluation of the westering experience there is more than just frontier boosterism; there is the promise of another chance for economic and social advancement, a new life for those who will fight and keep on fighting. The promise of Western opportunity carried with it the notion that the struggle would be physically and emotionally demanding, but it would not be meaningless or futile, and that although the environment would be harsh, it was not by definition an amoral natural world. Scarborough's naturalistic description posed a threat to the banker's optimistic satisfaction; he could not accept her portrayal of defeat, a defeat that was unjustified and unearned.[8]

For her fiction, Scarborough deliberately chose Texas settings because she knew the region thoroughly and because as a self-conscious regionalist she felt there were many aspects of Texas life that previously had never been treated by novelists:

> . . .I naturally choose Texas settings and incidents for my stories, since I am a Texan and a thorough one. . . .our great state offers such varied, unlimited and almost untouched possibilities for fiction, poetry, and the drama, her native sons and daughters would be foolish to look elsewhere for literary inspiration.[9]

Born at Mt. Carmel in 1878, Scarborough as a child had lived near Sweetwater, although she spent most of her youth in Waco. Receiving her bachelor's and master's degrees from Baylor University, she taught there before completing her Ph.D. at Columbia University and moving to New York City. She was also a charter member of the Texas Folklore Society; in *On the Trail of Negro Folk-songs*, published the same year as *The Wind*, she collected many of the songs and variants she had first heard from black singers during her Waco childhood. Scarborough's career thus combined three aspects: she was teacher, author, and folklorist, and all three aspects are parts of *The Wind*.

An early short story, "The Drought," will serve as an introduction to both the subject matter and the technique of Scarborough's novels dealing with Texas life.[10] In the story a newly married couple watch helplessly as the incessant, hot summer winds sear their garden and threaten to destroy the cotton, their only cash crop as tenant farmers. With their credit exhausted and their food supplies gradually depleted, the couple face starvation. From the point of view of the wife, Scarborough traces the psychological effects and the character changes slowly brought about by an impoverished life and the intense heat. The environment, "an unseen force that menaced and derided" them, finally provokes a violent quarrel in which the young man tries to strike his pregnant wife and she collapses. The story concludes with the long-awaited rainstorm, but the young woman, regaining consciousness, can only look at her husband with

fear and revulsion. In *The Wind* Scarborough returned to a
naturalistic focus on the overwhelming effects of a harsh environment on a young woman, expanding the psychological
drama that she had introduced in the short story and again creating a tragic ending.

                              II

    In an inquiry as to why Scarborough chose West Texas
as the setting for her novel, then, the vital question is not her
loyalty as a Texan but instead her literary motives. West Texas
provided the historical and geographical necessities for the
story: during the 1880's the countryside was sparsely settled,
there were years of extreme drought, and the arid land came
well-equipped with sandstorms, cyclones, and northers. In a
letter to a Dallas bookstore owner Scarborough explained her
choice:

> Now that the country is built up, civilization would offer
> any Letty many ways of escape. Only the savage isolation
> of the past would offer a situation where she would have
> no defenses. And former residents of the section assured
> me that the great drought of the late eighties, 86-7, would
> furnish conditions most trying. That was a time of ex-
> ceptional hardship. . . . [11]

In short, Scarborough selected a time when the "untamed
frontier" was the daily environment of early ranchers.

    As the phrase "savage isolation" indicates, Scarborough
approached her materials from the perspective of literary naturalism, that is, the physical environment exerts a power, often
destructive, over the individual lives of characters, defining their
possibilities and molding their responses. In the brief, opening
chapter of the novel Scarborough paid tribute to the natural
elements:

> The wind was the cause of it all. The sand, too, had a
> share in it, and human beings were involved, but the wind
> was the primal force. . . . Civilization has taken from
> them [the winds] something of their fiery, elemental
> force, has humbled their spirit. . . . But long ago it was

different. The winds were wild and free, and they were
more powerful than human beings.[12]

Scarborough intensified the force of the winds by selecting a
severe drought year when not even a few spring flowers bright-
ened the surroundings or softened the view of a barren landscape.   Another important choice shows when one compares
Scarborough's carefully researched notes with the novel. One of
the early West Texas residents she interviewed had mentioned,
"A Westerner thinks of wind differently. It is life-giving. How
should we have any water in our windmills if there was not wind.
We should die and our cattle should die."[13] The late nineteenth
century setting on the plains should have included windmills,
but these inventions for controlling the environment were not
appropriate to Scarborough's theme.   In her novel the primal
force of the wind is relentlessly destructive; a windmill would
have rescued the heroine from her fate.

The main character in this contest between humans and
the West Texas setting is a young girl, Letty, who at eighteen
travels from her family home in Virginia to live near Sweetwater.   The other characters are easily recognized Western figures, familiar as dime novels and melodramas: in addition to
the innocent, pretty heroine there is a swaggering, handsome
cattleman, described as tall, dark-haired and a "skirt-chaser."
The two cowboys who are main characters represent contrasting
types: one the lanky, taciturn, good-hearted, true-blue sort;
the other a boisterous raconteur, flamboyantly dressed.   The
heroine journeys to the West to live on a ranch with her nearest
relative, a cousin.   His wife exemplifies the vigorous, pioneer
mother. These characters, with the addition of Texas scenery, a
house-warming dance, round-ups, cattle drives, etc., would be
the ingredients for a situation comedy on the Western plains.
But Scarborough used these typical characters in a very different story.

First of all, the point of view in *The Wind* is narrowed to
the first person: the events are all presented through the consciousness of the young girl who has been orphaned and forced
to leave her home in a settled Virginia community.   Too, the
most common treatment of the westering experience has been
the picaresque; however, in this novel the journey west and the

introduction to life on the frontier are developed as a psychological drama.   Instead of the usual episodic action and emphasis on adventure and discovery, Scarborough constructs her heroine's "Tour of the Prairies" as an internalized narrative.   The descriptions are of the effects of frontier life on the young woman's emotional development and stability; the outcome of Letty's initiation journey is not success but madness.

A second factor that distinguishes *The Wind* from most other treatments of a young protagonist out West is the view of the environment as antagonist.   Letty is manipulated by circumstances and the West Texas weather and terrain: she feels driven into a loveless marriage; she has to endure the poverty and physical hardships of a drought year; terrified by sandstorms and northers, she gradually becomes hysterical in the isolated ranch shack.   In the final section of the novel the reader witnesses a violent disintegration of character. With a Texas norther shrieking around her, Letty is seduced by the cattleman; then she shoots him, attempting to bury his body in the large sand drifts.   By this time the wind has become a malevolent force of torture to the young woman; when she sees the wind uncovering the murdered man's body and revealing her crime, she runs wildly out into the storm to her suicide.

In Scarborough's papers the development of the novel from an initial set of impressions can be clearly followed. The success of *The Wind* indeed depends on the fact that Scarborough never modified the controlling idea, but rather molded all her carefully researched details on the region's history and landscapes, its local speech patterns and customs, to fit her heroine's struggle and defeat.   In her letter to the friendly Dallas bookseller, Scarborough explained:

> I used to live in West Texas, when I was about as big as a ground-squirrel. . . .   I went back for frequent visits in my early childhood and girlhood, and so I know her northers and sandstorms and droughts. . . .
>
> But *The Wind* had its real origin in the impressions I got from hearing my mother's vivid accounts of her struggles with the climate of the west. She loved the people out there, but she didn't care for the weather. My father had taken her there to that high dry climate, be-

cause her lungs were weak. . . .

> So in the back of my mind has been for a long time
> the purpose to write a story which would show the effects
> of the wind and sand on a nervous, sensitive woman, of a
> type not prepared to cope with it.[14]

In this letter Scarborough also recreates the conversation which encouraged her to begin writing the novel when she did:

> I had invited Edna Ferber to speak to the Writer's
> Club at Columbia University, and I was coming up to the
> hall with her in a taxicab. She said, "I'm nervous today,
> and I don't know why."

> "Probably because of the high wind that's blowing,"
> I told her. "That affects one's nerves decidedly."

> She looked surprised and said, "I had never thought
> of that."

> Then I told her of our Texas winds and sands, and
> how hard they are on women. I told her of the story
> I meant to write, of the effect of wind and sand and
> drought on a nervous, sensitive woman not used to the en-
> vironment. I quoted our Texas saying, "Never mind the
> weather so the wind didn't blow."

> "What perfectly wonderful material for a story!"
> she cried. "I'd give anything for it!"

> "But you can't have it." I laughed. "It's my story.
> And any way, no one could write it who hadn't lived in
> Texas."

> "It is folk-material of the richest sort," she went on.
> "Don't fail to write that story."[15]

When Ferber labelled Scarborough's sketch as folk-material, she had pointed to the experience of an entire region: the cyclones and the northers of West Texas are the winds of folk-legends. As such they are comparable to the mistral of southern

France and the sirocco of northern Africa, other violent winds which are said to drive individuals to extreme and uncharacteristic actions.[16]

For her novel Scarborough drew upon the descriptions of the northers retold and elaborated by generations of Texans. An important difference must be noted, however, between the tales recorded in the collections of the Texas Folklore Society which are humorous, tall-tale descriptions of the northers and the emphasis in *The Wind* on the terrifying and destructive powers of the winds. In her research notes Scarborough had recorded an informant's typical story of the changeable winds that one day blew tumbleweeds and five-gallon oil cans out of town and two days later, when the wind shifted, blew them all back. In her novel there is nothing comic about the storms and winds which as amoral, natural forces subdue men, women, and ranch animals alike. Although Scarborough duplicates the atmosphere of the familiar poem and song, "Hell in Texas," she does not write of the environment with the same tone of bravado. Implied in the "Hell in Texas" catalog is the fact that the narrator has survived the scorpions, rattlers, sandstorms, etc., by being just as mean, ornery, or at the very least, as tough. "Hell in Texas," after all, is an epic boast by a surviving warrior.[17] On the other hand, *The Wind* chronicles defeat.

One of Scarborough's major accomplishments in the novel is her adaptation of elements of the Texas folk-materials to her vision of an alien physical world. In the young heroine's mind the aggressive, brutal force of the sandstorms and winds become meshed with the legends of the pacing white stallion and its counterpart in the swift, wild black horse. The sound of the cyclones and the wind at night remind her of the neighing of a demonic beast that could never be tamed. The stallion becomes emblematic of an evil force in nature: "mighty in power, cruel in spirit, more to be feared than man" (p. 3). Commentators such as J. Frank Dobie and Walter Prescott Webb have seen in the wild stallion legends a defiant love of freedom and liberty, an untamable beauty and power, and a vanishing glimpse of unspoiled American wilderness.[18] But in Scarborough's novel the supernatural aspects of the legends only intensify the heroine's terror:

> She saw the wind as a black stallion with mane a-stream,
> and hoofs of fire, speeding across the trackless plains,

> deathless, defiant!   What if she were out on this prairie
> this night?   He would trample her down to her death
> with fiery hoofs. . . .   A phantom, riderless horse, whom
> no mortal would ever ride. . . . (p. 175).

In *The Wind* the heroine's state of mind determines how the folk
legends are interpreted, how they are really experienced.

The weather-lore of the region seems to confirm Letty's
nightmarish existence: as she experiences the unnatural seasons
in Texas and compares the sights and smells with her memories
of Virginia's predictable and verdant changes from winter to
spring and summer, Letty learns that indeed "All signs fail in
Texas."   None of the charms for bringing rain work.   Rattle-
snake rattles placed on every fencepost in the countryside give
witness to the optimism of some ranchers, but nevertheless, the
drought continues.

A house-warming dance with its folk-dances and tunes only
serves to demonstrate the powerlessness of the feeble social life
in Texas to save when compared with Letty's childhood community in Virginia.   The night of gaiety accentuates the endless
days of isolation.   The cowboys' laconic descriptions and humorous boasting at first delight the young woman with what to her
seems new and eccentric humor, but later she realizes that the
Western humor is no defense against the drought and does not
compensate for the dry water holes littered with carcasses of
bloated cattle.   The cowboys "facing hard luck with a joke, laugh
to hide despair" (p. 245).   The Western humorous stance has
become "tragic buffoonery" to Letty.

The cowboy songs, too, take on the shadows of this alien
world.   One example, "The Dying Cowboy," illustrates how folk-
song becomes an effective statement of theme.   When Letty first
hears the song, she thinks the melody "weird and haunting."
The lines "In a narrow grave, just six by three,/Oh, bury me not
on the lone prairie!" remind her of her mother's death and increase her sadness (p. 23).   The second time, when the cattleman
taunts her with the song, she wonders if her fate is to be buried
on the plains.   He sneeringly tells her that the song like life isn't
cheerful.   Letty has gradually realized that life is cruel and holds
no rosy future for her, but in her thoughts she struggles to dis-

prove such a definition of the world. The message of the song precludes any reasons for hope and reawakens her fears (pp. 213-4). Then in the final scene of the novel Letty imagines that she hears the cattleman's corpse singing "Oh bury me not on the lone prairie" and that this mournful voice was there to haunt her as she tries to bury the body. The tune of the song swirls in her mind along with her fear of the wind and her increasing hysteria (p. 328). All elements in the Texas milieu have become destructive.

In *Literature of the Great Plains* Walter Prescott Webb notes that *The Wind* is the only novel of cattle country he found that has a tragic ending. The literary naturalists Hamlin Garland, Theodore Dreiser, and Frank Norris, in their works published before 1925, had explored the impact of the physical and social environment on character.[19] Thus Scarborough in focusing on the overwhelming force of circumstance and environment did not introduce a new theme to American literature, but her naturalistic novel is unique in that it treated what one might term an older, wilder West than that in Norris's *The Octopus.* That is, she examined the complex set of values identified as Western and arrived at a thoroughly pessimistic interpretation.

At the beginning of the novel as Letty watches the Texas landscape from her train window, she notices the carcasses of cattle, and then, after she sees a crippled cow, she learns that the train had hit the animal. All the justifications she hears—fences are too expensive out here, it's too time-consuming to stop the train, the cattle are scrawny things anyway—only repulse her and she cries, "And is this the trail to your West—the bodies of the poor creatures you've killed?" (p. 32). For the heroine the West becomes a land of indifference and cruelty, a land of action without the ethical examination of consequences: "All the old values seemed left behind. Ahead lay the path to the West, with its trail of broken bodies. . . ." (p. 32).

Individual freedom and liberty, adventure and excitement—these features of Western life have drawn many from the East, but in Scarborough's novel the acceptance of a violent world means that individuals have little power and that they become victims not adventurers. The Westerners have as much control over their destiny as the pitiful cattle that stray in front of the train: Letty concludes, "Life didn't leave you much choice, but just shoved you around as if you hadn't any right to feelings" (p. 11). Powerlessness is a refrain throughout the novel:

> Life was a strange, queer, twisted thing, that left you no choice at all (p. 184). Life had got her in a corner and had driven her to do things she hadn't wanted to, and that didn't rightly represent her (p. 290).

No person could "make something" of his or her life because the impact of any individual in this frontier setting is negligible. The traditional virtues of Western heroes—fortitude, determination, courage—do not provide Scarborough's characters with the strengths to change their situation. The drought conditions force everyone to wait and suffer the heat and windstorms.

Letty also discovers that the West is a land of deception and illusion. Scarborough had kept the name Sweetwater because it was too interesting imaginatively to change. The heroine thinks of her destination as a delightful place with houses and trees, "One thing she was sure of—there would be water, sweet and cool and pure, for wasn't the place named Sweetwater?" (p. 6). Yet once she sees the town, she discovers that, like many Western land promotion deals, the name is an outrageous fake. A cowboy explains, "Names is like dreams—they go by contraries most times. I reckon the early settlers named this spot what they did because there ain't no water here, and the nearest is brackish, lime, you know" (p. 49).

In Scarborough's naturalistic West, then, dreams quickly develop into nightmares. The usual identification of the West with the good life, an escape from a confined existence, or the land of one's dreams turns out to be as inaccurate as the name Sweetwater. Letty, watching the splendor of a Western sunset, has wondered, "Would it [the West] be a land of glory as well as a land of fear and cruelty, perhaps?" (p. 35). The golden glow, however, mirrors Letty's false hopes. On this frontier no harmonious relationship with the natural world is possible:

> [Letty] felt oppressed by the solitude of nature, which was so different from the friendly countrysides she had known at home—these vast, distressing stretches of tree-

less plains, with nothing to see but a few stunted mesquite
bushes, and samples of cactus that would repel the touch.
(p. 56)

Indeed Letty soon learns that "[There is] no refuge in nature!"
(p. 105).

III

In her reply to the West Texas critics of *The Wind* Scarborough had explained, "I was trying to show the woman's side
of pioneer life, because most of the western fiction had been
about men and their struggles."[20] Beginning with her mother's
impressions of early life in the region, Scarborough developed a
woman's view of the West that emphasized the detrimental effects of the frontier on the human spirit. In her accounts of the
novel's original idea Scarborough always quickly explained that
her mother did not go mad and that she was happily married and
lived a long life; yet the destructive possibilities of the climate
and the isolation her mother had experienced intrigued Scarborough. Folk-wisdom also confirmed her thematic interest:
early in the novel Letty was reminded of the saying, "Folks say
the West is good enough for a man or a dog, but no place for a
woman or a cat" (p. 20).

In Scarborough's prologue to the novel, the physical effect
of the winds and sand on women is emphasized:

> The winds were cruel to women that came under their
> tyranny. They were at them ceaselessly, buffeting them
> with icy blasts in winter, burning them with hot breath
> in summer, parching their skins and roughening their hair,
> and trying to wear down their nerves by attrition, and
> drive them away. (p. 3)

But the isolation on the frontier and the lack of community
also exact their price; in essence, the West is a sterile land with
little social and cultural development to meet the needs of mind
and spirit. The adventure, the new sights, and the thrill of being
tested by physical danger do not compensate Letty for the loss
of family, loss of the sense of home and security, and loss of
values she had taken for granted during her Virginia childhood.

Scarborough suggests that,

> In the old days, the winds were the enemies of
> women. Did they hate them because they saw in them
> the symbols of that civilization which might gradually
> lessen their own power? Because it was for women that
> men would build houses as once they made dugouts?
> (p. 3)

Still within the novel the answer to these questions is neither a simple yes nor an agreement with the conventional dichotomy identifying men with wilderness and women with civilization. Instead Scarborough juxtaposes two kinds of women: one possesses the strength, physical energy, and the insensitivity to survive in the harsh world; the other longs for a world in which survival needs have been met and the society can offer a religious life, participation in a social group, and above all, the affection and comfort of friends. Scarborough selects the woman who is victimized by the Western environment as the main character, dramatizing the dark side of frontier experience.

Letty is eighteen, pretty, slender, and lively; she is reluctant to assume all the responsibilities of an adult and retains a naive, childlike manner. Isolated from anyone or any group that could provide advice or assist in her initiation, Letty struggles to meet each crisis and survive it. Her cousin's wife, on the other hand, is a self-sufficient woman who accepts the challenges of the environment. As Letty first describes Cora, she embodies the same natural vigor as Cather's pioneer women or Hilma Tree in *The Octopus:*

> Such a magnificent woman! Tall, like some goddess of
> the prairie, deep-bosomed, with noble, softly flowing lines
> like a statue; erect, instinct with vibrant, magnetic life!
> Her eyes were golden-brown, with slumbering fires in
> them. . . . (p. 69)

A few dry years and loss of income do not affect Cora's self-confidence and her optimistic commitment to life in the West: she will not give up but simply move on and start again. However, Letty sees the insensitivity and potential cruelty in Cora's strengths:

> It was as if the boundless energy of the plains, the stored-
> up vigor of the long centuries that had waited for human
> life to inhabit these prairies, had expressed themselves
> in her.   Yet was she like nature herself, contemptuous
> of weaklings, impatient and disregardful of others less
> capable than herself?   Could one who had never suffered
> sympathize with another's pang of body or mind or soul?
> (pp. 77-78)

Letty, who felt like a "lost soul," can find no sisterly relationship with Cora whose energy was as "wild and limitless as the
force of the wind on the prairies" (p. 116).

Letty seeks friendship and understanding, but Cora imagines
her a rival for the attention of her family:

> Cora was thoroughly a woman, though with a slashing
> selfishness by some considered masculine.   She didn't
> mind work. . . .   What she was not willing to do without
> . . .was a continual recognition of her personality.   She
> wished every one to be always aware of her existence, of
> her sex, of her ideas.   She forced herself into the fore-
> front of every one's thoughts, with her overpowering
> personality like a battering ram of beauty and sex and
> self-assertiveness. (p. 94)

As Scarborough sees her, the strong pioneer mother was not always admirable.   Letty cannot meet life aggressively as Cora
does; and when Letty finds no compassion in Cora's treatment,
instead of confronting the issue, Letty must leave her cousin's
home.

Letty's marriage to a cowboy provides no companionship
either, for he accepts hard times as an ordinary part of ranching
in West Texas.   When Letty searches for answers in conversations
with the older women of the region, she discovers that they have
made compromises and sacrifices that are not possible for her:

> The women of the plains were philosophic souls that had
> learned to bear their hardships with fortitude, and they
> showed that they expected Letty to do the same. Yet in
> their faces she read strange secrets without their knowing
> it, stories of their struggles and adjustments and their

longings. (p. 192)

In *The Wind* the battle of the pioneers in settling the West becomes another struggle for the survival of the fittest, but through
the eyes of Letty, Scarborough examines the devastation of that
battle. Although the struggle may bring out admirable traits
such as endurance, more often the life in the West is a deaden-
ing process that encourages a crassness and a contempt for the
weakling. In the final stages of the drought the humans are reduced to a level little better than the dying cattle: "Gaunt,
cadaverous beasts staggered about, tortured by heel-flies that
nagged them constantly, bawling in distress, searching everywhere for food and water" (p. 263).

There is one aspect of Letty's plight, however, that Scarborough does not attribute to the physical environment. In the
year following *The Wind* Scarborough's third novel *The Unfair
Sex* was published serially in the Houston magazine *The Woman's
Viewpoint.* In this work, as the title plainly states, Scarborough
protests the systematic discrimination by men against women.
For the fiery young heroine the unequal treatment began early
as she was excluded from games and skills, such as hunting, that
were supposed to be for boys only. Scarborough traces the influence of male prejudice at all ages of the heroine's life and
most emphatically condemns the discrimination against women
in hiring, salaries, and promotion in secondary and university
education. (Scarborough included as well the outrageous sexism
she herself had discovered at Oxford University, and one sus-
pects, the discrimination the heroine encountered in Texas
schools is based on Scarborough's personal experience, too.)

In *The Wind* this feminist viewpoint is a secondary theme.
While on the train from Virginia, Letty laments, "Oh, why aren't
girls taught to make their living and take care of themselves,
the same as men?" (p. 22). Letty's victimization is attributable,
in part, to the cultural attitudes that kept women economically
helpless and dependent: ". . .Letty told herself for the hun-
dredth time that girls ought to be trained to work, to support
themselves, so that misfortune couldn't overwhelm them as it
had her" (p. 230). In Cora's little daughter Alice, Letty has seen
a kindred sensitivity, and when the girl announces, "I'm goin'
to make a living my self when I'm grown. . ." (p. 232), Letty

hopes that there will be a way out of the stifling ranch life for this next generation of women.

Because of Letty's dim awareness of the cultural bonds on women, she can briefly sympathize with Cora, too: "She was a woman who so loved social gaiety, and life gave her so little! She, whose beauty and vivacity would attract attention in any assembly, spent her days cooped up in a shack in a remote ranch" (p. 121). Although Cora feels happy and successful in her life, Letty wonders what Cora could have accomplished if "she had had a wider training and culture, a broader opportunity, so that her native abilities might have developed more." Cora, also, has been blighted by the limited choices on the frontier: "How queer a thing was life that shut this heady creature with her wild, rich possibilities up in a little box-house on the prairie!" (p. 117). Even the successful pioneer women lead circumscribed lives.

IV

In 1927 M. G. M. made a silent film of *The Wind*, starring Lillian Gish as Letty and directed by Victor Seastrom. Gish, in her autobiography *The Movies, Mr. Griffith & Me,* describes the arduous filming conditions in the heat and sandstorms of the Mojave Desert location. After the film was completed, Gish and other members of the cast were extremely pleased with the results. However, eight of the largest film exhibitors insisted that the ending of the movie had to be changed—instead of Letty's suicidal disappearance into the sandstorm, she and her cowboy were happily reunited. Gish recorded the intense disappointment all the principals connected with the filming felt when this happy ending was tacked on to their finely drawn story.[21]

By the time Scarborough saw the completed version of the film, she had become reconciled as the novelist to the happy ending demanded by the movie arbiters of the popular taste. But as a folklorist she was disturbed by the music:

> . . .I do wish that a Texan might have been consulted as
> to the tune and the pronunciation of "Bury me not on the
> lone prairie!" No cowboy would recognize the song.

> And the sentimental ballad hooked on at the end of the
> last scene most incongruously! I had accepted with phi-
> losophic resignation the change which turned my tragedy
> into a happy ending, but I'd like to throw a West Texas
> cactus at the person who put that Broadway ballad in
> to ruin the end.[22]

Scarborough insisted that the production should have been true
to the regional atmosphere she had so carefully constructed.
Sentimental taste had already forced a reversal of the logical
plot outcome; Scarborough was angered that another concession
had been made—a Broadway ballad, not a folk ballad, had been
added. It is clear that the movie distributors had a commercial-
ized view of Western materials: for entertaining a mass audience,
cowboys in a sagebrush setting were a matter for comedy not
tragedy.

Scarborough probably was not surprised by the demand for
what she called the "happy ender." When her short story "The
Drought" was first published, the editor of *The Century* magz-
zine insisted that readers would not like the depressing ending,
and Scarborough did add three paragraphs to the story that
reconciled the couple and "converted the storm into a neighbor-
ly rain that saved the crop from imminent ruin."[23] In *The Wind*,
though, Scarborough excluded any possibility of the "happy
ender." Although Letty dreams of a chivalrous knight of the
plains that will rescue her, she soon admits that life is quite different from popular romances.[24] In popular Western fiction the
young man often goes West to find his fortune, the young
woman to find her true love, but in *The Wind,* no Virginian woos
a Molly Wood to live happily ever after.

In summary, when Scarborough published her novel over
fifty years ago, her tragic Western was an uncommon interpretation and a very unpopular one. Critics who glorified their
regional heritage rejected Scarborough's view of the Texas setting; the entertainment industry feared that a story of defeat
would not sell. But no one noticed a more disquieting suggestion
in Scarborough's definition of the West. Soon after Letty arrived in Sweetwater, she was told the story of Cynthia Ann
Parker, one of the few historical incidents mentioned in the
novel (pp. 58-9). Parker had been captured as a child by the

Comanche Indians, and then later, after she had married an Indian chief and was the mother of two children, she was recaptured and returned to the white society. Letty, like Parker, found herself culturally displaced through a violent, inexplicable, and uncontrollable series of events. Although Scarborough's heroine's life-change was less sensational than Parker's, it was as destructive.

The reference to Parker is appropriate also because of its link to the Indian captivity narratives which have traditionally been a treatment of evil in the wilderness. Scarborough's novel ultimately explores the existence of evil in the golden West—the force that Melville saw in the same prancing white stallion legends.

In *The Wind* evil is perceived through the mirage of the interior mind; it is the mirage that is madness, clear-sighted and supernatural. Letty shifts from the unbearable reality of her daily life to the memories of an abundant life in Virginia and then back to the forces terrifying and overwhelming her: "...a naked, unbodied wind—like a ghost more terrible because invisible—that wailed to her across waste places in the night, calling to her like a demon lover."[25] In the final scene of the novel Letty runs out into the raging storm, into the arms of the norther, for the force of evil which destroys is also a force preeminently seductive: "She fled across the prairies like a leaf blown in a gale, borne along in the force of the wind that was at last to have its way with her."[26]

NOTES

I would like to thank those who helped me in this study: the American Philosophical Society for a grant which financed my research in Scarborough's manuscripts and personal papers; the librarians and staff of the Texas Collection at Baylor University, Waco, Texas, for their generous assistance; Dorothy Brewster, professor emeritus of Columbia University and Mrs. Emma Shirley and Mrs. Nancy Marrs of Waco, Texas, for sharing their reminiscences of Scarborough; and Dr. Don Walker, professor of American Literature at the University of Utah, for his encouragement of my project.

[1]*The Wind* was first published anonymously, but not because Scarborough was trying to avoid personal abuse brought on by the novel's description of West Texas or because she wanted the freedom of an anonymous critic. Her publisher, Harper & Brothers, suggested bringing out the novel anonymously as a publicity maneuver. A recent novel *West of the Water Tower* by Homer Croy had been published anonymously, and the discussion over who the author was and why he wanted his name secret had greatly helped the novel's sales: "The mystery of anonymity is still strong, and we believe that it would greatly focus interest on *The Wind*." (William Briggs to Scarborough, April 27, 1925). However, by the end of 1925 Scarborough felt the publicity gimmick was not working, and she requested that other copies be printed with her name. (Acknowledgement by William Briggs in a letter to Scarborough, December 30, 1925). Scarborough concluded that the publicity for *The Wind* had been inexcusably bungled by Harper & Bros., with the result that the novel's sales never met her expectations. In letters concerning other novels Scarborough continued to remind Harpers of their failure in advertising *The Wind*. (Scarborough to Briggs, n.d. ?1926, letter beginning "IMPATIENT GRISELDA is finished. . . ."; Scarborough to Briggs, September 5, 1927; Scarborough to Harry Hoyns, Harper & Bros., August 27, 1927).

The account of the anonymous publication has been confused by the news releases that attempted to explain the reasons: ". . .the publishers felt that it might be well to await the reaction of readers to some of the strongly localized situations in the book before revealing the name of the author." DSP, Box 19. Some of the news releases were written by Scarborough as she tried to promote the sales of her novel: "As yet, the author has refused to disclose his identity. Why? Is it because he thinks he might be handled roughly for too much realism in his pictures of life down there? At any rate, he is keeping quiet, and his friends, if he has any, are helping him hide." DSP, "Waco Roundup," Box 4.

The source for all unpublished letters, notes, and manuscripts referred to in this study is the Emily Dorothy Scarborough Papers, The Texas Collection, Baylor University, Waco, Texas; listed as DSP.

[2]For more details on the West Texas reaction to *The Wind* see the dissertation of James W. Neatherlin, "Dorothy Scarborough: Form and Milieu in the Work of a Texas Writer," University of Iowa, 1973.

[3]"Anonymous to R. C. Crane," DSP, Box 19, published as "Unknown Author of WIND Answers Crane Criticism," in the Sweetwater, Texas, *Daily Reporter,* 15 December 1925, p. 6.

[4]*Ibid.*

[5]In Scarborough's papers there are three versions of a letter to Heywood Broun, dated September 30, 1925: one in Scarborough's handwriting, another in a disguised script, and the last version in typescript. The letter purports to be from a Texas oilman visiting New York City who had read *The Wind* and complained about the image of West Texas he found in the novel. His complaints about the vivid descriptions inadvertently praise the veracity of Scarborough's novel. The oilman thinks that the emphasis in literature should be on the "nice and cheerful" because "there's no sense in being all gormed up with gloom." DSP, Boxes 19 & 75. A close family friend in a letter to Scarborough commented, "Tom told me in detail your plan for advertising this book but, my dear, I do not believe that anyone can be found to adversely criticize it" (letter from J. B. Cranfill, October 15, 1925). Later he told Scarborough that he had read R. C. Crane's "screed against your book": "He takes your book awfully hard. . . . It will take a lot of wind to blow him away, believe me, my dear, but I know you will enjoy his philippic against 'The Wind.' Keep on, my dear, you are raising a lot of dust." (J. B. Canfill to Scarborough, November 23, 1925, both letters DSP, Box 5). The West Texas Chamber of Commerce with their own sincerely formed disgust at the treatment of Sweetwater in *The Wind* apparently did not know how well they carried out Scarborough's publicity idea.

[6]MSS beginning "I have often been asked why my novel THE WIND

. . . .," DSP, Box 19.

[7]Ex. S. Hughes to Harper Bros., November 3, 1925, DSP, Box 4.

[8]Hughes explained, "The story is certainly gripping but I cannot help feeling indignation that with all the Romance of West Texas the writer should be so cruel and heartless as to make every environment, contact and circumstance stronger than 'Lettie' could combat without any chance of escape or redemption." Other readers also challenged Scarborough's view. The questions that Mrs. Fannie Willis Pogue asked on behalf of the Beaumont Woman's Reading Club were typical: "Did you intend to exaggerate the wind storms, or was this severity your childhood impression, or is it really that bad? We wondered why you did not put even one noble character in the whole book?" (letter to Scarborough, October 24,1926, DSP, Box 6).

[9]Scarborough to Mrs. Polly Lobdell, February 15, 1926, DSP, Box 6. In a speech "Why Not a Literary Boom in Texas?" Scarborough reiterated the importance of Texans developing a regional literature: "There is an elemental vastness about Texas that challenges us to prove worthy of it in our writing. . . . Yet greatness is in our blood, the driving force of our pioneer ancestors that. . .won this empire for themselves will make us great in the arts when we once fiercely put our hearts into it." DSP, Box 62. (Scarborough's interest in the cotton growing regions of Texas and especially in the hardships of tenant farmers developed into what she called her cotton trilogy: *In the Land of Cotton* (1923), published two years before *The Wind; Can't Catch a Redbird* (1929); and *The Stretch-berry Smile* (1932).

[10]*The Century*, 100 (May 1920), pp. 13-22. The version that Scarborough preferred was published in *Best Short Stories from the Southwest*, ed. Hilton Ross Greer (Dallas: Southwest Press, 1928), pp. 73-99. See also footnote 23.

[11]Scarborough to Lobdell.

[12]*The Wind* (New York & London: Harper and Brothers, 1925), p. 1. All quotations will be taken from this volume and hereafter listed in the text.

[13]DSP, Box 61.

[14]Scarborough to Lobdell.

[15]*Ibid.*

[16]Norman Douglas's famous novel *South Wind* in which the sirocco dominates the action had been published eight years before *The Wind.* Scarborough in an introduction to a Modern Reader's edition of Douglas's novel explained that only after friends had commented on the similarities between the novels had she read *South Wind.* See "Introduction," *South Wind* (New York: Macmillan Co., 1929). Her praise for Douglas's book is enthusiastic.

[17]For a discussion of E. U. Cook who wrote the poem/song see Mody Boatwright, *Folk Laughter on the American Frontier* (New York: Macmillan Co., 1949), pp. 72-74.

[18]W. P. Webb, "The White Steed of the Prairies," *Legends of Texas,* ed. J. Frank Dobie (1924; rept. Hatboro, Penn.: Folklore Assoc., Inc., 1964), pp. 223-226; and J. Frank Dobie, "The Deathless Pacing White Stallion," *Mustangs & Cow Horses* (1940; rpt. Dallas: Southern Methodist University Press, 1965), pp. 171-179.

[19]Scarborough's study of these authors can be traced in her class notes for the courses in "The Modern Novel" and creative writing (novel and short story) that she taught. The opening scene of Letty and the cattleman on the train parallels the beginning situation in Dreiser's *Sister Carrie;* in a manuscript version of *The Wind* the similarity is more striking because Scarborough at first referred to the cattleman as a drummer and had named her heroine Annie.

[20]"Anonymous to R. C. Crane."

[21]Lillian Gish with Ann Pinchot, *The Movies, Mr. Griffith & Me* (Englewood, N. J.: Prentice-Hall, Inc., 1969), pp. 292-295.

[22]MSS beginning, "I was delighted when I knew that Lillian Gish was to star. . . ," DSP, Box 58.

[23]"An Apology to Goats," *Bookman,* 56 (1922-1923), p. 191.

[24]See the following pages in *The Wind:* 111-112, 125, 180, 188.

[25]The quotation is from page 4; see also the same phrasing on pages

312 and 330. Supernaturalism, especially in Scarborough's treatment of Letty's fear and daydreaming, amplifies the naturalistic plot. Scarborough's doctoral dissertation was published as *The Supernatural in Modern English Fiction* (New York: G. P. Putnam's Sons, 1917). Many of the examples Scarborough discusses in the chapter "The Supernatural in Folk-Tales" show the animation of natural phenomena with supernatural qualities and powers.

[26]*The Wind*, p. 337. In manuscript notes for the novel Scarborough wrote, "So the wind was a terrible power that she could not escape. The wind had its will with her. The wind spoken of as *he*, male, dominant." DSP, Box 61.

FOLK NARRATIVE IN CAROLINE GORDON'S FRONTIER FICTION

M. Lou Rodenberger
Texas A & M University

Forced to provide the daily food and fuel needs of a band of Shawnee and Cherokee Indians, captive Jinny Wiley keeps her senses by reminiscing about her early life in Harman's Station, a Kentucky frontier settlement in the Big Sandy Valley. Camped with her captors near the legendary Big Salt Licks in northern Kentucky, Jinny, who is narrator of Caroline Gordon's short story, "The Captive," recalls how back home folks laughed at Vard Wiley when he "told tall tales about a lick bigger'n any licks around those parts, where the beasts come up in tens of thousands."[1] Renowned for his tall tales, Vard was also a practical joker. Jinny is startled by the echo of her own laughter through the forest when she remembers one of Vard's pranks. She thinks

> Of the time he borrowed my dress and sunbonnet and shawl and went and sat on the creek bank when the schoolmaster was in swimming. He sat there all evening with the sunbonnet hiding his face and old Mister Daugherty shaking his fist at him. "You hussy! You brazen hussy! Don't you know I'm naked?" and finally when he comes up out of the water naked as the day he was born Vard took out after him and run him clean to the house. Old Mister Daugherty went around saying there was a woman ought to be run out of the settlements, and Vard would talk to him and make out it was me. But Old Man Daugherty knew wouldn't none of Hezekiah Sellard's daughters be carrying on like that. (pp. 236-37)

Several years ago, her interviewers asked Caroline Gordon what purpose Jinny's recall of events in her early life had in the story of her miserable life with the Indians. Miss Gordon pointed out that "one way of asserting your individuality is through your memories."[2]   In the interview, too, she says that Vard Wiley's joke on Old Man Daugherty was a tale she had heard her father tell during her own childhood.   An examination of "The Captive" and Miss Gordon's novel, *Green Centuries*,[3] reveals that much of the author's own Southern family saga, as well as folk life and legend indigenous to the early Western frontier, are used freely to delineate character and to develop theme in these works.

For the adventuresome colonist in the 1770's the westering experience he so avidly sought culminated ideally in his establishing a homestead as near the fabulous land of Kaintuck as the Cherokees, the Shawnees, and the British government would tolerate.   Caroline Gordon explores this frontier experience during the time of the American Revolution in both "The Captive" and *Green Centuries.*   In these works Miss Gordon demonstrates a comprehensive knowledge of the history of both the Indians and the borderers of that era, but the vitality of her frontier fiction originates in her use of folk narrative.

Folk narrative in Miss Gordon's fiction serves two purposes. Structure of plot depends upon folk history to provide the events which control the action of both the short story and the novel. The protagonists of these folk tales are the prototypes upon whom Miss Gordon bases many of her characterizations.   Although neither of these uses of folk narrative is unique among fiction writers, Miss Gordon's portrayal of folk character is singular in its technique.

In her critical study of fiction, *How to Read a Novel,* Miss Gordon says that folk tales, fairy tales, and good novels show that the "one true subject for fiction" is "the adventures of a hero or heroine—that is, the story of what happened to some man or woman who, through answering the call to the adventure which constitutes the action of the story, comes to stand out from his or her fellows as a remarkable person."[4]   She depicts folk characters as made of heroic stuff.   They are already portrayed as people of action in folk legend, but the perpetuation of stereotypical folk characters—borderers or Indians—is not Miss Gordon's aim.   With a sure intuitive understanding of human motivation and human weakness, the writer humanizes the folk hero and endows him with personality and passion. She accomplishes her creation of three-dimensional folk heroes and heroines by incorporation of both the materials of well-known legends surrounding her characters and her inherited store of Southern family stories, customs, and speech. With these materials as resources, Miss Gordon often chooses the techniques of the folk narrator to reveal character.

The legendary materials Miss Gordon employs originated in the historically factual activities of the borderers and the Indians on the Holston, Clinch, and Watauga Rivers in Northeastern Tennessee and eastern Kentucky between 1769 and 1787. At Harman's Station, Kentucky, in 1787, Jennie Wiley watched a war party of Shawnee and Cherokee Indians murder and scalp her brother and five of her children. With her youngest child in her arms, Jennie was forced to accompany the warriors on a long, arduous hike to northern Kentucky. One of the band bashed her crying baby's head against a tree, but she survived to serve as her captor's slave for almost a year. When the old Shawnee chief, who had been her self-appointed guardian, sold Jennie to the ruthless young Cherokee leader, Jennie escaped, and, after a frantic flight, finally found refuge in a blockhouse near her old home. She lived to rejoin her husband and produce another large family. She told her story many times.

When Caroline Gordon casually thumbed through William Elsey Connelley's account of Jennie's adventures[5] in the Vanderbilt library stacks, she became fascinated with Jennie Wiley's story. Connelley was a local historian who valued oral tradition. His account of Jennie's ordeal originated in the stories told him by Jennie's son, Adam, when he was an old man. According to Connelley, Adam was a storyteller whose "mind was a storehouse of history and border story."[6] Miss Gordon says that when she read Connelley's narration, she knew that she had to write the story.[7] In "The Captive," Connelley's courageous Jennie becomes brash, witty Jinny, who tells her own story.

Local historians also furnish much of the material for the novel *Green Centuries*.[8] The novelist creates Rion Outlaw and his brother Archy as heroes of this work. But the fictional Rion has explored eastern Tennessee with Daniel Boone, and early in the novel, he watches with envy when Daniel leaves Salisbury, North Carolina, with trader John Findley to explore the land of

Kentucky. The venture is financed by Judge Richard Henderson. When Rion's activities with the rebel Regulators against the King's militia are discovered, he goes west and settles with his young wife Cassy and her bookish brother Frank near the stations of James Robertson and Amos Eaton, historically among the first settlers on the Holston River. Young Archy Outlaw, who follows his brother, is captured by the Cherokees, and becomes the adopted son of one of the best-known Cherokee chiefs, Atta Kulla Kulla, head of the Cherokee town, Chota.

Historical events vividly recreated in the novel include the meeting between the Cherokee and Judge Henderson's associates at Sycamore Shoals in 1755. There, Atta Kulla Kulla accepted several loads of clothing and guns for his people and, in turn, agreed to give Kentucky to the land speculators. When Dragging Canoe, Atta Kulla Kulla's son, leads dissident Cherokees against the settlers at Eaton's Station in July, 1776, Rion participates in the Battle of Island Flats, where history records that the Cherokees were defeated and forced back to Chota.

These are well-documented episodes in a dramatic chapter of America's westering experience, but the men and women who played leading roles in these events were to become heroes and heroines of regional folk narrative. Although usually based on true occurrences, their stories became the material for storytellers, who embellished their exploits to aggrandize their subjects and to entertain their hearers. Protagonists of these narratives fulfill Miss Gordon's criteria for the heroic character. She recreates a number of them as fully rounded characters. Adventurer John Findley, who drifted down to the Yadkin from Pennsylvania and inspired Daniel Boone to make the 1769 surveying trip to Kentucky, is characterized as Rion sees him: ". . .a blatherskite, and by his own account a vagrant, yet Daniel seemed to think a lot of him" (p. 16). It is from Findley that Rion first hears about ducks and geese so numerous in Kentucky that they crowd together in the Ohio and swim over falls, stunning themselves so that a hunter can pick them up without effort (p. 18).

Scotch trader James Adair, who lived for a time with the Indians and whose *History of the American Indians* was published in London in 1775, spends an evening with Rion and his family on the Holston. While the men watch Cassy cook supper,

Adair and Frank discuss at length Adair's theory, which he develops in his book, that the Indians descended from a Hebrew tribe. Adair's origins and his beliefs are revealed in the conversation. When he mourns his estrangement from his Indian friends, brought about by the French, he says that he is destined "to fall in the woods and no man know where James Adair's bones lie," Frank holds up Adair's books and asks, "What do you care where your bones lie? James Adair's grave is here. . .and all men will visit it." And then Adair laughs and "throwing his head back gazed at the ceiling. With his wide grin and his eyes shining he looked like a man drunk on wine" (p. 406).

Even more fully developed are those characterizations of borderers Jennie Wiley and Daniel Boone and Indians Atta Kulla Kulla and Nancy Ward. In Connelley's account of the day the Indians captured Jennie, the reader learns that "Thomas Wiley was absent from home that day. Before daylight he had set out for some trading station with a horse laden with ginseng and other marketable commodities which he could barter for domestic necessaries."[9] In Miss Gordon's version, Jinny blames Tom's absence on her own stubborn insistence. "I was bound he should make the trip, Indians or no Indians," she says (p. 213). When daytime owl hoots begin to worry her, she remembers what a man once said to her when she was hunting bear with him. "You're brash, Jinny. . .and you always been lucky, but one of these times you going to be too brash," he warned (p. 215).

Miss Gordon's skill as a taleteller is given full play as Jinny reveals her personality, her background, and her values through what she tells about her ordeal. Her captors camped for the winter under an overhanging ledge, called a rockhouse, near the salt licks which had so intrigued early explorers and historians. In his account of the discovery of Kentucky, John Filson describes seven-foot rib bones and other hugh skeleton parts belonging to "quadrupeds now unknown" scattered around the licks.[10] Jinny knows now that Vard Wiley's yarn is not a tall tale. She says, "I couldn't keep my eyes off the bones. I would take them up in my hand and turn them over and over, wondering what manner of beasts they had belonged to" (p. 235).

Jinny goes to the licks for her salt supply and remembers Vard, then home, and then the songs her old granny used to sing back at the settlement:

Pa'tridge in the pea patch
Pickin'up the peas
'Long comes the bell cow
Kickin' up her heels. (p. 235)

Jinny "calls to mind" other events in her early life as she goes
about her monotonous daily drudgery. She remembers the
mighty hunter Lance Rayburn who came a-courting her, and who
threw his gift of a fine beaver pelt into the creek when she re-
buffed his advances. She dreams one evening that Tice Harman,
who is described by historians as a tough little Indian stalker, will
come rescue her because she knows that "he loved to fight Indians better'n eat when he was hungry" (p. 239). She dreams
another time of seeing all of her family dancing to fiddle music
and singing at a party. All through the difficult winter Jinny
keeps her senses by recalling episodes, stories, songs, and advice
which were a part of her frontier upbringing. Her native intelligence and knowledge of woods lore keep her alive when she flees
from the savages. She wades down streams to hide her tracks
and boils wild greens to give her strength. Her hunger sets her
thinking about the smoked herring she once stole out of the
smokehouse to feast on with her brothers. She berates herself
for ever wasting food, remembering the day she went hunting
with the Sellards and Damron boys and shot eighteen gobblers,
which they left lying. "I thought about them gobblers more'n
once that day and, Lord, how I wished I could git my hands on a
rifle butt one more time," she says (p. 252).

Revelation through her memories of her early life realistically delineates Jinny's character. She is stubborn, brash, and im-
pulsive; she is also brave, intelligent, and self-reliant. In the
interview Miss Gordon granted to discuss this story, she describes
her concept of Jinny this way:

> The woman is human. She has seen all her children
> killed. She saw a man tortured to death. She herself
> was in danger of being tortured. . . . She's frightened to
> death. . . . I would have been dead or nuts by this time,
> and I think most modern women would be. She is of
> heroic stature, but still is a human being.[11]

True to this concept, Miss Gordon creates a remarkable woman
and makes her believable through a blending of history, legend,

and family saga. Her taletelling genius is also evident. Jinny is a storyteller, and when she concludes her story, it is with the raconteur's talent for wry understatement. Succinctly, she concludes, "Lord God, I was lucky to git away from them Indians" (p. 256)!

Many popular legends, of course, are incorporated into Miss Gordon's creation of Daniel Boone's role in *Green Centuries.* Most of the novel is narrated from Rion's point of view—and Daniel is his friend, as well as his hero. Rion knows Daniel is the best shot and the best trapper in Rowan County. Daniel has taught him woodcraft and trapping techniques. Rion admires Rebecca Boone, who is so patient with her restless husband, and he does not believe the story that Daniel's brother, Squire, fathered one of her children. He thinks, "If she was a whore Daniel wouldn't think as much of her as he did. He was as crazy about that woman as if she was a young girl" (p. 34).

Rion is soon tied down with a young family, but as he cuts trees and plants corn in his new ground, he thinks of how he always wanted to go to Kentuck with Daniel. Finally, Daniel visits overnight with Rion and Cassy, and right away, Daniel takes out a book to show Frank. It is *Gulliver's Travels,* which legend insists Daniel carried with him on one of his trips into Indian country. He tells Rion's family how he lost the book in an Indian fracas. He swam a creek to recover it and named the creek Lulbegrud [sic]. He explains that he was reading about the Lulbegruds when the Indians came.

Boone gently teases the baby Sarah. "Cat's got her tongue and I don't believe she's got no teeth either," he laughs. Then he sings to Sarah:

> Oh you little dear,
> Who made your breeches?
> Daddy cut'em out
> And mommy sewed the stitches. (p. 318)

As the evening wanes, the men discuss the agreement made with Atta Kulla Kulla at Sycamore Shoals. Then, Daniel tells them of his son Jamie's untimely death when he was tortured and scalped by Shawnees on his way to get supplies for the family. Folk history describes Daniel's deep depression after that incident, and now he tells Rion and Frank, "I had one of my spells, the worst one I ever had in my life. . . . Profound melancholy. I've had those spells three or four times in my life. While they last I'm not a natural man" (p. 325).

In this chapter, Daniel Boone becomes, as did Jinny Wiley, a human being, who loves his Rebecca, mourns his son's death still, and wonders about man's spirit. He compliments Cassy, who "minds" him of his Rebecca. And, finally, Rion looks at this man Boone, whom he has always thought "the finest looking fellow he had ever seen," and mentally sizes him up. Rion's evaluation not only describes Daniel but all restless westering borderers who were to move farther west every decade of their lives:

> A vagrant he heard his mother call him once. Daniel hadn't changed much in these six years, but looking into his face tonight he saw something that he had never seen before—had they seen it all along? That look he had, almost too bold for a human. When a beast was set on going its way you couldn't stop it, short of killing it. Daniel talked about Kentuck and likely it was all he said it was, but if it wasn't he wouldn't care. He'd be off over the next range to see if the land there wasn't better. Or if Kentuck turned out to be the richest land ever was anywhere, something would take him away from it. He didn't have any choice. He was one of those men had to keep moving on. . . (p. 327).

As graphically depicted as Boone are Atta Kulla Kulla and Nancy Ward. Atta Kulla Kulla earned his name Little Carpenter as a peace treaty maker between the settlers and his people. As a young man, he had been one of several Indians who went to England as guests of Sir Alexander Cuming, a Scotch Baronet with interest in Cherokee trade. In *Green Centuries* he is an old man, still influential and still beloved by his wife, the Dark Lanthorn. Characteristic of Miss Gordon's long fiction, the chapter in which the Lanthorn sets about painting the history of her husband's life on her newly-woven carpet is a short story within the novel. There is both pathos and humor in the Lanthorn's reminiscences about her husband's long associations with the whites. Whites were different in her eyes from the Real People. A Cherokee physician had told her that they were not even human beings and that his grandfather had told him that in the old days it took "ten of the short-tailed eunuchs (as the old people called them) to make up the life of one man of the Real People" (p. 236). But she trusts her husband's judgment in his dealings with whites, and "as always when she thought of that small wrinkled man, her heart grew warm."

A little later, Archy Outlaw, now the adopted son of Atta Kulla Kulla, wanders down to the town square where the old men talk. When Atta Kulla Kulla begins to tell once again about his trip to London, the young men yawn. As old man often do, Atta Kulla Kulla mentions this great event in his life whenever the opportunity arises. But, he is also portrayed as a forceful little man, able yet to command the respect of both his council members and the borderers.

It is through the Lanthorn's eyes that the reader sees Nancy Ward for the first time. The Lanthorn is not so impressed with this influential woman as the folk narrators have been. She thinks of Ghigau, or the beloved woman, as one "whom in the last few years it was the fashion to praise above all other women." Later, as the Lanthorn talks to the Ghigau, she mentally recounts Nancy's story, including details which historians have recorded. Nancy officiates with great dignity in the Chota council meetings, but the Lanthorn remembers when the Ghigau's white husband, Brian Ward, left her, and she screamed and raged all through one night. Heroine though she has become in folk narrative because she often befriended the white man, Nancy Ward is depicted by Miss Gordon as having not so favorable an image among her own people, particularly the women and the young warriors. One remarks, "Our grandmother, the Ghigau, moves more like a cow these days" (p. 244). Dragging Canoe notes harshly, "She drinks the milk of the cow. Perhaps it makes her heavy—or it may be the heaviness comes from lying with white men" (p. 244). No idealized goddess is Nancy in this novel, but a real human being, who is admired by some and criticized by others.

Caroline Gordon's folk heroes and heroines lead daily lives. Her knowledge of folk legend, folk life and regional dialect links the outstanding figures in the historical westering movement with their stories which oral tradition has preserved both dramatically and effectively. In his introduction to *The Longhorns,*

J. Frank Dobie says, "I am a teller of folk tales, and as a historian I have not hesitated to use scraps of folklore to enforce truth and reality." The same may be said of Caroline Gordon as a fiction writer when her subject is the frontier experience.

NOTES

[1]*Old Red and Other Stories* (1963; rept. New York: Cooper Square Publishers, 1971), p. 236. Subsequent references to this short story will be made in the text. "The Captive" originally appeared in *Hound and Horn,* 6 (October-November 1932), pp. 63-107.

[2]Catherine B. Baum and Floyd C. Watkins, eds., "Caroline Gordon and 'The Captive': An Interview," *Southern Review,* 7 (Spring 1971), p. 456.

[3]1941; rept. New York: Coopers Square Publishers, 1971. Subsequent references to this work will be made in the text.

[4]1953; rpt. New York: Viking Press, 1964, p. 171.

[5]*The Founding of Harman's Station* (New York: The Torch Press, 1910).

[6]Connelley says also in his "Preface" that Adam Wiley "possessed fine oratorical and conversational powers."

[7]Baum and Watkins, p. 449. Harry M. Caudill also tells Jennie's story in his novel, *Dark Hills to Westward* (Boston: Little, Brown, 1969).

[8]Miss Gordon acknowledges as one source, John P. Brown, *Old Frontiers* (Kingsport, Tenn.: Southern Publishers, 1938). She mentions, too, that she is endebted to works by Judge Samuel C. Williams and A. V. Goodpasture.

[9]Connelley, p. 36.

[10]*The Discovery, Settlement and Present State of Kentucke* (New York: Corinth Books, 1962), pp. 34-36. This work was originally published in 1784.

[11]Baum and Watkins, pp. 460-461.

THE MORMON NOVEL: VIRGINIA SORENSEN'S
THE EVENING AND THE MORNING

Sylvia B. Lee
Whatcom Community College

It was only in the 1940's, one might say, that the Mormon novel was invented. True, within ten years of Joseph Smith's death in 1844, the first "literary" works reflecting his life and his church, the Church of Jesus Christ of Latter-day Saints, were published. But the very melodrama of Joseph Smith's life and death, the strangeness, to the larger community, of some of the doctrines he taught, and the peculiar social structure of the Mormon community almost necessarily forced those first literary treatments to be propaganda, some kind of strained symbolism, one way or the other, for or against. And then the fascination of the Mormon story held writers' eyes on the past, on that which had been, so that they could only see the present as a flatter continuation of that past. That is, if the first writers on Mormonism saw it as a contemporary thing, they, including Mormon writers, saw it nevertheless as exotic and therefore melodramatic; later writers concentrated only on the history, for it was there that the interest in Mormons lay. (All this is not to deny the history, for Mormon history is vividly alive to Mormons still; it is a living part of their daily world and must be a powerful element in the literature that images that world.)

In the 1930's Vardis Fisher's autobiographical tetralogy about Vridar Hunter was perhaps the first really successful literary vision of the Mormon world as it was, i.e., is. But Fisher's work concentrated more on Hunter than on the society that Vridar grew up in; that is, Fisher's work belongs to that long tradition of the romantic prose fiction that Richard Chase sees as characteristic of the American novel (*The American Novel and Its Tradition*) rather than being a novel based upon society. And Mormonism is, above all, a society.

In his gigantic *Children of God,* in 1939, Fisher turned back
to the past to tell the Mormon story once again and, although
it is not, then, a picture of contemporary Mormonism, this work
is a seminal work. For Fisher's history does try to explain why
Mormons are what they are. Too, he manages to see the actuality of the Mormon past: his Joseph Smith, his Brigham Young,
are not mere symbols of good or evil, but, rather, men, human
beings (and striking personalities). Fisher rejected Mormonism
as a system of belief (and rejected what he regarded as its narrowness), but he did not write mere abstraction in order to prove a
point.

Then, in 1941, Maureen Whipple published *The Giant
Joshua;* in 1942 Virginia Sorensen published *A Little Lower
Than the Angels;* in 1945 Richard Scowcroft published *Children
of the Covenant.* And, in 1947, after *The Neighbors,* a novel in
which Mormonism was peripheral, Sorensen, in 1949, printed
The Evening and the Morning. These are the key novels about
Mormons. And Whipple, Sorensen, and Scowcroft were all three
from Mormon families, a significant fact (indeed, during the
1940's there was a burst of novels about Mormonism written
by Mormons or ex-Mormons, novels that were attempts to understand the realities, not just the myths, of the Mormon society).
But one must note, too, that most of these novels were written
by women. There was a clear reason.

That reason was both literary and social. The American,
i.e., European-American movement west has invariably been
treated in our literature as the act of individual people, driven
either by a desire to conquer the land and civilize it or led by a
desire to escape civilization. And, certainly, the actuality of our
movement westward has been "individualistic," for most of the
west was explored and then settled by individuals, even if they
sometimes travelled in groups. And so the literature, reflecting
the actuality, took its form from its subject; it tended to be, that
is, "romantic," emphasizing the individual and, so, emphasizing
the role of men, for it was the men who *acted* in the West.

But not all the West was settled that way. The very center
of the West is Utah—and Utah means the Mormons. The Mormons from their beginnings were a community, not just a group.
And their community was built on the family, both theological-
ly, for Mormon doctrine holds that the family is eternal, lasting

after death, and socially. If they "conquered" the land, it was as farmers, not as city-builders, although they were also city-builders. The community was male-dominated, certainly, and so reflected the prevailing American male value system; it was also a closed community, built upon a common religious and moral system, which is not necessarily "male" or "female."

But a community built upon the family cannot be *lived* in simply as a scene for the *actions* of men. It must be lived *in*. And it is the conflict of lives, of values, between men and women, and of an open or a closed society, that automatically must structure any work of literature that attempts to reflect that Mormon actuality. That is, such novels, if they are to be successful works of art *and* successful re-creations of their subject matter, i.e., the life of the community, must be, as I have suggested, realistic, social novels.

Value systems can be seen purely in terms of symbolic actions and figures: Natty Bumppo is literarily "real," but "unreal" in actuality. Literary treatments of the male role in Mormonism have tended towards that kind of image in order to emphasize either male acceptance of Church doctrines or rejection of them, expressed in terms of action. And, therefore, because men tend to write about men, men writing about Mormonism have usually made use of the conventions of the romantic novel; their works have gone towards symbolic melodrama, not towards a picture of the society. Women, though, *have* lived *in* the society and so have seen it, not too oddly, more clearly than the men; and so their characters have been less symbolic, less external.

Maureen Whipple's *The Giant Joshua* was still historical, a retelling of the story of polygamy—or, more exactly and significantly, one should say "polygyny." This re-telling was not only from the side of the women (there had been plenty of such before, of course), but the woman and her world were fully realized, an actual woman in an actual society. Sorensen's first novel was also historical, and polygamy plays its part; but her heroine too is a brilliantly alive person—and the Mormon society of the 1840's, including Joseph Smith and Brigham Young once more, is made integral to the novel, not a decoration or falsification on the top of it. Scowcroft's *Children of the Covenant* is a "modern" novel in that it gives us a description of the Mormon society of the twentieth century. And his male protagonist is seen in the round.

However, Whipple published little more. And Scowcroft's interest in Mormonism has not been often expressed in his novels—although his 1973 *The Ordeal of Dudley Dean,* in which the hero is an ex-Mormon English professor, is one of the few and perhaps the best of comic Mormon novels—twentieth century Mormonism has not lent itself to comedy; Mark Harris' delightful *Wake Up, Stupid* has Mormons in it, but Mormonism is not central. Diane Johnson's 1968 *Loving Hands at Home* is, in a sense, a comedy about Mormons, but these Mormons are rather too secular, that is, they are California Mormons who are more Californian than Mormon.

Virginia Sorensen, then, has perhaps most successfully realized the Mormon experience. She has covered the whole range of that experience: her first novel, as I have noted, is historical; her last novel about Mormons, *Kingdom Come* (1962) is also historical. But in between she wrote her novels about Mormons of the twentieth century, letting us see the results of that history, giving the society in all its simplicities and complexities.

When, in 1949, Sorensen published *The Evening and the Morning,*[1] she made the definitive Mormon novel; that is, the novel can indeed be seen as the very type of social novel required by the Mormon community. Of course, the novel is more complex than that, i.e., it is not a mere photograph of a culture. It has its elements, necessary elements, of the romantic novel: the individual, a woman, in this case, is set against the community and must struggle for her own self—and will, in the end, win a kind of victory, an acceptance of life, in the name of love. But love is more than an expression of the individual self. It continues life, it continues lives, it continues the community. The victory is of the alone, lonely individual, but it is also an affirmation that human love is by necessity social: "There has been a woman and she loved a man and through this love men and loves were multiplied" (p. 341).

The title of *The Evening,* as well as the title of Sorensen's first novel, *A Little Lower Than the Angels,* is drawn from the Old Testament. And these titles themselves are thematic—and somewhat ironic. Both suggest something about the place of

humankind in the universe.   Humankind is somewhat lower
than the angels, but it is capable of creativity.   But, too, if here
we have images of heroism, Sorensen's images are not necessarily
of *heroes.*   And so, if we remember that the Old Testament society was a patriarchal one, we must see that Sorensen is playing
against that fact.

More important, the title of *The Evening,* using those words
of Genesis that describe the creation of the world, is a way of relating the act of the artist, the work of art, to the subject matter.
Structurally, this novel is perhaps Sorensen's most experimental:
the stories of the central figure, Kate Black Alexander (on whom
I shall concentrate), of her daughter, Dessie, and of her granddaughter, Jean, is told by a series of flashbacks, set against the
gradual resolution of those stories during six days in July. The
artist is creating her world, as God created his; but hers is not
ex nihilo—it is, rather, from his, and his is a world of men in
interrelation, i.e., in society.   One should note, too, that the
flashbacks, either memories of Kate's or narrations by the
authorial voice, are Sorensen's way of bringing Kate's past and
the Mormon past into the present so that each moment of the
past clarifies the present.

Kate Alexander is not, of course, a typical Mormon; indeed,
she is an apostate, a word that had and still has a peculiarly
powerful meaning for Mormons.   For apostasy is not merely the
rejection of the Church; it is the rejection of the community.
In the Mormon world, one belongs or one is cut off, isolated.
And yet Sorensen must present Kate as an outsider in order for
the reader to understand *why* Kate has become one: that is,
through the eyes of the outsider who was once within one can
see what Mormonism is, both objectively and subjectively.

Kate, when the novel begins, is sitting on her daughter
Dessie's back porch; she has just returned to the small town in
central Utah (Manti, where Sorensen herself spent her formative
years); here Kate grew up and here she married Karl Alexander.
And here she had the affair with Peter Jansen, married to a sister
of her husband's first wife, that was to form the rest of Kate's
life; Dessie is the child of that relationship.   Now, after an absence of many years, Kate, aging but still vulnerable, returns to
her past.   She has never forgotten Peter: ". . .one expected—
even hoped—as long as breath went in and out. . ." (p. 4).   But

she will find that, unlike herself who feels the need to see Peter in order to end the "ragged, unfinished feeling she had about life," (p. 64), Peter's life, within the Church and within the community, has been fulfilled.

Yet Kate must relive her past in order to live beyond it. And that past is quintessentially Mormon. Kate was reared as a member of a polygamous household; her mother was the second of four wives. Kate, then, lived in a world of women, her mother and her "aunts" and all their children. She hated that household, for there was no privacy in it, no escape from others; yet at the same time, as she admits later, there was a sense of sharing. However, Kate's early rebelliousness is directly from her mother, a woman who read and wrote poetry (the artist figure in American literature is inevitably set against the prevailing value system, either as fool or as suffering hero).

Still, it is the male value system, realized in Mormon doctrine and practice, then, against which Kate rebels. Oddly though, Kate does not, even as an aging woman, blame her father, a man she saw little of as a child but whom she loved (this is no doubt psychologically accurate and explainable): her father "came home only between journeys freighting and bringing immigrants, on his brief visits scattering a munificent seed. . . ." (p. 19). Instead, Kate blamed Brigham Young, the archetypal Mormon male. And indeed she is still somewhat proud of the moment when, as a child, she had, instead of throwing flowers before the carriage of the passing Young, thrown them on the ground rather and stomped on them.

This episode is more than a sign of simplistic rebellion, though. Sorensen uses it to show the complexity of reactions to the Mormon world. Kate had told her own children this story when they were young. Dessie (short for Deseret, the Mormon name for their western territories) could not comprehend the meaning of Kate's act except to interpret it as a willful rejection of one's very self. And Dessie has, within limits, accepted her Mormon world. She hopes her mother will not retell her children the story; it had given her "a curious uncertainty among good neighbors to whom she dared not speak of it, and she wanted to spare her children every possible uncertainty" (p. 20). And later Dessie will protest, reminding her mother that some people must remain in place: "You see—we live here" (p. 27).

When at sixteen Kate married the widower Karl, she did not do so necessarily out of love but in order to escape the restrictions, the suffocation of living in that huge, polygamous household of her family. And, if one ignores her adultery, Kate was a good wife by the definitions of the community. She is not a rebel for rebellion's sake.

However, that adultery *is* an action of rebellion. But its meanings are multiplex, ambiguous. It is with some justification that Kate began her affair with Peter. She felt a great hurt when she accidentally saw Karl kissing her sister Verna. For Karl—and Verna—it was an innocent act, a thing of the moment, quickly forgotten; but for Kate it "was the true beginning of herself as a woman. . .and she began to build about the painful kernel of a new knowledge a smooth and rationalized rebellion." Too, "she perceived at last some of the reasons for rebellion, in herself, in her mother before her, in many others." But she also sees "some of the reasons why rebellion failed" (p. 42). Yet Kate also says to Dessie that rebels are "simply the natural ones who refuse to bother to pretend" (p. 30). Her love for Peter, then, has its element of "naturalness"; it is not just an act of rejection.

Peter Jansen himself was at a moment a rebel; he blamed his father's poverty on the father's too easy willingness to give up everything in order to obey his church's commands. But Peter in time returns to the fold, becomes, indeed, a minor member of the establishment. And, although he fathers Kate's child, he cannot stop pretending; he is forever afraid. He cannot, in brief, accept any definition for himself except as the community perceives him.

Kate and Peter's adultery had been suspected by Marya, Karl's former sister-in-law, the sister of Peter's wife. After Karl's death, Marya tells Karl's son by his first wife of his stepmother's acts. Karlie, the stepson, confronts Kate, telling her with vehement hatred that he knows of her betrayal of his father—and that he also "knows" on legal authority that because of her conduct she has no rights to Karl's property. Frightened, alone, and desperate, Kate turns to Peter for help. But he cannot openly defend or support her—he will never divulge his part—but rather he seeks protection for himself through his position in the Church. Kate understands that she must carry the burden of guilt alone: Marya has spoken the attitude of the community when she cried, "If you think I think Peter is responsible! *When a woman is like that. . .!*" (p. 290).

Kate departs, leaving Dessie and another daughter, Martha, behind to be raised by Kate's sisters, and joins her two older sons in the railroad town of Thistle. Still, it is the community that has, even if indirectly, driven her out. And so it is in these years that she makes, in her way, her protest most explicitly against that community. In Thistle she runs a boardinghouse—and there was, still is, an odd Utah-Mormon prejudice against boarding-houses, perhaps because they represent a parody of the family without the stability of the family. And later Kate lives in the mining town of Tintic; and the Mormon world has rejected mining (a male enough occupation, true) as a way of living in the world, mostly because mining towns inevitably bring in the very riff-raff of the world. (Later Kate will defend Dessie's husband, Ike, who occasionally drinks and smokes *and* works on the railroad; the railroad is the visible threat of the outside world and has never quite been accepted in Utah as safe.)

Still, all her life, Kate stays in love with Peter, still believing in him—and, perversely, willing to "serve" him. She would have been a rather conventional person if her emotions had been satisfied. And so Sorensen does not present a flat, misunder-stood or perfect type in order to suggest that the Mormon cul-ture is simply repressive. Certainly Kate is blameworthy herself; as a small instance, she is too often insensitive to people around her. At one moment Dessie worries about whether some visitors ("teachers" from the church) might have smelled the coffee she had made for Kate (coffee, as well as liquor, is frowned upon in the "Word of Wisdom," the set of dietary rules promulgated by Joseph Smith and having nearly the weight of doctrine in the Church). Kate remarks, "Oh, dear, I'm sorry. I'd forgotten. Maybe when people go away they forget those little things and only remember the mountains" (p. 6). The episode is a bit comic, a bit satirical of a narrow Mormon attitude. But those little things *are* mountains to Dessie; she *does* live there.

Still, Dessie's own experience in the novel will be one of recognizing that a certain kind of narrowness is unbearable, al-though it is not necessarily the narrowness of Mormonism but, rather, the narrowness of the closed community, i.e., the small American town. When Dessie learns the story of her own conception, she is almost shattered; but, recovering somewhat with Ike's help, she finds she can, and must, resent the attitude of Marya, who represents that small town thinness of spirit. In the end, Dessie and her family will leave, not the Mormon world, for they go only towards Salt Lake City, but the small town, escaping into a freer atmosphere.

The adolescent granddaughter, Jean, has her own "growth" to undergo in the novel; she must become aware of the possibility of evil in the world, as well as of the fact that all people are not to be relied on. And so, although her initiation into "adulthood" seems a small thing, it too has a thematic importance: one night, invited to play with the boys, she is pawed by one of them and not defended by the boy whom she has liked. All this is not "Mormon," but it does reflect a set of societal attitudes that derive from a largely male dominated world.

Kate, then, must also give up her final illusion, her vague hope that Peter, now a widower, will at last relate to her as a human being. She takes the child Jean with her when, at last, she visits him, perhaps using the child, Peter's granddaughter, as a kind of offering; she thinks, almost hopefully, that "he could see we [he and Kate] had come to a kind of perfection after all" (p. 64). Peter is, in his way, a gentleman; he rather feebly offers Kate marriage, but "she hears the fear in it; his determination to pay the price for his youth stood upon it like. . .thorns . . . ." (p. 335). Marriage to Kate would upset the fine adjustment he has made to his world.

And so Kate knows now that she alone has made and can, must, make her own life. There *is* a quiet tragedy here, the tragedy of a life that has been misshapen by a society that is unwilling to allow a certain kind of freedom. But there is also a kind of hope. As Kate and Jean ride back home on the train, Kate remembers the words of Genesis: *"And He rested. . .And God saw everything that he had made, and behold, it was very good."* She *has* made her own life, based on love (p. 341). And so, as I have suggested, the novel is in the end an affirmation of the individual, but in positive relation to others.

NOTE

[1]Virginia Sorensen, *The Evening and the Morning* (New York: Harcourt, Brace and Company, 1949). All following quotations from the novel will be noted by page numbers only.

V

OTHER VOICES, OTHER WESTS

"ON THE *OTHER* SIDE OF THE MOUNTAINS": THE WESTERING EXPERIENCE IN THE FICTION OF ETHEL WILSON

Beverley Mitchell, SSA
The University of Alberta, Edmonton

When one speaks of "the West" in reference to Canadian literature, it is generally understood to be the region occupied by the three prairie provinces and ending rather abruptly with the Rocky Mountains. Somehow, the term fails to include what lies on the *other* side of these mountains—and nearly 400,000 square miles of the most beautiful and varied land in Canada is vaguely and misleadingly dismissed as "the coast" or, more properly, referred to simply as "British Columbia".

As different from its fellow provinces to the east as it is from its neighbour, Washington, to the south, British Columbia has always been something of an anomaly and a world in itself. Bruce Hutchison has described it in *The Unknown Country* by saying

> life is good in British Columbia and unlike life on the prairies or the east—so unlike that, crossing the Rockies, you are in a new country, as if you had crossed a national frontier. Everyone feels it, even the stranger, feels the change of outlook, tempo, and attitude. What makes it so, I do not know. The size of everything, I suspect, the bulk of mountains, the space of valleys, the far glimpses of land and sea, the lakes and rivers, all cast in gigantic mold. They make a man feel bigger, more free, as if he had come out of a crowded room.[1]

Because these qualities are reflected by its writers, what has been said of "western" or prairie literature in particular, and of Canadian literature in general, does not always apply here. Both the literature and the art of this province are distinctive for what historian Margaret Ormsby defined (perhaps in desperation) as "some elusive shining quality,"[2] and both show that life on "the *other* side of the mountains" is indeed different from that in the rest of Canada. Therefore, in the following paper I will extend the geographical limits of Canadian literature to include the "westering experience" unique to this province as it is revealed in the fiction of Ethel Wilson.

First, however, a brief introduction to Ethel Wilson herself. Although English critics acclaimed her one of the most exquisite stylists of this century and her Canadian peers recognized her immediately as a "writer's writer", for various reasons her work has yet to receive the critical attention it deserves. For one, her books were published between 1947 and 1961, before Canadian literature was admitted to academic respectability and before the current plethora of "Canlit" courses created both market and demand for paperbacks. (Although some of her works have been re-issued in paperback, others are now out of print.) For another, because the apparent simplicity of her style and her mordant wit often mask the profundity and consistency of her themes, her work must be read *in toto* before it can be recognized for what it is: a view of the human predicament which is wise, compassionate, witty, ironic, and even, at times, mildly cynical—based on more than half a century of experience and observation of life in British Columbia. (Ethel Wilson was nearly sixty when her first book was published; she was seventy-three when the sixth and last appeared.) Suffice it to say that Ethel Wilson has lived in Vancouver almost continuously since 1898, that British Columbia has been both her "sphere of consciousness" and the setting for her fiction, and that more clearly and more completely than any other writer, she has shown both the literal and metaphorical meanings which "westering" has for a people who live on the periphery of this continent.

In the literal sense of "movement in a westward direction", that in British Columbia was a somewhat staid and decorous procession, especially towards the end of the 19th century when the colony had achieved provincial status and when most of those "westering" were English—or from the United Kingdom. Unlike many immigrants to Canada, these people were not victims of religious or political persecutions seeking freedom in a new land. Neither were they impoverished by economic conditions in their mother country. Reasonably affluent, and compelled neither by desperation nor by romantic anticipation, they came from a society remarkable for its stability and its complacency—and they came to a society which they knew would be very similar to the one they had left. Because Ethel Wilson's own family was typical of those "westering" to British Columbia in the 1890's, *The Innocent Traveller*—a "family chronicle" thinly-disguised as fiction—not only preserves the record of four generations of her own family but also serves as a social history for the people of this province.

In part the smugness, insularity, and decidedly "English" character which distinguished British Columbians until the last few decades, were the legacy of a middle-class Victorian society which had been "transplanted" in the province almost intact. While peoples other than middle-class English also migrated at this time, the influence of those from the United Kingdom was so powerful, so concerted, and so complete that it effected, as it were, an "instant society", making British Columbia indeed a world in itself. Like the Edgeworths described in *The Innocent Traveller,* these transplanted families bore the indelible imprint of a generation of Victorian patriarchs. Describing the last days of Great-Grandfather Edgeworth, Ethel Wilson writes:

> He sat there, sleeping in security in the sunshine. His world was a good world. His Queen was a good Queen. His country was a good country. His business was good. His health was good. His family was a good family and God was good. . . . His imagination, which flew beyond the bright blue sky to the Invisible, did not pierce the squalor of the Poor so near at hand in the grim town. The Poor took their familiar deplorable place in the squalor, and it would have seemed a novel and disturbing idea to Great-Grandfather Edgeworth that the poor should reasonably aspire to eat well, live well, and die well. Not wrong of course, but chimerical. Each age, like our own, has its blind spots. The social conscience was stirring but not awake. Great-Grandfather Edgeworth was a product of the ages which preceded the young Victoria. Here he was, sleeping in the garden, ninety years old, an upright old man in a world which he really thought was upright.[3]

This passage partially explains why "westering" in British Columbia has had none of the characteristics one associates with the raw frontier the American West, nor the challenge, bitterness, frustration, and struggle one associates with settlement of the prairie "west" in Canada. For better or worse, the securities, convictions, and blindnesses of Victorian England—personified here by Great-Grandfather Edgeworth—travelled very smoothly and en masse to British Columbia and adapted themselves comfortably to life in this new land, stabilizing and ordering what might easily have been a frontier in the finest wild tradition.

Most accounts of "westering" on the Canadian prairies present the literal journey in terms of an epic struggle, stressing physical hardships and psychological difficulties which test the limits of human endurance.   As Henry Kreisel has observed, "man, the giant conqueror, and man, the insignificant dwarf threatened by defeat, form the two polarities of the state of mind produced by the sheer physical fact of the prairie."[4]   In prairie literature, "westering" was accomplished on horseback, in covered wagon, or in crowded and uncomfortable third-class railway coaches.   In *The Innocent Traveller,* however, Ethel Wilson shows that for the mid-Victorian English, the literal journey to British Columbia was made under rather different circumstances.

Like many English families coming to the province at this time, Grandmother Edgeworth and the two spinster aunts "westered" in comfort and dignity in their drawing-room on the train. At least, the Grandmother and Aunt Rachel did. For a few brief shining hours Great-Aunt Topaz (the "innocent traveller" of the title) had a much more interesting time in the gentlemen's smoking room, thereby shocking the Grandmother and Aunt Rachel to the very depths of their Victorian sensibilities:

> "Well, what a fuss, I do declare!" said Topaz swaying in the doorway of the swaying coach. "This is a free country, isn't it? We've come to a free country, haven't we? I didn't say I was smoking, did I? Really, Annie, and you too, Rachel—It's no good looking at me like that—now that you've come to Canada, you know, you'll have to be less conventional, you know. You're both very conventional, I don't mind telling you. The gentlemen were very nice indeed and I think they were pleased to see me."[5]

Marshalling her stunned and outraged proprieties to order, the Grandmother mounted her counter-attack:

> "Topaz," said Sister Annie, "you are right. This is a free country. And gentlemen are free to gather together, if they wish to, without intrusion by you or anyone else. Let this be the last occasion. I do beg of you. . ."[6]

While this sort of "westering" makes deliciously funny reading, it does not constitute the stuff from which an epic literature is fashioned. Despite the very real hardships which earlier travellers to British Columbia suffered, "westering" in this province is generally associated with the adventures and mis-adventures of the English who travelled "innocently" like the Edgeworths. Their stories do not cast man in epic proportions—consequently, while there is a mythical "west" in British Columbia, it is not the "west" of heroic struggle against inexorable odds.

The Innocent Traveller is the only work of Ethel Wilson which treats of "westering" in the literal sense. Nevertheless, it is sufficient to establish the historical reasons why the west in British Columbia is viewed differently from the "West" in the Canadian prairies or that of the American frontier. The works which followed *The Innocent Traveller*[7] (*Hetty Dorval*, 1947; *The Equations of Love*, 1952; *Swamp Angel*, 1954; *Love and Salt Water*, 1956; *Mrs. Golightly and other stories*, 1961) illustrate the rapidity with which Victorian "virtues" deteriorated in this province and how succeeding generations replaced spirituality with token church attendance, moral good with "propriety", and family integrity with smug, self-righteous complacency and snobishness. While the human predicament which is the concern of Ethel Wilson's fiction is universal, it is also particular in its application to life in British Columbia—and although this fiction does not cast man in heroic mold, struggling with blind forces outside himself, it does show the quieter heroism involved when one's opponent is himself. In keeping with F. R. Leavis' "great tradition", it promotes "awareness of the possibilities of life" for vulnerable humanity—even in British Columbia. It also shows that this awareness frequently involves another kind of "westering", one which has nothing whatsoever to do with movement towards the geographical west—although it does not necessarily exclude this.

Uniquely British Columbian, this metaphorical "westering" involves the quest for what Ethel Wilson has described in *The Equations of Love* as "something which transcends and heightens ordinary life and is its complement,"[8] inherent in the unspoiled landscape of this province. Evident even today, it shows most clearly why life in British Columbia is viewed so differently by its writers from that in the prairies or the rest of Canada. While prairie literature may be seen in the context of the classical heroic tradition, that of British Columbia belongs more properly with the tradition of mystical literature.

Perhaps because man here is rarely pitted against nature in a struggle for survival—or perhaps because there is a quality intrinsic to the land itself, nature is never regarded as something to be battled with. Unlike the prairie landscape which either elevates man to the status of "conquering giant" or reduces him to that of "insignificant dwarf", the landscape of British Columbia is as remarkable for its tolerance of man as it is for its natural beauty. More significantly, it is remarkable for a mysterious quality which transcends these. Both the literature and art of this province suggest that there is something in the remote and untamed beauty of this landscape which exists as a world in itself, something which is separate and distinct from the human world and essentially different from the human world, but somehow necessary to it and compellingly attractive—something which is *tremendum et fascinans.*

This mysterious entity which Ethel Wilson refers to in her various works as the "timeless and impersonal world", the "world which is powerful and close", or the "world of the invisible senses", becomes the goal of metaphorical westering for many of her characters. Without awareness of it, she writes in *Lilly's Story,* "life is uninformed, without poetry or ecstasy or anguish, with little divination in human relations."[9] Unlike literal westering which is usually a group endeavour and results in the establishment of human community, metaphorical westering of necessity is an intensely private and personal quest which establishes the individual as an individual. Somewhat paradoxically, at times it also re-establishes the individual as a member of the human community, for contact with the natural world in this setting somehow enables the individual to place human affairs in their proper perspective.

Because the natural world has been almost "obliterated by every modern convenience" in the city, metaphorical westering is usually directed eastwards to British Columbia's Interior. Nevertheless, even in Vancouver there are reminders of "another kind of place":[10]

> Sometimes the sea-gulls fly over the city streets and their mewing cries disturb the busy or abstracted townspeople going about their business. Something shakes for an instant the calm of a man crossing the street when he hears the cry of a gull above the traffic, something that is not sound but a disturbing, forgotten, unnamed desire, a memory.... What is it?[11]

Similarly, because evidence of a timeless and impersonal world may still be seen in the "inlet, and forest, and mountains" of Vancouver's North Shore, Mrs. Gormley in the short story "A Drink with Adolphus" stops her taxi for "ten cents' worth of view":

> In ten cents' worth of time, she thought—and she was very happy islanded, lost, alone in this sight—there's nearly all the glory of the world and no despair, and then she told the taxi-man to drive on.[12]

It is clear even from these examples that the physical landscape in British Columbia has not produced the "garrison mentality" Northrop Frye ascribes to Canadians in other parts of the country. Neither is there any evidence in Ethel Wilson's fiction of the "tone of deep terror in regard to nature" which Frye finds characteristic of Canadian literature.

In his conclusion to the *Literary History of Canada*, Frye describes this "terror":

> It is not a terror of the dangers or discomforts or even the mysteries of nature, but a terror of the soul at something these things manifest. The human mind has nothing but human and moral values to cling to if it is to preserve its integrity or even its sanity, yet the vast unconsciousness of nature in front of it seems an unanswerable denial of these values.

The importance which Ethel Wilson attaches to nature in her fiction and the significance which metaphorical westering has for her characters demonstrate that, for the British Columbian, nature inspires not "terror" but a vague longing; not an "unanswerable denial" but an affirmation, a strengthening, and an illumination of human values. Indeed, contemplation of the North Shore mountains leads the protagonist in the short story "The Window" to the realization that "a man needs humanity. . .and if he ceases to be in touch with man and is not in touch with God, he does not matter."[13]

Although nature is always an integral part of Ethel Wilson's fiction and is used to play a variety of roles—for example, it is used to reveal a character's inner thoughts and feelings, to parallel or contrast human situations, or to provide analogies by which these situations may be understood—metaphorical westering invariably results in self-awareness and "divination of human relations". The most important aspect of this natural world, however, is not its reflected view of the human situation but its reflected view of something "unexpressed and inexpressible" that transcends the human. Ethel Wison's insistence that man belongs to this "timeless and impersonal world" is ultimately explained only by her own experience, for her fiction reveals that she heard much more than the "still, sad music of humanity" in the remote and lonely beauty of British Columbia.

In her preface to the Alcuin edition of *Hetty Dorval* published in 1967 when she was well into her seventies, Ethel Wilson wrote:

> From the first year of our marriage until the last year of our happy travels and activities, my husband and I sought the remote beauties of British Columbia. Here were those beauties which do not change, except for the exquisite and surreptitious signatures of the seasons, the surface and movement of waters, the glory of the skies, the seasonal flighting of birds, the great isolated ponderosa pines each with its solitary tall shadow that moves with the sun, the pale virginal trembling aspens, the laughter of the loon on the lake. . .the beauty of British Columbia became an un-lose-able permanent part of me.

There is an echo of Augustine's "O Beauty ever ancient ever

new" in this catalogue, for both here and in her fiction Ethel Wilson suggests that the beauty and mystery of the natural world in this setting led her to an experiential knowledge of the beauty and mystery of the Supreme Being. Indeed, there are similarities between her works and those of the Old Testament writers and of the mystics—and with some qualification, the following general description applies to her:

> All mystics have groped in the dark in their efforts to describe what they experienced when they felt God. At best, they took refuge in symbols, allegories, and analogies taken, as in poetry, from natural and visible things.[14]

However, the essential difference between Ethel Wilson and the mystics described here is that "natural and visible things" are not used as "symbols, allegories, and analogies" for her experience of God—rather, they appear to be inextricably involved with it.

While a mystical experience, by definition, has a spiritual character or reality beyond the comprehension of reason and therefore beyond complete expression in words, it is not necessarily esoteric. The mystical experience is simply the felt presence of the Divine and, as such, is neither unusual nor limited to a select few. Furthermore, the characteristics which have been identified as "the universal core of mystical experience" (unitary consciousness; timelessness and spacelessness; sense of objectivity or reality; blessedness, peace; feeling of the holy, sacred, or divine; sense of paradoxicality; alleged by mystics to be ineffable[15]) may be found not only in Ethel Wilson's fiction but in that of other writers from British Columbia as well. It would seem, therefore, that this most western of Canada's provinces is, to borrow a phrase from *The Compleat Angler,* the "quietest and fittest place for contemplation"—at least, for many.

In her careful and varied descriptions of the natural world, particularly those of the Interior, it is clear that here Ethel Wilson found not only the "quietest and fittest place for contemplation" but also an experiential knowledge of a Being "perfect in beauty", paradoxically changeless but changing, of infinite variety and inference. Essentially mysterious—even, at times frightening—this Being is seemingly inseparable from natural and visible things, yet somehow transcends them. Not only is the Presence felt here supra-anthropomorphic, like the God-figure of the

Old Testament, in its remote beauties the land itself is like that
described in Genesis before the creation of man, with no evidence of man or of God-become-man.

For someone like Ethel Wilson whose childhood has been
permeated with religious influence—her father was a Methodist
minister, her Grandmother a Methodist "saint"—the mystical
experience complements and supersedes what has been learned
in the institutional church. Like Job, such an individual realizes
"I had heard of you by word of mouth, but now my eye has
seen you" (Job 42:5). The institutional church has little or
nothing to do with the mystical experience itself, however, and
like other writers from western Canada (for example, W. O.
Mitchell or Margaret Laurence), Ethel Wilson implies a certain
incongruity—if not a dichotomy—between God as presented by
the institutional church and God as experienced in the natural
world. Consequently, because the institutional church (or
churches, for this applies to all denominations) has somehow
reduced God to man's image and likeness, the mystical experience frequently goes undefined. (Not that this matters in the
least. The important· thing is to *experience,* not to *define.*)
Nevertheless, although Ethel Wilson usually implies this felt
Presence, she also uses· Biblical imagery and allusions which define it in conventional terms. As Nell Severance says in *Swamp
Angel,*

> It seems to me that one has to move on to the. . .ultimate
> . . .that's God. . .it makes things very complicated but
> quite simple. . . .[16]

Therefore, the westering experience on the "*other* side of the
mountains", described in Ethel Wilson's fiction, is unique to this
province, for the literal journey which has brought the individual
to the edge of the continent appears to be symptomatic of a
more basic "questing". When one has come as far "west" as is
possible physically, this quest becomes metaphorical. (Perhaps
it is necessary for man to reach the physical limit of the literal
journey to realize that the initial impulse to "wester" is inspired
by his need to know himself, his relationship to his fellow man
and to his physical surroundings and, ultimately, to God. Perhaps, too, the vague dissatisfaction inherent in accounts of
"westering" on the Canadian prairies or in the American West
lies in a failure to recognize this.) At any rate, metaphorical

westering in British Columbia brings the individual to self-awareness and to awareness of a Being who is greater than the self,
for he finds himself not only on the "margin" of the continent
but also on the "margin of a world which is powerful and close."

There are, of course, individuals in this fiction whose lives
lack any direction, either metaphorical or literal. Somehow, the
absence of "westering" in these characters appears as the absence
of a necessary human quality. Apparently, after more than half
a century of experience and observation of life in British Columbia, Ethel Wilson has concluded that "westering" is essential
if one is to be fully aware of the "possibilities of life".

NOTES

[1]Bruce Hutchison, *The Unknown Country* (Toronto, 1965), p. 266.

[2]Margaret Ormsby, *British Columbia: A History* (Toronto, 1958), p. 494.

[3]Ethel Wilson, *The Innocent Traveller* (Toronto, 1960), p. 73.

[4]Henry Kreisel, "The Prairie: A State of Mind," *Contexts of Canadian Criticism*, ed. Eli Mandel (Toronto, 1971), p. 257.

[5]*The Innocent Traveller*, p. 109.

[6]*The Innocent Traveller*, p. 110.

[7]*The Innocent Traveller* was published after *Hetty Dorval* although it was written first.

[8]Ethel Wilson, *The Equations of Love* (London, 1952), p. 194.

[9]*Ibid.*

[10]Ethel Wilson, *Swamp Angel* (Toronto, 1967), p. 21.

[11]*The Innocent Traveller*, p. 261.

[12]Ethel Wilson, *Mrs. Golightly and other stories* (Toronto, 1961), p. 68.

[13]*Ibid.*, p. 197.

[14]*The Soul Afire: Revelations of the Mystics,* ed. H. A. Reinhold (New York, 1973), p. 22. One wonders if the mystics themselves thought they were using "natural and visible things figuratively"—or if the careful explanation above is a non-mystic's attempt to forestall charges of panthe-

ism.

15Walter Houston Clark, "Mysticism as a Basic Concept in Defining the Religious Self", *From religious experience to a religious attitude,* ed. A. Godin, S. J. (Chicago, 1965), p. 35. (The criteria are those formulated by W. J. Stace.)

16*Swamp Angel,* p. 103.

TRADITION OF THE EXILE:
JUDITH WRIGHT'S AUSTRALIAN "WEST"

Stephen Tatum
University of Utah

> Old Man River is not a conceivable
> figure in Australian folklore.
>
> —H. C. Allen, *Bush
> and Backwoods*, 1959.

Since we often talk of regional differences in authors and works originating in the United States, it is perhaps patently obvious that any discussion of the traditions found in two separate countries, let alone continents, will emphasize the differences rather than the likenesses. Yet the essential point underlying any worthy comparative endeavor—whether it be to compare a Turkish bandit with an American outlaw or an Argentinian gaucho with an American cowboy—is aptly stated by Laura Trevelyan, a fictional character in Patrick White's novel *Voss*: "Knowledge was never a matter of geography. Quite the contrary; it overflows all maps that exist."[1] Unlike the commentator who devotes his efforts to the Turkish-American outlaw traditions, however, the writer interested in exploring Austral-American relationships can at least discover added points of departure in more than mental landscapes. Roy W. Meyer, for instance, in his article "The Outback and the West: Australian and American Frontier Fiction," refers at one point to Herman Melville's statement characterizing Australia as "that other America"[2]; on the other hand, Robert G. Athearn, in his book *Westward the Briton,* records British traveler Foster Barham Zincke's verdict that Western America is the "Australia of North America."[3]

On a more general level, Wallace Stegner's statement that "the confrontation between empty land and imported populations, which is the salient historical fact about the West, as about America at large,"[4] applies equally well to the Australian experience. Australia was settled, as was America, by pioneers and convicts from Great Britain, and the Australian landscape offered, as did America's frontier, its share of deserts, mountains, and forests inhabited by a native race. While Frederick Jackson Turner imaginatively appealed to his audience to "stand at the Cumberland Gap" and watch the passage of the various frontiers, here is how historian W. K. Hancock, as John Greenway reports in his book *Australia: The Last Frontier,* adopted Turner's thesis in his historical assessment of Australia's settlement: "Stand at this gap [in Australia's Blue Mountains] and watch the frontiers following each other westward—the squatter's frontier which filled the western plains with sheep and laid the foundations of Australia's economy, the miner's frontier which brought Australia population and made her a radical democracy, the farmer's frontier which gradually and painfully tested and proved the controls of Australia's soil and climate."[5]   What is interesting here is the rather early occurrence of the pastoral frontier and the somewhat conspicuous absence of the fur trader and mountain man in the Australian pioneering experience; at the same time, one could point to the mining frontiers during the California gold rush of 1849 and the Ballarat, Victoria gold rush of 1851 as not only comparable events, but also as the arena of closest physical contact between the two countries during the westward push. While an Australian was among the first to be hung by the vigilantes in San Francisco, an American was the first to be tried for treason during Australia's only major revolutionary incident, the Eureka Stockade rebellion.[6]

In her poem "South of My Days" (1946), Judith Wright endows the historian's prose with concrete shapes and illustrates at the same time the universality of Stegner's comment:

> Droving that year, Charleville to the Hunter,
> nineteen-one it was, and the drought beginning;
> sixty head left at the McIntyre, the mud round them
> hardened like iron; and the yellow boy died
> in the sulky ahead with the gear, but the horse went on,
> stopped at the Sandy Camp and waited in the evening.

It was the flies we seen first, swarming like bees.
Came to the Hunter, three-hundred head of a thousand—
cruel to keep them alive—and the river was dust.

Or mustering up in the Bogongs in the autumn
when the blizzards came early. Brought them down; we
   brought them
down, what aren't there yet. Or driving for Cobb's on the
   run
up from Tamworth—Thunderbolt at the top of Hungry
   Hill,
and I give him a wink. I wouldn't wait long, Fred,
not if I was you; the troopers are just behind,
coming for that job at the Hillgrove. He went like a luny,
him on his big black horse.[7]

While the spirit of place lending a vivid flavor to "old Dan's" yarns is truly Australian—as it should be, for Judith Wright was born and reared on the property established by her family in 1828—the experiences of the drover and stockman enduring environmental hardships and of the stagecoach driver facing a dangerous outlaw are, of course, such that Charles Russell or Frederick Remington could have painted without undue cultural shock, such that Charles Goodnight could have recalled as occurring during a particularly dry year, and such that a Wells Fargo driver could have recaptured when describing a meeting with Black Bart. While the sympathetic wink bestowed on the bandit by the coach-driver is perhaps only truly characteristic of a country whose convict heritage engendered an intense hatred of authority, the mud hardening in the intense heat, the buzzing flies, the riderless horse, the anguished encounter with a river of dust or the sudden blizzard during round-up constitute an integral part of our "blood's country." And while the historian may echo Turner, the novelist may at times echo the poet: Larry McMurtry, for instance, included portions of the opening and concluding statements in "South of My Days" as an epigraph to part one of *Leaving Cheyenne.*

Yet no matter how much one focuses on the instructive similarities between the Australian and American pioneering experiences—however much one focuses on the equation of the bushranger and the outlaw, the drover and the cowboy, the Aborigine and the Indian, the brumby and the mustang—the knowledge which overflows the map of existence in the sunburnt space of Australia is not that of living in the "garden of the world" but rather that of experiencing, as Judith Wright states, "the stunned shock of those who cross the seas and find themselves, as the Australian ballad puts it, in a 'hut that's up-side-down.' "[8] Instead of prolonged contact with an open frontier symbolizing regeneration, a new life in new space, the Australian —as resident in this country that possesses birds unable to fly, dogs unable to bark, animals unable to walk on all fours, and trees unable to shed their leaves—too often confronted a closed frontier after crossing the dividing range; instead of furs, forests, rivers, and agricultural lands, Australia offered deserts and semi-deserts to her explorers and immigrants.[9] Ultimately, this is the country, as Judith Wright depicts it, which "has been the outer equivalent of an inner reality—first, and persistently, the reality of exile."[10]

The point here is not to deny or diminish the physical and mental sufferings that confronted American explorers and immigrants but rather to disclose a distinctive philosophical difference permeating these experiences in the two continents—a difference which also affects Australian and American literary heritages. In America, "since the myth affirmed the impossibility of disaster or suffering within the garden," writes Henry Nash Smith in *Virgin Land*, "it was unable to deal with any of the dark or tragic outcomes of human experience."[11] If, as in Australia, the desert remains a desert and can not be transformed into an image of the garden by physical or imaginary means, the corollary is obvious: there is no reason to assume "the impossibility of disaster or suffering." Australian pastoralists who did not encounter the myth of the agrarian utopia during their yearly battles with drought and flood were spared the added disillusionment faced by the American farmers who endured the late nineteenth century divergence of fact and ideal.

This historical reality enables us to understand two major distinctions in the literature of the outback and the literature of the American West. While Americans are discovering in this century of the closed frontier, as Harold Simonson relates in his *The Closed Frontier: Studies in American Literary Tragedy*, "the tragic realities that nations, like men, are only mortal; that the truth comes chiefly through tragedy and paradox; and that the old inheritance of pride still carries its inexorable consequences,"[12] Australian authors have written of this truth since the beginning of their residence on the last continent: idealism, under the environmental controls of distance and dryness, is— or has been—always tinged with a darker strain of naturalism. Instead of being extraordinary events, the droughts, blizzards, rivers of dust that Wright's "old Dan" recalls, for instance, are all too ordinary, all too real, reflecting what critic H. P. Heseltine has found to be the true subject of the Australian writer throughout the years: "the individual human being confronting the primal energies at the centre of his being on the stage of the Australian continent."[13]   Furthermore, as the second distinction reveals, "it was not the lonely, highly individual rider of the range, with his heroic cowboy honor, that captured Australian imagination to create both legend and ideal; it was the hard, unspoken, unsentimental devotion of man for man, united in the face of nature or other men, and derived from all the 'mates' at sea and onshore, who attend a job together."[14]   Although one could choose to contrast a Henry Lawson short story with a story by Owen Wister to illustrate this point quite forcefully, one can discover in a novel as recent as Patrick White's *Voss* not only an imaginative, highly successful exploration of, to use Heseltine's words, "the individual human being confronting the primal energies at the centre of his being on the stage of the Australian continent," but also an imaginative portrayal of the shifting demands of membership in a societal grouping within the crucible of the outback.   While McTeague dies in utter loneliness in the Death Valley desert—handcuffed to a corpse; accompanied by a half-dead canary—Voss's death in the outback is linked thematically with the breaking of Laura Trevelyan's fever during a night in her Sydney bedroom.

While the above generalizations possess the virtues and vices of any generalized statements, the above emphasis on the desert and the community, instead of the garden and the individual, provides an entry into not only a study of a country's literary heritage but also the study of an important contributor to that heritage.   As one might expect of a poet whose country's historical heritage has been beset by the two realities of distance and dryness, and whose country's literary heritage has been described as being "suckled by a wolf" or sounding like "the cry of the crow,"[15] Judith Wright's poetic vision of the pioneering past reflects the brooding presence of the landscape and its effects on its inhabitants.   Instead of heroic, individual figures of triumph like a Daniel Boone or a Jim Bridger, Wright presents —especially in her first two volumes *The Moving Image* (1946) and *Woman to Man* (1949)—a panorama of nameless outback figures "caught in the endless circle of time and star/that never chime with the blood" ("The Moving Image"):   there is the bullock-team driver whose sojourn in the bush results in "mad, apocalyptic dreams" in the manner of Moses ("Bullocky"); there is the disinherited son from England tramping the dusty outback tracks and letting "everything but life slip through his fingers" ("Remittance Man"); there is the ignored half-caste girl "buried under the bright sun" ("Half-Caste Girl"); there is the poet's great-great grandfather who "moved in that mindless country like a red ant" ("Old House"); and there are the white men and women at a country dance unable to enjoy themselves because of the rats that "nibble at the cords of our nerves" ("The Blind Man"), and the black men and women whose record is "a dream the world breathed sleeping and forgot" ("Bora Ring").

In these poems Wright's vision of isolation, madness, betrayal, death, and broken dreams effectively unites natural symbols of her country with perennial human concerns to record a saga of endurance, not grandeur. In "Trapped Dingo," a female dingo wailing for her running mate—hurling "woes at the moon, that old cleaned bone, till the white shorn mobs of stars on the hill of the sky/huddled and trembled"—becomes not only a "desperate poet" but also an "insane Andromache," whose pacing around the steel trap recalls the human figure's pacing in her prison towers; in "Bullocky," a driver filling the "steepled cone of night/with shouted prayers and prophecies" evokes the figure of Moses, another prophet who dies before reaching the Promised Land. In "The Harp and the King" (1955), the harp's reply to the King's desire for a music to quench the despair of "night and the soul's terror coming on" serves as a metaphor for not only the experience of the Australian exile in "that harsh biblical country of the scapegoat" ("Remittance Man") but also the international human exile living in the shadow of a world at war or acting out the purely materialistic dream in the suburb:

> Wounded we cross the desert's emptiness
> and must be false to what would make us whole.
> For only change and distance shape for us
> some new tremendous symbol for the soul.
>
> ("The Harp and the King")

The appropriateness of the setting here, as in White's novel *Voss,* is that while the desert's wasteland stands as a symbolic complement of the soul's sterility, the desert's uncluttered, barren landscape also frees the individual from distraction, allowing the traveler to explore the layers of his or her being. Since "change" and "distance" connote forms of death—the possible discarding of a wounded egocentric self that views the bush as an antagonist; the further distancing in space and time from European origins—then perhaps a "new" life will rise out of the dust and sand. I say "perhaps" for it is Wright's view that Australians inevitably speak "from the state of mind that describes, rather than expresses, its surroundings, or from the state of mind that imposes itself upon rather than lives through, landscape and event."[16]

With her recognition that in both mental and physical landscapes the classical European and the local Aboriginal traditions are defunct—that, in short, "Achilles is overcome and Hector dead,/and clay stops many a warrior's mouth" ("Trapped Dingo")—Wright attempts to forge "some new tremendous symbol for the soul." "What finally I am trying to express," as she states in a letter to critic T. Inglis Moore, "is my own experience that the modern 'journey into darkness' is, if it is honestly and completely taken, a journey into a new kind of light."[17] I find that symbol and that journey into a new kind of light poetically expressed in the image of the great green fig-tree rising out of the outback dust in her long poem "The Blind Man."

> No one has loved or sung of the unregarded dust.
> Dance upright in the wind, dry-voiced and humble dust
> out of whose breast the great green fig-tree springs,
> and the proud man, and the singer, and the outcast.

Furthermore, in that conjunction of brown and green, death and life, proud man and the outcast, there are three roots in Wright's work that nourish the future harvest: the belief, as expressed in "Nigger's Leap, New England," that "all men are one man at last," that, as Wright states in her critical book *Pre-occupations in Australian Poetry,* "the past holds the clue to the present,"[18] and that the entire spectrum of the human being must be acknowledged—not just the brain but also the blood, not just the practical but also the spiritual.

These thematic concerns, all of which have their kinship
with the typical themes of sacrality Max Westbrook outlines in
his article "The Practical Spirit: Sacrality and the American
West,"[19] are all the more valuable as truths because they arise
out of, to use the poet's own words, "the result of hardship and
endurance, of sacrifice of personal ease, sacrifice perhaps of life
itself."[20]   These glimmers of redemption which balance the
moving image of time and the ravaging effect of the environment
are highlighted, appropriately enough, in the lives of a man who
has sacrificed his sight and a man who has sacrificed his sanity.
Instead of the hero who transcends society because of physical
and mental exploits, we are presented the exile who is separated
from society because of physical or mental deformities.   Even
though the exile's separation is a necessary one for Wright—the
outcast's distance from society provides for a truer perspective
and commentary—it is, ultimately, a superficial separation: the
madman and the blind man represent the spirit of love and life
which can unite the human community and rekindle the devotion of man for man—a task all the harder to achieve because
it is performed amid the swirling dust and howling wind of the
heath and outback.

In her volume *Woman to Man* it is blind Jimmy Delaney,
the half-caste fourth-generation descendant of the pioneering
Delaney family, who rambles the truth of legends to an unsym-
pathetic audience, and who, along with a crying child, represents the spirit of Eros in its struggle against Thanatos:

> We two, the singer and the crying child, must feed
> that whirling phantom on the wind of the world's end.
> Only these two can join the sperm to the golden seed—
> the tears of a child that fall for the dust at the world's end
> and the song of the singer of love, whom the wasps of
>   dust made blind.
>
>   ("The Blind Man")

It is important to recognize that there is more here than the
somewhat standard association of an Australian country town
with "the world's end," that there is more here than the familiar
relation—we remember Sophocles and Flannery O'Connor among
others—of blindness and true vision, that there is more here than
the fusion of innocence and experience in the figures of the blind
man and the child, and, finally, that there is more here than the

notion of creativity resulting from the union of the water (tears) and the earth under the guidance of love's song. At her very best, Wright imbues a common object with profound implications in order to poetically state a prevailing theme without resorting to the didactic impulse. Here in this stanza, as well as the entire poem, the pervading presence of dust operates on at least three levels of meaning. Literally, of course, particles of dust lodged in anyone's eye can produce a momentary blindness; yet when the decomposed remnants of Delaney's forebears are said to permeate the dancing dust, then the paradoxical assertion that the man who was born blind can also be blinded by dust is cleared up—the dust is symbolic of a permanent, genetic blindness also. Beyond this association of one man's genetic blindness and everyman's potential blindness, however, is the recognition that the dust symbolizes the lives and works of all the past pioneers, and that the dust is a "whirling phantom" because the wisdom of the past has been neglected by all residents of the newer order—neglected, that is, by all but the exile. If we recall the blind Oedipus along with Jimmy Delaney, then we should also recall the Furies who, like the early Australian pioneers, were deposed by younger gods. Still, as Wright carefully points out, the dust's symbolic capacity for regeneration balances its destructive aspects: it is not only the golden particle of blindness but also the golden seed of the future community of past and present, exile and everyman.[21]

In her earlier volume and poem of the same title, *The Moving Image,* Wright places beside the blind man the figure of "poor Tom of Bedlam through whose feverish blood life poured like thunder/till the frail floodgates burst within his brain" ("The Moving Image"). Standing in an airfield "that was once the world's end," the poet discovers—amid the swirling columns of dust blotting out the darkening sky—the continuous source of life embodied in the figure of the mental exile whose heath resembles the poet's rural environment:

> The first birth and the first cry and the first death,
> the world of the first cell and the first man,
> every sound and motion forgotten, remembered,
> left their trace in his body, their voice in his speech.
>
> ("The Moving Image")

While "The Blind Man" acknowledges the community of time,

"The Moving Image" realizes the essential community of man-
kind since each of us not only partake of the original essence, but
also retain traces of the madman as well as the sane man. These
twin concerns actually coincide in Wright's work, for the tension
between past and present is often reflected in the symbolic tension between Wright's juxtaposition of figures of the past with
figures of the poem's present: the poet in "The Moving Image"
remembers the struggles of Tom of Bedlam, the bullocky recalls
the spirit of Moses, and the dingo resembles an "'insane Andromache."

We remain finally with the instinctual knowledge of the
blood demanding equal time with the instinctive knowledge of
the *brain*. Significantly, blood wisdom is not recreated in the
lives of kings and generals and scientists, but in the dreams of
sleepers, the world of lovers, and the rebirth of the Wise Old
Child. As Wright concludes "The Moving Image,"

> . . . .We are dwarfed by the dark
> We inherit a handful of dust and a fragment of stone.
> Yet listen, the music grows around us, before us, behind,
> there is sound in the silence; the dark is a tremor of light.
> It is the corn rising when winter is done.
> It is the madmen singing, the lovers, the blind;
> the cry of Tom of Bedlam, naked under the sun.
>
> ("The Moving Image")

The movement here from dark to light, silence to sound, winter
to spring, the death to life implies the wedding of the human and
the nonhuman worlds. The sound of the corn rising is identified
with the sounds uttered by the "madmen singing, the lovers, the
blind"; the newly-sprouted plants are merged with the image of a
nude Tom of Bedlam receiving the sun's rays. This community
of the natural and the human environments is complemented,
furthermore by the union of the past and the future into the
present. As we have seen in "The Blind Man," music for Judith
Wright connotes the spirit of love and fertility that elevates the
narrator's aural perception of rebirth in a particular time and
place to a perception of the spirit of love that will always bind
together humanity "around us" (the present), "before us" (the
future), and "behind us" (the past). Ultimately, as in the last
three statements of the stanza, the presence of Time "that like a
bushranger held its guns on us/and forced our choice" ("The

Moving Image") serves to signify the reality of growth as well as that of decay, and to hold out hope for a "home" in the life of the exile.

If the literature of the Australian "West" is truly characterized by a disregard for a romantic hero and a romantic setting—if we are as likely to read of the drover's wife as of Ned Kelly—and a corresponding high regard for an exploration of the individual's bout with his or her primal energies and an examination of the forces that make society cohere,[22] then Judith Wright's "western" work can be placed squarely in that tradition. Although she has certainly produced accomplished poems worthy of inclusion in any anthology of feminine verse, and although she has written of the Australian "West" in an insightful way that avoids nostalgia and sentimentality, Wright's work—which is still an ongoing concern—transcends purely genetic or national interests. She possesses, on the one hand, the basic virtue which she herself finds present in the world's great poets: "a kind of humility that makes the poet capable of true sympathy with all that is human";[23] on the other hand, her use of her country's frontier heritage is instructive not merely for its visual imagery of stockman and aborigines, droughts and floods, kangeroos and koalas, but because of what these sences of the past express about the human condition, about man and woman in the cosmos.

After all, as critic H. P. Heseltine states, "if our literary heritage offers us nothing but the simple virtues appropriate to a simple frontier society, what can we do but reject it?"[24] Though he is referring to Australia's literary heritage, the same question could and should be asked of our own heritage in the American West. Are we solely interested in *American Western poetry* or are we more truly interested in *poetry in the American West?* Or, we can drop the question mark and consider Judith Wright's caution to the old stockman who worked her family's property during her childhood and who filled her head with tales of "bush" people and animals:

> For the country I travelled through was not your kind of
> country
> and when I grew I lost the sound of your stories
> and heard only at night in my dreams the sound of dogs
> and cattle and galloping horses. I am not you,
> but you are part of me. Go easy with me, old man;

I am helping clear a track to unknown water.
                                        ("Unknown Water")

In her quest for the water necessary to quench the soul's "raging drought," Judith Wright travels beside the waterholes of the past, but they are essential trail markers now on the way to her final destination. Perhaps it requires an extreme suspension of disbelief to accept the transformation of a cursing bullock-team driver into a secular Moses, or a trapped dingo into an "insane Andromache," but the effort does move us beyond the level of authenticity alone, and nearer to a wedding of the personal and universal that Melville likewise sought in his yarns.

NOTES

[1]*Voss* (New York: Viking, 1957), p. 440.

[2]"The Outback and the West: Australian and American Frontier Fiction," *Western American Literature,* 6 (Spring 1971), p. 3.

[3]*Westward the Briton* (New York: Scribner's, 1953), p. 156.

[4]"Born a Square—The Westerner's Dilemma," *Atlantic Monthly,* 213 (January 1964), p. 48.

[5]*Australia: The Last Frontier* (New York: Dodd, Mead & Co., 1972), pp. 121-122.

[6]For the particulars of American involvement in the Eureka Stockade rebellion see John Greenway, "The Austra-American West," *American West,* 5 (January 1968), p. 37.

[7]*Collected Poems, 1942-1970* (Sydney: Angus & Robertson, 1971), p. 20. Further references to the poems will be designated by poem title.

[8]"The Upside-Down Hut," *Australian Letters,* 4 (1961), rpt. in *The Writer in Australia,* ed. John Barnes (Melbourne: Oxford University Press, 1969), p. 331.

[9]As Marcus Clarke writes, "in Australia alone is to be found the Grotesque, the Weird, the strange scribblings of nature learning how to write. Some see no beauty in our trees without shade, our flowers without perfume, our birds who cannot fly, and our beasts who have not yet learned to walk on all fours. . . . The phantasmagoria of that wild dream-land termed the Bush interprets itself, and the Poet of our desolation begins to comprehend why free Esau loved his heritage of desert sand better than all the bountiful richness of Egypt." See his "Preface to Gordon's *Poems*" (1876), rpt. in *The Writer in Australia,* p. 36. I have summarized here also Judith Wright's contrast between the two countries' experiences in "The

Upside-Down Hut," p. 332.

[10]"The Upside-Down Hut," p. 331.

[11]*Virgin Land: The American West as Symbol and Myth* (1950; rpt. Cambridge, Mass.: Harvard University Press, 1971), p. 188.

[12](New York: Holt, Rinehart & Winston, 1970), p. 5.

[13]"The Australian Image: The Literary Heritage," *Meanjin*, 1 (1962), rpt. in *Twentieth Century Australian Literary Criticism*, ed. Clement Semmler (Melbourne: Oxford University Press, 1967), p. 95.

[14]Henrietta Drake-Brockman, "Domesticating a Continent," *Texas Quarterly*, 5 (1962), p. 46.

[15]Colin Roderick, *Suckled by a Wolf* (Sydney: Angus & Robertson, 1968); T. Inglis Moore, "The Cry of the Crow: Sombreness in Australian Literature," *Meanjin*, 30 (1971), pp. 5-26.

[16]"The Upside-Down Hut," p. 331.

[17]T. Inglis Moore, "The Quest of Judith Wright," rpt. in *On Native Grounds: Australian Writing from Meanjin Quarterly*, ed. C. B. Christesen (Sydney: Angus & Robertson, 1968), p. 146.

[18](Melbourne: Oxford University Press, 1965), p. xix.

[19]*Western American Literature*, 3 (1968), pp. 193-205.

[20]*Preoccupations in Australian Poetry*, p. 55.

[21]By way of contrast, we should notice here that Wright, unlike A. B. Guthrie in *The Big Sky*, focuses her narrative and hope for the future on the blind, half-breed legacy, rather than emphasizing the exploits of a Horrie Delaney, the stockman "who came here first with cattle/and shook the dust out of its golden sleep," or a Dick Delaney who cleared the hills of timber, or a Yellow Delaney, the swagman who "went wandering with his despised white girl, and left no track/but the black mark of a campfire." It would be as if the half-breed child of Teal-Eye and Boone—and not Boone himself—was the principal actor in *The Big Sky*.

[22]Wright herself states that whereas "the American dream made use

of the competitive individualistic element in life, the freedom of any man to become richer and better than his fellows by hard work and emulation, the Australian dream emphasizes man's duty to his brother, and man's basic equality, the mutual trust which is the force that makes society cohere." See *Preoccupations in Australian Poetry*, p. xxi.

[23]*Preoccupations in Australian Poetry*, p. 92.

[24]"The Australian Image: The Literary Heritage," p. 87.

CONTRIBUTORS' NOTES

KERRY AHEARN earned his Ph.D. from Ohio University with a dissertation on modern western fiction writers, including Wallace Stegner. He is presently on leave from Oregon State University as a Fulbright Scholar at the University of Ghana in Africa.

SUSAN H. ARMITAGE is Visiting Assistant Professor of History at the University of Colorado. She is one of 15 national participants in the MLA-sponsored project, "Teaching Women's Literature From A Regional Perspective," with special interest in frontier women, oral history, and the development of methodologies to incorporate women's experience into local history.

CAROL J. BANGS received her Ph.D. from the University of Oregon in March of 1977. She spent 1977-78 in England, doing research on Modern British fiction at Cambridge and the University of East Anglia. Her poems and reviews have appeared in numerous periodicals, including *Concerning Poetry, College English, Poetry Now*, and *Northwest Review.* Her first book of poetry is published by Copper Canyon Press.

ROGER E. CARP, born in Los Angeles, received his B.A. from Duke University in 1973 and his M.A. from the University of North Carolina—Chapel Hill, where he is now pursuing a doctorate in American History.

JOSEPH M. FLORA is Professor of English and Associate Dean of the Graduate School at the University of North Carolina at Chapel Hill. He is the author of *Vardis Fisher; William Ernest Henley;* and *Frederick Manfred.* He has edited James Branch Cabell's *The Cream of the Jest,* and co-edited *A Biographical Guide to Southern Literature* (forthcoming). He is currently working on an edition of the letters of Vardis Fisher and Frederick Manfred.

SYLVIA GRIDER was born and raised in Pampa, Texas, where she learned to love the Great Plains—one of her earliest childhood memories is that of the constantly blowing wind. Specializing in oral tradition, she is active in both The Texas Folklore Society and the American Folklore Society. She received her Ph.D. in Folklore from Indiana University, and is currently Assistant Professor of English at Texas A & M University.

L. L. LEE, Professor of English at Western Washington University, is the author of *Vladimir Nabokov* (Twayne) and *Walter Van Tilburg Clark* (Boise State University Western Writers Series); co-author of *Virginia Sorensen* (BSU WWS); and co-editor of *The Westering Experience in American Literature* (Western Washington University). He was editor of *Concerning Poetry,* 1968-1977.

SYLVIA B. LEE teaches English as a second language at Whatcom Community College in Bellingham, Washington. She is co-author of *Virginia Sorensen,* published by Boise State University in 1978.

ELINOR LENZ, presently coordinator of Special Programs, University Extension, University of California at Los Angeles, was director of the Western Humanities Center, funded by the National Endowment for the Humanities. She is co-author of the book, *So You Want To Go Back To School,* McGraw Hill, 1977. She is also a free-lance author, published in many journals.

MERRILL LEWIS, Professor of English and Director of American Studies at Western Washington University, is co-author of *Wallace Stegner* (Boise State University Western Writers Series) and co-editor of *The Westering Experience in American Literature* (Western Washington University, 1977). He is presently working on a critical study of writing in the Pacific Northwest.

CHARLOTTE S. McCLURE has written bibliographic and critical articles on Gertrude Atherton which have appeared in *American Literary Realism* and in the Western Writer's Series (Boise State University). An essay and a book-length critical-analytical study of Atherton will appear respectively in *Itinerary Seven* (Bowling Green St. University) and in the Twayne United States Author Series. She is currently director of the Honors Program at Georgia State University at Atlanta.

JEANNIE McKNIGHT is a Visiting Assistant Professor at Lewis and Clark College where she teaches courses in Women on the Frontier, Women and Literature, Modern British Literature and James Joyce. She has published an article in the *James Joyce Quarterly*, "Unlocking the Word-Hoard: Madness, Identity and Creativity in James Joyce," and is currently completing a study of women's lives and writings on the Western Frontier.

BARBARA MELDRUM, Professor of English at the University of Idaho, has published articles on Melville, Rølvaag, Vardis Fisher, S. K. Winther, and images of women in American literature among others. She has a continuing interest in American, western, and women's literature, expressed in her published works and in papers read.

BEVERLY MITCHELL, SSA, is Assistant Professor of English at the University of Alberta, Edmonton, Alberta, specializing in Canadian literature. Her critical articles have been published in *The Journal of Canadian Fiction, The Dalhousie Review, The Fiddlehead, Studies in Canadian Literature,* and *The Open Letter.* Her short story "Letter from Sakaye" was published in Martha Foley's *Best American Short Stories 1974* and has been requested for publication in Japan.

BARBARA QUISSELL, who did her graduate work at the University of Utah, teaches for Idaho State University in Idaho Falls. In addition to her interest in Dorothy Scarborough's *The Winds,* she has worked extensively on the Oregon Trail experience as reflected in the diaries of and novels by women.

M. LOU RODENBERGER, Assistant Professor of English at Texas A & M University, is currently teaching American Literature and Life and Literature of the Southwest. Her dissertation study was of Caroline Gordon's use of family saga and folk narrative in her fiction. Professor Rodenberger's scholarly interests also focus upon the trail driver in Southwestern history and literature.

ANN RONALD is an Associate Professor of English at the University of Nevada—Reno. She is the author of *Zane Grey* (1975) and of several articles about women writers from both America and England.

CLARICE SHORT, whose poem, "The Old One and the Wind," gives a thematic center to this book, died while the book was being prepared. She was a friend and teacher of both the editors; her death is a personal loss. Clarice did not publish many poems, but what she did was remarkable. A collection of her work, *The Old One and the Wind,* was put out by the University of Utah Press in 1973. Professor Emeritus of English at the University of Utah, she was an authority and writer on the works of the English authors of the Romantic and Victorian periods.

BERNICE SLOTE has to her credit numerous articles and books, including one volume on Keats, five on Willa Cather—*The Kingdom of Art, Willa Cather: A Pictorial Memoir,* and editions (with introductions) of *April Twilights* (1903), *Uncle Valentine and Other Stories,* and *Alexander's Bridge.* She is currently working on an extended biography of Cather. Professor of English at the University of Nebraska, she is also the editor of *Prairie Schooner.*

HELEN STAUFFER received her Ph.D. from the University of Nebraska. In the summer of 1976, she was awarded an NEH Individual Research Grant. She has been published in *Platte Valley Review, Midwestern Miscellany, Kansas Heritage, Nebraska Library Journal* and others. Professor of English at Kearny State College in Nebraska, she is currently on leave to finish her Sandoz biography.

STEPHEN TATUM is a graduate student/teaching fellow at the University of Utah who is currently working on the idea of the West in Victorian literary periodicals. He visited and worked in Australia in 1972, where he was introduced to Judith Wright's work by a Queensland cattle-station owner's wife.

Women, Women Writers, and the West

Composed in IBM Selectric Composer *Journal Roman* and printed offset, sewn and bound by Braun and Brumfield, Incorporated, Ann Arbor, Michigan. The paper on which the book is printed is Warren's "1854."

Women, Women Writers, and the West is a Trenowyth book, the scholarly publishing division of The Whitston Publishing Company.

This edition consists in 500 casebound copies.